Second International Workshop on Resources and Tools for Derivational Morphology (DeriMo 2019)

Prague, Czech Republic
19 – 20 September 2019

ISBN: 978-1-7138-0078-1

DeriMo 2019

**Proceedings of the Second International Workshop
on Resources and Tools for Derivational Morphology**

19–20 September, 2019
Charles University,
Faculty of Mathematics and Physics,
Institute of Formal and Applied Linguistics
Prague, Czechia
https://ufal.mff.cuni.cz/derimo2019

Introduction

This volume contains papers accepted for presentation at DeriMo 2019: The Second International Workshop on Resources and Tools for Derivational Morphology, held in Prague, Czechia, on 19-20 September 2019. DeriMo 2019 follows up on the first DeriMo workshop (DeriMo 2017), which took place in Milan, Italy, in October 2017.

The submission and reviewing processes have been handled by the EasyChair system. In total, there were 19 submitted contributions, each reviewed by 3 program committee members. The proceedings contains 12 papers selected according to the reviews. In addition, the proceedings include contributions of two invited speakers, Lívia Kőrtvélyessy and Fiammetta Namer. We thank the LINDAT/CLARIN project (LM2015071) and the LINDAT/CLARIAH-CZ project (LM2018101) for financial support for the workshop organization.

Zdeněk Žabokrtský

Magda Ševčíková

Eleonora Litta

Marco Passarotti

Organizers:

Magda Ševčíková	ÚFAL, Charles University, Prague, Czechia
Zdeněk Žabokrtský	ÚFAL, Charles University, Prague, Czechia
Eleonora Litta	CIRCSE, Università Cattolica del Sacro Cuore, Milan, Italy
Marco Passarotti	CIRCSE, Università Cattolica del Sacro Cuore, Milan, Italy

Program Committee Members:

Mark Aronoff	USA
Alexandra Bagasheva	Bulgaria
Jim Blevins	UK
Olivier Bonami	France
Nicola Grandi	Italy
Pius ten Hacken	Austria
Nabil Hathout	France
Andrew Hippisley	USA
Claudio Iacobini	Italy
Sandra Kübler	USA
Silvia Luraghi	Italy
Francesco Mambrini	Germany
Fabio Montermini	France
Fiammetta Namer	France
Sebastian Padó	Germany
Renáta Panocová	Slovakia
Vito Pirrelli	Italy
Lucie Pultrová	Czechia
Jan Radimský	Czechia
Andrew Spencer	UK
Pavol Štekauer	Slovakia
Pavel Štichauer	Czechia
Salvador Valera	Spain

Local Organizing Committee:

Magda Ševčíková
Zdeněk Žabokrtský
Jana Hamrlová

Table of Contents

Cross-linguistic research into derivational networks

Lívia Körtvélyessy
P.J.Šafárik University/Moyzesova 5, 04001 Košice, Slovakia
`livia.kortvelyessy@upjs.sk`

1 Introduction

In the past decades, word-formation vindicated its position in the system of linguistic sciences. More and more attention has been paid to phenomena which are typical of this field. Frequently, morphologists are in search for analogies between inflection and derivation. A good example of this are derivational paradigms. Even though they are not in the centre of theoretical considerations, they have already been discussed within various theoretical frameworks, e.g. Dokulil (1962), Horecký et al. (1989), Pounder (2000), Beecher (2004), Furdík (2004), Ševčíková and Žabokrtský (2014), Bonami and Strnadová (2016). The paper presents a new contribution to the discussion. The basic notion is the derivational network which differs from derivational paradigms by its three-dimensional nature.

2 Theoretical background

Derivational paradigms can be treated as a system of complex words derived from a single word-formation base. This includes all direct derivatives from a single word-formation base (first dimension), for example:

(1) (i)   dom   'house'
       (iii) dom-ček   'little house'
       (iv) dom-ík   'little house'
       (v)   dom-isko   'large house'
       (vi) dom-ov (adverb of direction)   'towards one's home'

In this case, we speak of the **paradigmatic capacity** of the word-formation base represented by the number of derivatives from the word-formation base.

In addition, there is another (second) dimension that should be taken into consideration, in particular, all **linear** derivations from a single word-formation base, as in (2):

(2) (a) dom   dom-ov   dom-ov-ina   dom-ov-in-ový
          'house'   'home'   'homeland'   'related to homeland'

     (b) dom   dom-ček   dom-ček-ový
          'house'   'little house' 'related to a little house'

     (c) dom   dom-ík   dom-ík-ový
          'house'   'little house' 'related to a little house'

     (d) dom   dom-isko   dom-isk-ový
          'house'   'large house' 'related to a large house'

This dimension enables us to identify the number of affixation operations available for a given basic underived word. Each affixation operation represents one order of derivation. By implication, this dimension identifies the number of linear derivations. In example (2), (2a) shows three orders of derivation, while (2b) through (2d) permit two orders of derivation from the same simple underived word *dom* 'house'.

Proceedings of the 2nd Int. Workshop on Resources and Tools for Derivational Morphology (DeriMo 2019), pages 1–4,
Prague, Czechia, 19-20 September 2019.

Each derivational step introduces (and therefore expresses and represents) a particular semantic category (third dimension). In (2a), these are, respectively, Location, Location and Quality, in (2b) and (2c) Diminutive and Quality, and in (2d) Augmentative and Quality. By implication, a combination of derivatives from the same base identifies a combination of semantic categories realized in the process of consecutive affixal derivations. It follows from example (2) that one and the same basic word can give rise to several paths of consecutive derivations, each of which has its specific number of derivatives representing specific semantic categories.

The paradigmatic capacity and orders of derivation establish a derivational network, that is, a network of derivatives derived from the same word-formation base (simple underived word) with the aim of formally representing specific semantic categories.

3 What was compared?

Derivational networks may substantially differ from language to language in their complexity. However, no major empirical, the less so cross-linguistic research has been implemented yet. For this reason, a research project was designed that is aimed at comparison of derivational networks in 40 languages of Europe. Two criteria for the selection of languages were applied: (i) each language presented a language of Europe. The primary source was the languages covered in the HSK Word-Formation; (ii) the number of languages was reduced on the basis of their data availability, i.e., according to the possibility to verify the existence of derived words by means of representative dictionaries and/or corpora. An important reference guide in this respect was *Ethnologue*, in particular, its *Expanded Graded Intergenerational Disruption Scale*.

Parallel to inflectional paradigms, derivational networks rely on word-classes. Our derivational networks include nouns, verbs and adjectives as basic words. Each of these word-classes is represented by 10 simple underived words. Words were selected from Swadesh's core vocabulary list.

4 Points of comparison

The primary objective of the project was to compare derivational networks in 40 languages of Europe. For any typological analysis a tertium comparationis is needed. For this purpose, we introduced the concept of saturation value as quantitative representation of structural richness. Saturation value calculations are based on the concept of the Maximum Derivational Network (MDN). The maximum derivational network results from the intersection of all implemented (actual) derivations found for all basic words of an examined sample within a particular word-class. For its computation, it is necessary to identify the highest number of derivatives for a given semantic category from among all ten sample words (in our research) of a given word-class. The MDN values enable us to calculate the saturation value for individual words by means of the formula:

$$SV = \frac{D}{MDN} \times 100(\%) \tag{1}$$

Legend: SV - Saturation value, D - Number of derivatives, MDN - Maximum derivational network

Saturation value is computed for each derivational network in each language. As explained above, in each language 30 derivational networks were constructed (10 for nouns, 10 for verbs, 10 for adjectives). The gained data enable us to compare languages in terms of the number of derivatives, the number of orders of derivation, the maximum derivational network, and the saturation value. Obviously, we also search for various associations between these parameters. Furthermore, the dimension of semantic categories is evaluated. This makes it possible to identify correlations between semantic categories and orders of derivation and typical combinations of semantic categories; to identify semantic categories with blocking effects, their multiple occurrences, and the reversibility of semantic categories.

5 Conclusions (selected)

i. There are considerable differences among languages in their derivational capacity, which is reflected in the number of derivatives in derivational networks.

ii. If we compare the average MDN values by word-classes and by orders of derivation it is obvious that the derivational potential of simple underived nouns and adjectives is very similar, in some orders almost identical. Verbs have clearly the highest MDN value in every order of derivation, significantly higher than the other two word-classes. This is especially due to an extreme derivational potential of those languages which employ prefixes for the expression of the category of Aktionsart.

iii. The richness of derivational networks is sensitive to the word-class of the basic word. This means that for the majority of languages the richness of derivational networks varies depending on the word-class of the basic words. A high consistency across all three orders in all three word-classes is rare but does occur in Bulgarian and Serbian. If restricted to order 1, highly consistent networks in all three word-classes have been identified for Croatian, Turkish and Basque, and, partly, Bulgarian, Polish and Welsh.

iv. The richness of derivational networks is sensitive to the order of derivation.

v. There is a tendency for languages to actualize 20-29.99 % of the derivational potential of a word-class. This tendency is almost identical for all three word-classes and is represented by 67.5 % of languages for nouns and 62.5 % of languages for both verbs and adjectives.

vi. There is a core group of languages that keep high saturation values across all three word-classes. They include Greek, Dutch, North Saami and Dargwa. They might be completed with German, Turkish and Lithuanian which have high values in two word-classes and a medium SV in the third word-class.

vii. There is an unambiguous tendency for saturation values to fall gradually with the rising order of derivation in all three word-classes.

viii. The saturation values do not vary for the examined genera in a significant way in any of the word-classes which indicates that it is possible to predict the level of richness of derivational networks for language genera.

ix. A medium saturation value (20-30 %) can be considered the most typical saturation value for all word-classes and the first three orders of derivation.

x. There is no geographically homogeneous territory on which the languages of topmost saturation values are spoken. These languages are of various genetical origins and are scattered across Europe. What, however, can be considered as a general tendency is the use of low- saturation values languages at geographically peripheral areas of Europe.

xi. The correlation between saturation value and paradigmatic capacity may significantly differ for the same language in different word-classes and different orders of derivation.

xii. The maximum number of orders of derivation, i.e., the maximum number of affixes attached to a simple underived word is five for all three word-classes. There are six languages reaching five orders of derivation in all three word-classes, none of them belonging to the Romance or Germanic genus. The average number of affixation steps is very similar for verb-based and adjective-based derivation (2.78 and 2.76, respectively). It is lower for nouns (2.46).

xiii. Also in terms of the total number of derivatives, the most prolific base is verb. The average of verb-based derivatives clearly outnumbers the figures for adjectives and nouns. This word-formation feature is dominated by Slavic and Uralic languages. The values for the adjective-based derivation are slightly higher than those for the noun-based derivation.

xiv. Inflectional and agglutinating languages tend to have a high number of derivational orders. However, the genetic factor might be influential, too. Romance inflectional languages have smaller number of derivational orders than Slavic. While Nakh-Daghestanian languages, classified as agglutinating, tend to have a very low number of derivation orders Uralic languages, also agglutinating, feature high numbers. Analytic languages are not consistent in their behaviour. Generally, they tend to have lower number of derivation orders, especially in the case of nouns.

xv. The most clearly correlated with the first order of derivation are the following semantic categories:

- Nominal bases: Diminutive, Quality, Privative, Relational and Action
- Verbal bases: Action, Agent, Resultative and Ability
- Adjectival bases: Manner and Stative

xvi. In the second order of derivation they are:

- Nominal bases: Action and Stative
- Verbal bases: Action and Agent.

xvii. No recurrent patterns could be established in terms of the combinability of semantic categories or the blocking capacity of semantic categories from a cross-linguistic point of view (with the exception of the blocking effect of Diminutive). This suggests that there is no universal cognitively founded succession of derivational operations.

xviii. Three semantic categories stand out in terms of their capacity to reoccur in successive orders of derivation: Quality, Action and Diminutive.

References

Henry Beecher. 2004. Derivational paradigm in word formation. http://citeseerx.ist.psu.edu/viewdoc/download?doi=10.1.1.94.9071&rep=rep1&type=pdf.

Olivier Bonami and Jana Strnadová. 2016. Derivational paradigms: pushing the analogy. A paper presented at the SLE conference, Naples, Italy, August- 3 September 2016.

Miloš Dokulil. 1962. *Tvoření slov v čestine. Teorie odvozování slov*. Academia, Prague.

Magda Ševčíková and Zdeněk Žabokrtský. 2014. Word-formation network for czech. In *Nicoletta Calzolari et al. (eds.), Proceedings of the 9th International Language Resources and Evaluation Conference (LREC 2014)*. ELRA, Paris, pages 1087–1093.

Juraj Furdík. 2004. *Slovenská slovotvorba*. Edited by Martin Ološtiak. Náuka, Prešov.

Ján Horecký, Klára Buzássyová, and Ján Bosák et al. 1989. *Dynamika slovnej zásoby súčasnej slovenčiny*. Veda, Bratislava.

Amanda Pounder. 2000. *Processes and Paradigms in Word-Formation Morphology*. Mouton de Gruyter, Berlin/New York.

ParaDis and Démonette
From Theory to Resources for Derivational Paradigms

Fiammetta Namer
UMR 7118 ATILF
CNRS & Université de Lorraine
Nancy, France
`fiammetta.namer@univ-lorraine.fr`

Nabil Hathout
UMR 5263 CLLE-ERSS - CNRS &
Université de Toulouse Jean-Jaurès
Toulouse, France
`nabil.hathout@univ-tlse.fr`

Abstract

This article traces the genesis of the French derivational database Démonette$_{v2}$ and shows how current architecture and content of derivational morphology resources result from theoretical developments in derivational morphology and from the users' need. The development of this large-scale resource began a year ago and is part of the Demonext project (ANR-17-CE23-0005). Its conception is adapted from theoretical approaches of derivational morphology where lexemes, units of analysis, are grouped into families that are organized into paradigms. More precisely, Démonette$_{v2}$ is basically an implementation of ParaDis, a paradigmatic model for representing morphologically complex lexical units, formed by regular processes or presenting discrepancies between form and meaning. The article focuses on the principles of morphological, structural and semantic encoding that reflect the methodological choices that have been made in Démonette$_{v2}$. Our proposal will be illustrated with various examples of non-canonical word formations.

1 Introduction

Morphological analysis is one of the initial steps in many NLP systems. Analyzers, most often based on machine learning and statistical methods, decompose words into morphemes in order to compensate for the limitations of lexicons. Let us mention Linguistica (Goldsmith 2001), Morfessor (Creutz and Lagus 2005), or, more recently, Cotterell and Schütze (2017)'s models. These systems are applicable to any language, however they are more effective for languages with concatenative morphology such as English, German and French. Morphological analysis can also be carried out by symbolic parsers, most of them developed by linguists; for a panorama, see (Bernhard et al. 2011).

Lexical resources with derivational annotations can replace or supplement morphological parsers in the NLP pipeline if their lexical coverage is large enough and if their features are sufficiently rich and varied. In its meticulous and exhaustive report, Kyjánek (2018) produces a typology describing the structure and coverage of 30 recent derivational resources for Romance (including Latin), Germanic and Slavic languages. The reader should refer to this work to get a clear idea of the existing derivational databases (DDBs) and lexicons with derivational annotations.

The lack of large-scale derivational resources of French motivated the development, from 2011, of a prototype database Démonette$_{v1}$ (Hathout and Namer 2014a, 2016). Démonette$_{v1}$ describes derivational families made up of verbs, agent and action nouns and modality adjectives. Three objectives were pursued: (1) use DériF's analyses (Namer 2009, 2013) to produce a resource whose inputs are derivational relations between two words W_1 and W_2, labelled with linguistically grounded fetures, including semantic annotations; (2) complete these $W_1 \rightarrow W_2$ derivations by relations between derivational family members provided by the analogic model implemented in Morphonette (Hathout 2009); (3) define an extensible and redundant architecture, which can be fed by varied and heterogeneous morphological resources. The design of the Démonette$_{v2}$ database (§.3) is based on the experience gained during the development of Démonette$_{v1}$. The aim is to produce a lexicon whose descriptions (morphological, phonological, frequency, and especially semantic) will be useful for NLP, but will also serve as a reference for several audiences (research in morphology, university teaching, academic or speech therapy practice, just to cite a few). The structure of the database must allow (semi-)automatic acquisition from existing resources, and must be robust enough to be able to include any new type of derivation. We therefore need an architecture based on theoretical principles that ensure a uniform representation of regular derivation (words where meaning and form deduce from each other) and non-canonic derivation, which infringe form-meaning compositionality. For this purpose, Démonette$_{v2}$ applies the theoretical principles borrowed from lexeme- and paradigm-based approaches to word formation (WF), summarized in §.2.

2 Démonette's theoretical background

Two major facts have independently contributed to recent evolution in WF, and have therefore influenced the content and organization of derivational resources: (1) the adoption of the lexeme as a unit, and (2) the structuration of the morphological lexicon into paradigms.

2.1 Morphemes, and form-meaning non-compositionality

Morpheme-based morphological traditions, whether concatenative (Item and Arrangement) or functional (Item and Process) (Hockett 1954), have long been taken as models for the development of automatic derivation tools. However, the limits of morpheme-based morphology have been widely discussed in the literature (Aronoff 1976, Anderson 1992, Fradin 2003): the most significant drawback concerns the rigidity of the morpheme, a unique and minimal combination of form and meaning which cannot easily adapt to non canonical derivation (Corbett 2010). In these frameworks, the analysis of words whose meaning and form do not coincide becomes (very) complex. One example is *zero affixation* or *conversion* (Tab.1-a) (Tribout 2012), characterized as "formal undermarking" of the derivative with respect to its base by Hathout and Namer (2014b) (the derived form is identical to the base form but its semantic content is more complex). On the other hand, *parasynthetic* derivatives (Tab.1-b,c) (Hathout and Namer 2018), are said to be "over-marked" because one of their formal parts does not play a role in the construction of their meaning. Finally, the derivational relations obtained by *affix replacement* (Booij and Masini 2015) are both "under- and over-marked" with respect to each other: in Tab.1-d, Lex$_2$ is constructed by replacing *-ism* in Lex$_1$ by *-ist* (and vice versa). Non-canonical derivations also include processes that regularly produce two series of words with the same shape but different meanings, or with distinct forms but the same meaning. In the first case, (absence of formal markdown) the derivative is *polysemic* (in French, cf. Tab.1-e, *-eur* suffixed nouns denote either humans or artifacts). The second case corresponds to *morphological variation* or *competition*. Here, the absence of semantic markdown corresponds to what Thornton (2012) calls *overabundance*: for instance, in Italian, Tab.1-f, prefixes *s-* and *de-* compete to form adjective-based verbs, cf. (Todaro 2017).

	formation	lgge	Lex$_1$	Lex$_2$
a	conversion	eng	*nurse$_N$*	*nurse$_V$*
b	parasynthesis	fra	*banque$_N$* 'bank'	*interbancaire$_A$* 'between banks'
c			*département$_N$* 'department'	*interdépartemental$_A$* 'between departments'
d	affix replacement	eng	*altruism$_N$*	*altruist$_N$*
e	polysemy	fra	porter$_V$ 'carry'	*porteur$_{Nm,[hum]OR[artif]}$* 'carrier'
f	overabundance	ita	*compatto$_A$* 'compact'	*scompattare$_V$* or *decompattare$_V$* 'uncompact'

Table 1: Different types of meaning-form discrepancies in Lex$_1$/Lex$_2$ derivational relations.

2.2 Lexemes, and non-binary or non-oriented rules

Abandoning the morpheme in favour of the *lexeme* solves some problems that arise from meaning non-compositionality. Unlike the morpheme, lexeme is not a concrete minimal unit. It is actually an abstract object (an uninflected word, in the simplest cases) that records the common properties of the inflectional paradigm it stands for, in the form of an autonomous three-dimensional structure: (1) a phonological form (the stem); (2) a part-of-speech; (3) a meaning. Unlike morpheme concatenation rules which apply an affixal function to a morphological structure, *word formation rules* (WFRs) are oriented relations between two lexemes or schemas, as in (1). WFRs apply independently and simultaneously to all three levels of description allowing the formal exponent to vary for a same semantic type of derivative, and vice versa.

In particular, this evolution solves part of the problems illustrated in Tab.1. For conversion (Tab.1-a), as shown in (1), the rule only modifies the semantic content and the part-of-speech, leaving the formal values of the related lexemes unchanged; as for polysemy (Tab.1-e), nothing prevents two distinct rules to derive word-types with different semantic content using the same formal exponent; as for overabundance (Tab.1-f), two different WFRs can produce different formal realizations for the same semantic value.

$$(1) \quad \begin{bmatrix} /\text{n3:s}/ \\ \text{N} \\ \text{`nurse'} \end{bmatrix} \rightarrow \begin{bmatrix} /\text{n3:s}/ \\ \text{V} \\ \text{`ACTING as a nurse'} \end{bmatrix}$$

However WFRs are designed to connect a derivative to its base. They are not designed to describe indirect relations, such as (Tab.1-d). For the same reason, lexeme-based models are not able to describe parasynthetic derivation (Tab.1-b,c) where, for a given prefixation process (e.g. *inter-*), the suffix exponent is not unique (*-aire* in *banque* → *interbancaire*, but *-al* in *département* → *interdépartemental*), and the suffix value cannot be determined by neither the form or the meaning of the base.

2.3 Paradigms, and partially motivated relations

Derivational paradigms overcomes the limitations of the lexeme-based morphology where derivational relations are restricted to binary and oriented base$_W$ → derived$_W$ connections (for a panorama, see Štekauer (2014)). In a paradigmatic framework (Bonami and Strnadová 2019), the central unit is the *derivational family*, i.e. a structured set of lexemes[1], whose form and meaning depend on each other: all the members of a family are interconnected. Two families belong to the same paradigm when they line up; in this alignment, members of the same rank or position maintain in their respective families the same form and meaning relations with the other members of their family, and are therefore part of the same *derivational series* (Hathout 2011). Families may align partially. In such a framework, directly and indirectly related word pairs are both described in the same way by means of non-oriented schemata as in (2). This schema decribes the relation between *altruist* and *altruism* of Tab.1-d, where X is set for their common subsequence /æltrʊ/. Semantically, the mutual motivation of the two nouns is described by means of the "@1" and "@2" indexes: *altruism* is the "IDEOLOGY DEFENDED by (an) altruist", which in turn is a "FOLLOWER of altruism".

$$(2) \quad \begin{bmatrix} /\text{X}\text{ɪst}/ \\ \text{N} \\ \text{@1:`FOLLOWER of @2'} \end{bmatrix} \leftrightarrow \begin{bmatrix} /\text{X}\text{ɪzm}/ \\ \text{N} \\ \text{@2: `IDEOLOGY DEFENDED by @1'} \end{bmatrix}$$

(*altruist, altruism*) is a partial family that belongs to a sub-paradigm of the paradigm resulting from the stacking of triplets like the ones presented in Tab.2. Each triplet connects a (proper) noun denoting an entity (X), a noun of ideology (Xism) valuing that entity, and a human noun (Xist) denoting a person supporting that ideology. In his *Cumulative Patterns* Bochner (1993) represents these paradigmatic relations in the form of ternary schemata as in (3)[2].

$$(3) \quad \left\{ \begin{bmatrix} /\text{X}\text{ɪst}/ \\ \text{N} \\ \text{@1:`FOLLOWER of @2,} \\ \text{ENDORSING @3'} \end{bmatrix}, \begin{bmatrix} /\text{X}\text{ɪzm}/ \\ \text{N} \\ \text{@2: `IDEOLOGY} \\ \text{DEFENDED by @1,} \\ \text{PROMOTING @3'} \end{bmatrix}, \begin{bmatrix} /\text{X}/ \\ \text{PrN or N} \\ \text{@3: `ENTITY} \\ \text{PROMOTED by @2,} \\ \text{ENDORSED by @1'} \end{bmatrix} \right\}$$

---

[1]The notion of paradigm does not necessarily imply that of lexeme. Nevertheless, we are only interested here in this type of unit.

[2]Various other theoretical approaches have been proposed to represent paradigms in derivation by Koenig (1999), Booij (2010), Spencer (2013), Antoniova and Štekauer (2015) to only cite a few.

X: Valued Entity	Xist: Follower	Xism: Ideology
Calvin	calvinist	calvinism
race	racist	racism

Table 2: (X, Xist, Xism) paradigm in English.

However, some questions raised by the derivations in Tab.1-(b,c) remain unanswered. One of them is the variable value of the suffix on the adjective prefixed by *inter-*: *interbancaire*, *interdépartemental*, but also *interocéanique* 'between oceans' or *intercorallien* 'between corals'. Moreover, there is a meaning-form asymetry because the suffix does not contribute to the adjectival meaning, basically, a spatial interval between two or more concrete entities ('between several X') where X is, respectively, *banque*, *département*, *océan* and *corail*. When observing the derivational family of these adjectives (Tab.3), we can see that the suffix that shows up in the prefixed adjective is the same as the one of the relational adjective ('of X') of all these nouns.

In a way, the adjective in *inter-* has two bases: the noun X is its semantic base, and the adjective Xsuf its formal base. In other words, the construction of $inter\text{Xsuf}_A$ requires simultaneous access to the semantic properties of X_N, and the formal properties of Xsuf_A.

X_N	Xsuf_A: 'of X'	$inter\text{Xsuf}_A$: 'between several Xs'
banque	*bancaire*	*interbancaire*
département	*départemental*	*interdépartemental*
océan	*océanique*	*interocéanique*
corail	*corallien*	*intercorallien*

Table 3: (X, Xsuf, *inter*Xsuf) paradigm in French.

An access to the derivational family of the prefixed adjective is therefore necessary for the description and prediction of its properties. However, "classical" paradigmatic organizations such as the ones we have just presented are too rigid to express the double ascendancy of the *inter*Xsuf adjectives. Classical paradigmatic systems are actually designed to describe regularities that hold at all three levels: formal, categorial and semantic. These paradigms are therefore unable to capture the regularities that involve lexemes with a mismatch between form and meaning, like the ternary relations in Tab.3. To properly describe and predict this type of discrepancy, the semantic and formal relations must be described and accessed separately, as they do in ParaDis.

2.4 ParaDis

As shown in the previous section, the principles of lexeme-based and paradigmatic approaches to derivation are both required in order to provide WF models and resources with sufficient descriptive and predictive power. However, they remain unable to account for asymmetrical formations as in Tab.3-b,c. Far from being exceptional, such formations occur in a large part of the prefixed denominal adjectives of French (and other European languages): they describe a spatial relation (*inter-*, *intra-*, *sous-*, *sur-*, ...), adversativity (*anti-*), quantification (*mono-*, *bi-*, *pluri-*,...), etc. Other types of derived words display comparable over-marks with respect to their bases: for example, in French, verbs like $scolariser_v$ 'get into school' are formally formed by suffixation in *-iser* on an adjectival base ($scolaire_A$ 'of school') while their semantic content is built on the meaning of the base noun of this adjective ($école_N$ 'school').

We therefore need a model that grasps the paradigmatic regularities blurred by the many form-meaning discrepancies, by transposing the main contribution of lexeme-based morphology (independent formal, categorial and semantic levels do representations) to the paradigmatic organization of the lexicon (access to all the members of a derivational family). In other words, the model must combine a morpho-phonological paradigmatic network (in order for example to predict the formal motivation of *inter*Xsuf

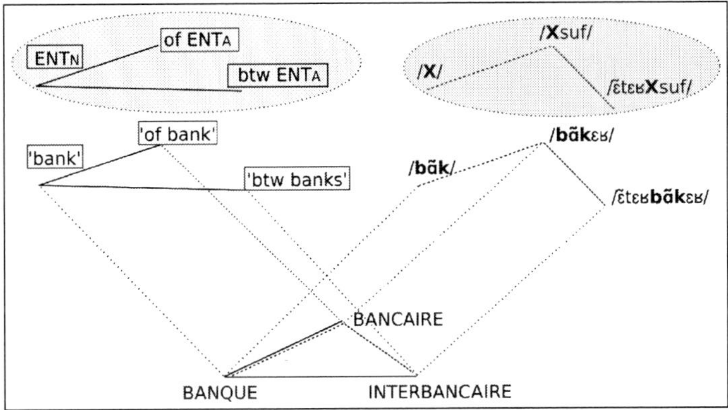

Figure 1: ParaDis: Representation of the (X, Xsuf, *inter*Xsuf) unbalanced paradigm.

with respect to Xsuf) and a morpho-semantic paradigmatic network (able for instance to predict the semantic motivation of *inter*Xsuf with respect to X) in order to properly describe and predict these adjectives.

This is precisely what we propose in ParaDis "Paradigms vs Discrepancies" (Hathout and Namer 2018). The model is based on the assumption that a derivational paradigm behaves as a kind of generalization of the lexeme's ternary structure: it contains the same three-level organization. The premise is that, if morphological regularities are paradigmatic, then the morpho-semantic, morpho-categorial and morpho-formal levels in correspondence with these paradigms are themselves paradigms. In other words, ParaDis brings to the semantic, categorial and formal levels the organizational principles of classical paradigm-based WF models. This system therefore includes a (morpho-)formal paradigm, a (morpho-)categorial paradigm and a (morpho-)semantic paradigm, whose junction is the morphological paradigm they are in correspondence with. This morphological paradigm is the abstract combination of the other three components, just as the lexeme is the abstract combination of a formal, categorial and semantic descriptions.

The independence of the formal, categorial and semantic paradigms allows a three-dimensional description of asymetric derivations like *interbancaire*, cf. Fig.1. For sake of readability, we have merged the categorial and the semantic levels. The formal paradigm (gray oval on the right) is an alignment of families of forms; families are represented as connected graphs, where each edge expresses a formal motivation between two phonological sequences. The semantic paradigm (gray oval on the left) is an alignment of families of concepts; families are represented as connected graphs, where each edge expresses a semantic motivation between two semantic values. These graphs are incomplete and they differ from each other. In the semantic paradigm, the semantic values that represent the spatial interval ('btw ENTITIES') and the relation ('of ENTITY') are not deductible from each other, and therefore they are not related. Likewise, in the formal paradigm, the two unrelated formal patterns /X/ and /ɛ̃tɛʁXsuf/ are not interpredictable. In the morphological paradigm (bottom), the relation between *banque* and *bancaire* is regular (displayed by a double line): it inherits a semantic motivation from the semantic paradigm, and a formal motivation from the formal paradigm. Conversely, there is only a formal relation between *bancaire* and *interbancaire* (displayed by hyphens), and only a semantic relation (solid line) between *banque* and *interbancaire*. The other families of Tab.3 are analyzed in the same way.

In the next section, we show how Démonette$_{v2}$'s implements the main features of ParaDis.

3 The Démonette$_{v2}$ derivational database

The organization of Démonette$_{v2}$ is original: an entry in the DDB corresponds to a *derivational relation* between two lexemes belonging to the same family, but not necessarily in a base/derivative relationship. The DDB is thus based on the theoretical assumptions summarized in § 2 which consider that the lexeme is the fundamental morphological unit and that the derivational construction fulfills two functions: (1)

create new lexemes and (2) establish semantic and formal relations of motivation between the lexemes present in the lexicon.

In addition to the initial contribution of the 96,000 entries of Démonette$_{v1}$ (Hathout and Namer 2014a, Namer et al. 2017), the content of Démonette$_{v2}$ is obtained by migrating existing derivational resources, developed and validated by morphologists. These resources where selected because of their availability, complementarity and richness of description (morphological annotations and, for most of them, semantic and phonological features). Their processing is scaled according to the complexity of their migration in the format of Démonette$_{v2}$. These resources amount to 183,000 entries, most often in the form of annotated (base$_W$, derived$_W$) word pairs, corresponding to ca. 120 derivational processes by conversion, suffixation (*-ard*, *-ariat*, *-at*, *-âtre*, *-el*, *-aie*, *-iser*, *-erie*, *-esque*, *-esse*, *-eur*, *-eux*, *-iste*, ...), or prefixation (*a-*, *anti-*, *bi-*, *co-*, *contre-*, *dé-*, *é-*, *extra-*, *hyper-*, *hypo-*, *in-*, *infra-*, *inter-*, ...). The migration often involves a reanalysis of the original base/derivative connections in order to produce a description compatible with Démonette$_{v2}$'s principles. Moreover, new information, new connections and new lexemes may be added (semi-)automatically in order to extend derivational families.

3.1 Overview

Démonette$_{v2}$ implements the fundamental features of ParaDis. In other words, the structure of this database is based on the following principles, some of which being already implemented in the Démonette$_{v1}$ prototype.

- each *entry* describes a relation between two lexemes of a derivational family: the same lexeme therefore intervenes in as many entries of the base as it has relations within its family,

- each entry is *annotated* with respect to the relation and to each of the two related lexemes,

- the description of a *lexeme* is stable because it is independent of the connections it takes part. It consists of a standardized written form, a part-of-speech, an inflectional paradigm (in IPA format), and an ontological type, selected among the 25 WordNet *Unique Beginners (UB)* (Miller et al. 1990)),

- *relations* are defined by three independent sets of properties: structural ones (characterization of the morphological connection itself), formal ones (formal pattern of each lexeme and stem variation, if any) and semantic ones (semantic type of the relation and glosses that mutually defines the two lexemes).

The remaining of the paper presents the architecture of Démonette$_{v2}$ and its formal, structural and semantic parts. The reader can refer to (Namer et al. 2017) for a presentation of the morpho-phonological properties. We mainly show how this structure allows families to be grouped into formal, semantic and derivational networks and will ultimately provides a large-scale description of the paradigmatic organization of the morphologically complex lexicon that takes into account meaning-form discrepancies.

3.2 Regular Paradigms in Démonette$_{v2}$

Let us consider the five families of Tab.4. Each one is built around a verb predicate (*laver* 'wash'), and includes an iterative verb (*relaver* 're-wash'), the action nouns of the two predicates (*lavage* 'washing', *relavage* 're-washing'), and an adjective indicating potentiality (*lavable* 'wash-able'). In French, action nouns may be constructed by conversion rule (*découper* / *découpe*) or suffixation, in which case several exponents are available (*-age*, *-ment*, *-ion*, *-ure*, ...). However, the same formal process is used for the nominalization of the simple predicate and the iterative predicate. The derivational relations between the five members of each family in Tab.4 are all regular because they all are formally and semantically motivated. These relations form complete oriented graphs with 2×10 edges. Each edge is an entry in the Démonette$_{v2}$ DDB.

X_V	$X(suf)_N$	reX_V	$reX(suf)_N$	$Xable_A$
laver 'wash'	lav**age**	relaver	relav**age**	lavable
classer 'rank'	classe**ment**	reclasser	reclasse**ment**	classable
planter 'plant'	plant**ation**	replanter	replant**ation**	plantable
souder 'weld'	soud**ure**	resouder	resoud**ure**	soudable
découper 'cut (out)'	découpe	redécouper	redécoupe	découpable

Table 4: (X_V, reX_V, Xsuf, reXsuf, $Xable$) families in French.

Tab.5 describes the way each relation in the family of *laver* is labelled in Démonette$_{v2}$[3]. This description involves four features: `Ori(entation)` and `Co(mplexity)` identify the relation's structure, whereas `Sch(ema)`$_{L1}$ and `Sch(ema)`$_{L2}$ encode the formal patterns L1 and L2 match within this relation. For a given (L1, L2) entry, `Ori` indicates whether L1 is the ancestor of L2 (`a2d` value), whether L2 is the ancestor of L1 (`d2a` value) or whether there is an `ind(irect)` relation between them. Note that the feature `Ori=ind` characterizes formations with an affix replacement (Tab.1-d), for example in the follower/ideology relations as in Tab.2. The `Co` feature describes the number of morphological steps necessary to reach L2 from L1. In the case of a regular derivation, its value is `si(mple)` when one of the two lexemes is the base of the other, or when both have a common base; the value `co(mplex)` is used in the other cases. `Sch`$_{L1}$ and `Sch`$_{L2}$ indicate which exponents are needed in the relation to go from L1 to L2: X represents the sequence they have in common in this context.

L1	L2	Sch$_{L1}$	Sch$_{L2}$	Ori	Co	L1	L2	Sch$_{L1}$	Sch$_{L2}$	Ori	Co
laver	*lavage*	X	Xage	a2d	si	*laver*	*relavage*	X	reXage	a2d	co
laver	*relaver*	X	reX	a2d	si	*laver*	*lavable*	X	Xable	a2d	si
lavage	*relavage*	X	reX	a2d	si	*lavage*	*relaver*	Xage	reX	ind	si
lavage	*lavable*	Xage	Xable	ind	si	*relavage*	*relaver*	Xage	X	d2a	si
relavage	*lavable*	reXage	Xable	ind	co	*relaver*	*lavable*	reX	Xable	ind	si

Table 5: Démonette$_{v2}$ – Encoding structural and formal properties in the family of *laver*

When `Complexity=simple`, the formal description of the relation is coupled with a semantic annotation (Tab.6). This provides information on the semantic value of the relation (`RSem`), for instance `syn(onymy)`, `iter(ation)` or `pot(entiality)`, for the relations in Tab.4. Semantic descriptions also include a paraphrase defining the two related words with respect to each other. For instance, the gloss for (*lavage*, *lavable*) is: "`One can perform` lavage `on` something `if it is` lavable"). The generalization of such paraphrases (col. 6) is obtained by replacing the words L1 and L2 by their ontological types (cols. 3 and 4). The derivational relations in the other families of Tab.4 are annotated structurally, formally and semantically in the same way. The generalization made on all the features allows families to align and paradigmatic regularities to emerge.

3.3 Meaning-form discrepancies in Démonette$_{v2}$

So far, we have shown how the architecture of Démonette$_{v2}$ allows for the representation of classical and regular derivations (*laver/lavage*), but also derivations with some meaning-form mismatches summarized in the Tab.1: conversion and overabundance are dealt with by the autonomy of features in the (L1, L2) relation, the semantic types (`RelSem`) being independent from the formal structures (`Sch`$_{Li}$). It is also able to deal with polysemy and affix replacement, , the latter being identified by the feature `Orientation=indirect`.

---

[3]For reasons of space, word pair are listed in only one direction. The description of $L2 \rightarrow L1$ is symmetrical to that of $L1 \rightarrow L2$: the values of Sch$_{L1}$ and Sch$_{L2}$ and of TySem$_{L1}$ and TySem$_{L2}$ are inverted (Tab.5, Tab.6); the value `a2d` substitutes for `d2a` and vice-versa for the feature `Complexity` (Tab.5); the values of the other features are unchanged.

L1	L2	TySem$_{L1}$	TySem$_{L2}$	RSem	Def_abs
laver	*lavage*	Act$_{V1}$	Act$_{N2}$	syn	'To Act$_{V1}$ sth is to perform Act$_{N2}$'
relavage	*relaver*	Act$_{V1}$	Act$_{N2}$		'To Act$_{V2}$ sth is to perform Act$_{N1}$'
laver	*relaver*	Act$_{V1}$	Act$_{V2}$		'To Act$_{V1}$ smth several times is to Act$_{V2}$ it'
lavage	*relavage*	Act$_{N1}$	Act$_{N2}$	iter	'To perform several Act$_{N1}$ is to perform Act$_{N2}$'
lavage	*relaver*	Act$_{N1}$	Act$_{V2}$		'To perform several Act$_{N1}$ is to Act$_{V2}$'
laver	*lavable*	Act$_{V1}$	Mod$_{A2}$		'One can Act$_{V1}$ sth if it is Mod$_{A2}$'
lavage	*lavable*	Act$_{N1}$	Mod$_{A2}$	pot	'One can perform Act$_{N1}$ on sth if it is Mod$_{A2}$'
relaver	*lavable*	Act$_{V1}$	Mod$_{A2}$		'One can Act$_{V1}$ several times sth if it is Mod$_{A2}$'

Table 6: Démonette$_{v2}$ – Encoding semantic properties in the family of *laver*

In Démonette$_{v2}$, derivational families can be reconstructed from the network of direct and indirect relations that connect its members. Then, families can be grouped into semantic (resp. formal) paradigms if the (L1, L2) relations included in the families are aligned (Co and Ori values are identical), and belong to the same semantic (resp. formal) series, i.e. share the same values for TySem$_{L1}$, TySem$_{L2}$, RSem and Def_abs (resp. for Sch$_{L1}$ and Sch$_{L2}$). The paradigms may include sub-paradigms made up of partial families.

Démonette$_{v2}$ can also represent paradigms with heterogeneous connections, such as those in Tab.3. The set of features we use allows for the compartmentalization of the descriptions into formal, structural, semantic and phonological levels. The analysis of meaning-form discrepancies then does not require any modification in the architecture. We only need two additional values, f(ormal)-m(otivation) and s(emantic)-m(otivation), for the attribute Complexity. We illustrate their role with Tab.7. Each column corresponds to an entry of Démonette$_{v2}$. These entries connect the members of the morphological family of *banque$_N$*, as displayed in the lower part of Fig. 1. When the (L1, L2) relation is only formally motivated, it is encoded with the f-m value (col. 4) and does not involve a semantic description. On the other hand, the value s-m (col. 3) signals a semantically grounded relation with no formal motivation. Recall that regular relations like *banque/bancaire* are noted Co=simple (col.1): in other words, this value merges f-m and s-m [4].

L1 – L2	*banque – bancaire*	*banque – interbancaire*	*bancaire – interbancaire*
Sch$_1$/Sch$_2$	X$_N$/Xaire$_A$	X$_N$/interXaire$_A$	X$_A$/interX$_A$
Ori	a2d	a2d	a2d
Co	si	**s-m**	**f-m**
SemRel	relation	space interval	–
Def.	'Smth bancaire pertains to the bank'	'Smth interbancaire relates to several banks'	–

Table 7: Démonette$_{v2}$ entries for the family of *banque$_N$*

With s-m and f-m, Démonette$_{v2}$ can independently represent formal and semantic paradigms just as in ParaDis and thus becomes a large-scale formalization of this model: a relation with Complexity=f-m only belongs to the formal network (no semantic counterpart) while a relation with Complexity =s-m only belongs to the semantic network.

4 Conclusion

We have presented Démonette$_{v2}$ and its theoretical background. This resource is under development, and therefore the results we have presented are still partial. The WF principles we choose follow from the

---

[4]The same features are used for the description of the members of the other families in Tab.3.

objectives of the database. Our goal is to provide a semantically and formally homogeneous description of morphologically constructed French words, formed by regular derivations as well as non-canonical WFR. One way to achieve this goal is to combine the contributions of lexeme-based morphology and paradigmatic models of derivation.

This work also shows how a lexical resource and a theoretical model can cross-fertilize even if our presentation mainly focused on the theoretical foundations of Démonette$_{v2}$. We therefore omitted other aspects of the database: among them, the edition and visualization platform, the devices operating a (partial) automatisation for the semantic annotations of the lexemes and the relations, the elaboration of the glosses, the automatic extension of families. For the last task, several approaches are envisaged, including the formalization of linguistic reasoning, the implementation of neural networks or the application of formal concept analysis (Leeuwenberg et al. 2015). We have also left aside the conversion of the content of Démonette$_{v2}$ in order to meet the needs of the different uses of the database, by reseachers and students interested in morphology, elementary school teachers, speech-language pathologists specialized in language acquisition disorders. All these topics are ongoing research. Their results will be published in future.

Acknowledgments

This work benefited from the support of the project DEMONEXT ANR-17-CE23-0005 of the French National Research Agency (ANR). We wish to thank the partners of DEMONEXT, and especially Lucie Barque and Pauline Haas who have also taken part in the results presented in this paper.

References

Stephen R. Anderson. 1992. *A-Morphous Morphology*. Cambridge University Press, Cambridge, UK.

Vesna Antoniova and Pavol Štekauer. 2015. Derivational paradigms within selected conceptual fields – contrastive research. *Facta Universitatis, Series: Linguistics and Literature* 13(2):61–75.

Mark Aronoff. 1976. *Word Formation in Generative Grammar*. Linguistic Inquiry Monographs. MIT Press, Cambridge, MA.

Delphine Bernhard, Bruno Cartoni, and Delphine Tribout. 2011. A task-based evaluation of French morphological resources and tools. *Linguistic Issues in Language Technology* 5(2).

Harry Bochner. 1993. *Simplicity in generative morphology*. Mouton de Gruyter, Berlin & New-York.

Olivier Bonami and Jana Strnadová. 2019. Paradigm structure and predictability in derivational morphology. *Morphology* 29(2):167–197.

Geert Booij. 2010. *Construction Morphology*. Oxford University Press, Oxford.

Geert Booij and Francesca Masini. 2015. The role of second order schemas in the construction of complex words. In Laurie Bauer, Lívia Körtvélyessy, and Pavol Štekauer, editors, *Semantics of complex words*, Springer, Heidelberg, volume 47, pages 47–66.

Greville G. Corbett. 2010. Canonical derivational morphology. *Word Structure* 3(2):141–155.

Ryan Cotterell and Hinrich Schütze. 2017. Joint semantic synthesis and morphological analysis of the derived word. *CoRR* abs/1701.00946. http://arxiv.org/abs/1701.00946.

Mathias Creutz and Krista Lagus. 2005. Unsupervised morpheme segmentation and morphology induction from text corpora using Morfessor 1.0. Technical Report A81, Helsinki University of Technology.

Bernard Fradin. 2003. *Nouvelles approches en morphologie*. PUF, Paris.

John Goldsmith. 2001. Unsupervised learning of the morphology of natural language. *Computational Linguistics* 27(2):153–198.

Nabil Hathout. 2009. Acquisition of morphological families and derivational series from a machine readable dictionary. In Fabio Montermini, Gilles Boyé, and Jesse Tseng, editors, *Selected Proceedings of the 6th Décembrettes: Morphology in Bordeaux*. Cascadilla Proceedings Project, Somerville, MA.

Nabil Hathout. 2011. Une approche topologique de la construction des mots : propositions théoriques et application à la préfixation en *anti-*. In *Des unités morphologiques au lexique*, Hermès Science-Lavoisier, Paris, pages 251–318.

Nabil Hathout and Fiammetta Namer. 2014a. Démonette, a French derivational morpho-semantic network. *Linguistic Issues in Language Technology* 11(5):125–168.

Nabil Hathout and Fiammetta Namer. 2014b. Discrepancy between form and meaning in word formation: the case of over- and under-marking in French. In Franz Rainer, Wolfgang U. Dressler, Francesco Gardani, and Hans Christian Luschützky, editors, *Morphology and meaning*, John Benjamins, Amsterdam, pages 177–190.

Nabil Hathout and Fiammetta Namer. 2016. Giving lexical resources a second life: Démonette, a multi-sourced morpho-semantic network for french. In *Proceedings of the Tenth International Conference on Language Resources and Evaluation (LREC 2016)*.

Nabil Hathout and Fiammetta Namer. 2018. La parasynthèse à travers les modèles : des RCL au ParaDis. In Olivier Bonami, Gilles Boyé, Georgette Dal, Hélène Giraudo, and Fiammetta Namer, editors, *The lexeme in descriptive and theroretical morphology*, Language science Press, Berlin, Empirically Oriented Theoretical Morphology and Syntax, pages 365–399. http://langsci-press.org/catalog/book/165.

Charles Francis Hockett. 1954. Two models of linguistc descriptions. *Words* 10:210–234.

Jean-Pierre Koenig. 1999. *Lexical Relations*. CSLI Publications, Stanford, CA.

Lukáš Kyjánek. 2018. Morphological resources of derivational word-formation relations. Technical Report 61, ÚFAL - Charles University, Prague.

Artuur Leeuwenberg, Aleksey Buzmakov, Yannick Toussaint, and Amedeo Napoli. 2015. Exploring pattern structures of syntactic trees for relation extraction. *Lecture Notes in Artificial Intelligence (Subseries of Lecture Notes in Computer Science)* 9113:153–168. https://doi.org/10.1007/978-3-319-19545-2-10.

Georges A. Miller, Richard Beckwith, Christiane Fellbaum, Derek Gross, and Katherine J. Miller. 1990. Introduction to WordNet: An on-line lexical database. *International Journal of Lexicography* 3(4):335–391.

Fiammetta Namer. 2009. *Morphologie, lexique et traitement automatique des langues : L'analyseur DériF*. Hermès Science-Lavoisier, Paris.

Fiammetta Namer. 2013. A rule-based morphosemantic analyzer for French for a fine-grained semantic annotation of texts. In Cerstin Mahlow and Michael Piotrowski, editors, *SFCM 2013*, Springer, Heidelberg, CCIS 380, pages 93–115.

Fiammetta Namer, Nabil Hathout, and Stéphanie Lignon. 2017. Adding morpho-phonology into a french morpho-semantic resource: Demonette. In Eleonora Litta and Marco Passarotti, editors, *Proceedings of the First Workshop in Resources and Tools for Derivational Morphology (DeriMo),*. EDUCatt, Milano, Italy, pages 49–60.

Andrew Spencer. 2013. *Lexical relatedness*. Oxford University Press, Oxford.

Pavol Štekauer. 2014. Derivational paradigms. In Rochelle Lieber and Pavol Štekauer, editors, *The Oxford Handbook of Derivational Morphology*, Oxford, Oxford University Press, Oxford, pages 354–369.

Anna M Thornton. 2012. Reduction and maintenance of overabundance. a case study on italian verb paradigms. *Word Structure* 5(2):183–207.

Giuseppina Todaro. 2017. *Nomi (e aggettivi) che diventano verbi tramite prefissazione: quel che resta della parasintesi*. Ph.D. thesis, Tesi di dottorato, Università Roma Tre et Université Toulouse Jean-Jaurès.

Delphine Tribout. 2012. Verbal stem space and verb to noun conversion in french. *Word Structure* 5(1):109–128.

Semantic descriptions of French derivational relations in a families-and-paradigms framework

Daniele Sanacore
CLLE, CNRS
University of Toulouse
daniele.sanacore@univ-tlse2.fr

Nabil Hathout
CLLE, CNRS
University of Toulouse
Nabil.Hathout@univ-tlse2.fr

Fiammetta Namer
ATILF, CNRS
University of Lorraine
Fiammetta.Namer@univ-lorraine.fr

Abstract

This paper proposes a new way to represent morphosemantic regularities in derivational paradigms of French in the context of derivational morphology. Starting from what has already been done in Démonette, a derivational morphological lexical resource for French, we show how structures inspired by Frame Semantics and FrameNet could help with the problem of the efficient representation of morphosemantic regularities in derivational paradigms. This first phase of the experiment consisted in the representation of four French derivational subfamilies of the French lexicon with a frame-like structure in order to show how this approach could work.

1 Introduction

An increasing number of lexical resources containing word formation descriptions are currently developed for many languages. If we start from the basic assumption that morphology is the study of systematic covariation in the form and meaning of words (Haspelmath and Sims, 2013), one problem that remains unsolved in the context of derivational morphology is finding an efficient way to represent morphosemantic regularities that are present in the derivational lexicon. In this paper, we address this issue in the framework of paradigmatic morphology. The objective is to describe the morphosemantic relations contained in the lexicon and design semantic representations compatible with morphological resources that could be used in NLP and experimental linguistics. Starting from what has already been done with *Démonette* (Hathout and Namer, 2014, 2016), we propose a representation of paradigmatic regularities in the lexicon by using structures inspired by Frame Semantics (Fillmore et al., 2006) and used in resources like *FrameNet* (Baker et al., 1998). Although differences exist between the objectives of *FrameNet* (document the range of semantic and syntactic combinatory possibilities of each word in each of its senses through objects called "frames") and *Démonette* (representing morphological regularities in the lexicon) frame-like structures could help us achieve our objective.

2 Definitions

Derivational families.   A derivational family is a set of lexemes connected by morphological derivational relations (Hathout, 2009). This extensive definition includes also forms with suppletive stems (*hippodrome* 'racecourse' in the family of *cheval* 'horse'). An example of derivational family for French is the one built around the verb *laver* 'to wash' in (1):

(1) *laver* 'to wash'; *lavage* 'washing'; *lavoir* 'wash house'; *laverie* 'laundromat'; *laveur* 'washer (male)'; *laveuse* 'washer (female)'; *lavette* 'dishcloth'; *lavable* 'washable'; *lavement* 'enema'

In derivational families we can find two types of derivational relations between lexemes: direct relations and indirect relations. A **direct derivational relation** connects a lexeme directly

Proceedings of the 2nd Int. Workshop on Resources and Tools for Derivational Morphology (DeriMo 2019), pages 15–24,
Prague, Czechia, 19-20 September 2019.

with one of its descendants or ascendants in the derivational family, for instance *laver* 'to wash' and *laveur* 'washer (male)'. On the other hand, an **indirect derivational relation** connects more distant elements of the family, e.g *laveur* 'washer (male)' with *lavage* 'washing'. In fact, both *laveur* and *lavage* are derived from *laver*.

Paradigmatic systems. A paradigmatic system is a collection of (partial) families that are aligned in terms of the content-based relations that their members entertain (Bonami and Str-nadová, 2018). The CONTENT is the specification of the syntactic and semantic properties of a word, while the FORM is the specification of its phonology e/o orthography. The notion of paradigmatic system can be used both for inflectional and derivational morphology. An example of paradigmatic system can be illustrated by the following four subfamilies for the verbs *imprimer* 'to print', *souder* 'to weld', *laver* 'to wash' and *nettoyer* 'to clean':

(2)

verb	agent_m	adj	action noun
imprimer	imprimeur	imprimable	impression
souder	soudeur	soudable	soudage
laver	laveur	lavable	lavage
nettoyer	nettoyeur	nettoyable	nettoyage

The derivational relation between the verb *imprimer* and the masculine human agent noun *imprimeur* is the same as the derivational relations that link *souder* and *soudeur*, *laver* with *laveur* and *nettoyer* with *nettoyeur*. Another alignment can be found between the relations connecting the verbs with the derived modal adjective: the derivational relation between *imprimer* and *imprimable* is the same as the relation between *souder* and *soudable*, *laver* and *lavable* and *nettoyer* and *nettoyable*. Ultimately, a third alignment can be seen about the relations linking the verb (*imprimer, souder, laver, nettoyer*) with the respective action nouns (*impression, soudage, lavage, nettoyage*). It is important here to specify that the notion of alignment is based on content, rather than form. Pairs of words are aligned if they contrast in the same way. When an alignment of same derivational relations between couples of lexemes is found, these relations compose a **derivational series**.

3   Démonette

The problem of organizing morphosemantic description has been approached by resources like *Démonette* (Hathout et al., 2017; Hathout and Namer, 2014), a French derivational database. *Démonette* is a resource designed for the description of word formation in French. Its construction is based on the fundamental assumption that morphology is relational and each relation where a given word is involved contributes to its meaning. *Démonette* seeks a complete, redundant and explicit description of all the properties of each relation and each description of a relation is independent from the others. For this reason, entries in the *Démonette* database do not describe the properties of the derivatives, they describe instead properties of the derivational relations connecting two lexemes. Entries are thus pairs of morphologically related words (w_1,w_2) belonging to the same derivational family, such as *laver* → *laveur*.

Relations in *Démonette* are characterized by their orientation. *Démonette* is a directed graph where a relation (w_1 ← w_2) describes the morphological motivation of w_1 with respect to w_2. Most of the lexemes are connected with each other in both directions. (Hathout and Namer, 2016). Direct relations in *Démonette* may be descending or ascending: the first connect a derived lexeme to its base or to a more distant ascendant (*laver* ← *laveur*) while the latter connect a lexeme to its derivative or to a more distant descendant (*laveur* ← *laver*).

Among the existing fields used to describe derivational relations in the *Démonette* database, an important role is played by the four fields used for the semantic description. Currently, there are two fields expressing the semantic type of w_1 and w_2, one for the concrete definition giving the meaning of w_1 with respect to w_2 and one for the abstract definition where w_2 is replaced by its semantic type. Abstract definitions are important to highlight morphosemantic paradigms in the database. In fact, relations with the same abstract definition highlight regularities in the lexicon and form a derivational series, as in Table 1:

W1	W2	Type W1	Type W2	Concrete definition	Abstract definition
laveuse	laver	@AGF	@	"she who performs the action of laver "	"she who performs the action of @"
nettoyeuse	nettoyer	@AGF	@	"she who performs the action of nettoyer"	"she who performs the action of @"
imprimeuse	imprimer	@AGF	@	"she who performs the action of imprimer"	"she who performs the action of @"

Table 1: Semantic types, concrete and abstract definitions

For what concerns the semantic typing provided in Table 1, (e.g. @AGF for *laveuse, nettoyeuse* and *imprimeuse*), the problem is that it actually merges two levels of morphosemantic information: the ontological category of the described lexeme and its semantic role. Given that the ontological category of a lexeme is independent from the semantic role it plays with respect to the other member of the family, it is necessary to separate these two types of information. This is why the structure we propose in Section 6 is articulated on three levels: relational, argumental and ontological.

4   Frame Semantics and FrameNet

Frame Semantics is based on the fundamental assumption that people understand language by means of situations evoked in their mind by words. These representations of real world situations evoked in our mind are called **frames** (Fillmore et al., 1976). For instance, the *Apply_heat* frame describes a common situation involving a COOK, some FOOD and a COOKING_INSTRUMENT and is evoked by lexical units like *bake, blanch, boil, broil, brown, simmer* and *steam*. Lexical units are pairings of words with a meaning. Typically, each sense of a polysemous word belongs to a different frame (Ruppenhofer et al., 2006). For example, the lemma *bake.v* evokes three different frames:

- APPLY_HEAT: Michelle *baked* the potatoes for 45 minutes

- COOKING_CREATION: Michelle *baked* her mother a cake for her birthday

- ABSORB_HEAT: The potatoes have to *bake* for more than 30 minutes

The implementation of Frame Semantics is *FrameNet*, an English lexicon which relates words to their meanings (via the "frames" that they activate) and records the way in which sentences and phrases are structured around them. The main objectives of *FrameNet* are: characterize frames, find the words that evoke those frames, develop a descriptive terminology for each frame and extract sample sentences. Once a frame is defined, it can be used to annotate selected examples from a corpus and to derive valence descriptions for the lexical units involved in the frame itself.

Frames thus represent story fragments, which are evoked by a given set of lexical units (a pairing of a word with a given sense). Each frame is characterised by a certain number of participants involved in it, called **frame elements**. If we take for example the term *avenger* in *FrameNet*, we can see that it evokes the REVENGE frame, whose definition is provided in (3):

(3) An **Avenger** performs a **Punishment** on a **Offender** as a consequence of an earlier action by the Offender, the **Injury**. The **Avenger** inflicting the **Punishment** needs not be the same as the **Injured_party** who suffered the **Injury**, but the **Avenger** does have to share the judgment that the **Offender**'s action was wrong. The judgment that the **Offender** had inflicted an **Injury** is made without regard to the law.

Sentences instantiating this frame:

a. They took REVENGE for the deaths of two loyalist prisoners.
('They' realizes AVENGER and 'for the deaths of two loyalist prisoners' realizes INJURY)

b. Lachlan went out to AVENGE them.
('Lachlan' realizes AVENGER while 'them' realizes INJURED_ PARTY)

c. The next day, the Roman forces took REVENGE on their enemies.
('on their enemies' realizes OFFENDER)

As we can see in (3), the situation is presented by a global definition that shows the core frame elements involved and how they relate with each other. *FrameNet* also provides the non-core frame elements for each frame, which are optional frame elements. For the REVENGE frame, these elements are DEGREE, INSTRUMENT, MANNER, PLACE and PURPOSE. After the global definition of the frame, some example sentences as in (a, b, c) are usually provided in order to show the type of sentences that may instantiate the frame. The second part in the frame representation shown in (4) is composed by partial sentences describing the individual role of each core frame element.

(4) AVENGER: The **Avenger** exacts revenge from the **Offender** for the **Injury**.
e.g. We want to AVENGE her ('We' realizes AVENGER)

INJURED_PARTY: This frame element identifies the constituent that encodes who or what suffered the **Injury** at the hands of the **Offender**.
e.g. Sam's brothers AVENGED him ('him' realizes INJURED_PARTY)

INJURY: The **Injury** is the injurious action committed by the **Offender** against the **Injured_Party**. This Frame Element needs not always to be realized, although it is conceptually necessary.
e.g. The team sought REVENGE for their 4-1 defeat last night ('for their 4-1 defeat last night' realizes INJURY)

OFFENDER: The **Offender** has committed the earlier **Injury** for which the **Avenger** seeks revenge
e.g. Marie took terrible REVENGE on Trevor ('Trevor' realizes OFFENDER)

PUNISHMENT: The **Avenger** carries out a **Punishment** in order to exact revenge on the **Offender**
e.g. The team took REVENGE with a resounding victory ('with a resounding victory' realizes PUNISHMENT)

Frames also provide information for what concerns the semantic types of the frame elements, even though not all the elements are associated to a semantic category. As far as the REVENGE frame is concerned, the semantic types associated with frame elements (both core and non-core) are provided in (5).

	AVENGER	Sentient
	INSTRUMENT	Physical entity
(5)	PURPOSE	State_of_Affairs
	MANNER	Manner
	PLACE	Locative_relation

Last but not least, *FrameNet* also lists all the lexical units that can evoke the frame. For example, for the REVENGE frame, these lexical units are presented in (6):

(6) *avenge.v, avenger.n, get back (at).v, get even.v, payback.n, retaliate.v, retaliation.n, retribution.n, retributive.a, retributory.a, revenge.n, revenge.v, revengeful.a, revenger.n, sanction.n, vengeance.n, vengeful.a, vindictive.a*

5 How could frames be used for morphosemantic description?

As we have seen, *FrameNet* manages to represent a given conceptual situation in an unique object with frames. For what concerns us, our objective is to find a semantic representation for derivational families in a paradigmatic context. One aspect to keep in mind is that *FrameNet* is a resource for English, while *Démonette* is a lexical resource for French.

We can interpret the elements of the derivational family like frame elements in *FrameNet* and put the lexemes of a family in a frame-like structure. In a second moment, we can find other families that fit the same structure and align them, in order highlight regularities in the lexicon and represent a paradigmatic system.

(7) *FrameNet*:

An **Avenger** performs a **Punishment** on a **Offender** as a consequence of an earlier action by the Offender, the **Injury**...

(8) *Démonette*:

Un **laveur lave** quelque chose dans un **lavoir**...
'A washer washes something in a wash house...'

After having created frame-like structures with two or more elements of a derivational family like in (8), we can create an abstract definition by replacing the lexemes with their ontological type and semantic role in square brackets, as in (9):

(9) *Démonette*:

Un **[agent;human][predicate;activity]** quelque chose dans un **[place;artifact]**
'A [agent;human][predicate;activity] something in a [place;artifact]'

We would then have a number of other derivational subfamilies that fit the structure in (9), where the elements of the family would align with the abstract definition like in a paradigmatic system. The next section shows how four derivational families in French could be represented with a frame-like structure.

6 Building a frame-like structure for morphosemantic description

The first family taken as example is the partial family of *laver*, composed by the elements in (10), associated with a morphologically constructed meaning:

(10)	laver	-
	laveur, laveuse	person who washes
	lavoir, laverie	public place where people do the laundry
	lavette	hard sponge used for washing
	lavable	able to be washed
	lavement	procedure / medicinal product for the intestinal washing
	lavage	action or result of the action of washing

As explained in section 3, the description of the derivational family must be structured on three levels of analysis: ontological (which semantic types can be associated to the family elements), relational (how the family elements relate with each other in the sentence) and argumental (which kind of semantic roles are instantiated by the family elements).

6.1   Ontological level

In order to associate the member of the derivational families to a semantic type, a reference ontology needs to be chosen. The basic ontology we used are the **unique beginners for nouns** proposed by Wordnet (Miller, 1995), a large database of English that groups nouns, verbs and adjectives into sets of cognitive synonyms (synsets). In the taxonomy used by Wordnet for nouns, the unique beginners are 25 semantic primes that cover distinct conceptual and lexical domains (Miller et al., 1990). The complete list can be found in (11):

(11)			
act, activity	communication	motivation, motive	process
animal, fauna	event, happening	natural object	quantity, amount
artifact	feeling, emotion	natural phenomenon	relation
attribute	food	person, human being	shape
body	group, grouping	plant, flora	state
cognition, knowledge	location	possession	substance
time			

On the ontological level of the representation we propose, each lexeme in a family is associated with a unique beginner, as for the case of *laver* illustrated in (12):

(12)	**laver**	activity
	lavage	activity
	laveur, laveuse	human
	lavoir, laverie	artifact
	lavable	attribute
	lavette	artifact
	lavement	substance

6.2   Relational level

The information provided on the relational level shows how the family elements relate to each other by means of sentences like those of *FrameNet* including two or more members of a derivational family. Sentences in (13) contain two elements of the family:

(13) a. Un **laveur lave** quelque chose
　　 b. Une **laveuse lave** quelque chose
　　 'A washer washes something'

　　 c. Quelque chose est **lavable** si on peut la **laver**
　　 'Something is washable if it can be washed'

d. On **lave** quelque chose dans une **laverie**
'Something is washed in a laundromat'
e. On **lave** quelque chose dans un **lavoir**
'Something is washed in a wash house'

f. Un **laveur** procède au **lavage** de quelque chose
g. Une **laveuse** procède au **lavage** de quelque chose
'A washer does the washing of something'

h. On réalise un **lavage** quand on **lave** quelque chose
'A washing is realised when we wash something'

i. On pratique un **lavage** sur quelque chose qui est **lavable**
'The washing is done on something that can be washed'

j. Un **lavement lave** l'intestin
'An enema washes the intestine'

k. On realise le **lavage** de quelque chose avec une **lavette**
'We do the washing of something with a dishcloth'

If we take a look at the binary sentences we have constructed, we can see that certain elements will be easier to put together (LAVEUR, LAVEUSE, LAVAGE, LAVETTE), on the other hand it will be almost impossible to combine LAVEMENT with the others, being it a lexeme which refers to a specific medical procedure.

In (14) we present some examples of sentences with three or four elements we can compose:

(14) a. Un **laveur lave** quelque chose dans un **lavoir**
b. Une **laveuse lave** quelque chose dans un **lavoir**
'A washer washes something in a wash house'

c. Quelque chose est **lavable** si un **laveur** peut la **laver**
d. Quelque chose est **lavable** si une **laveuse** peut la **laver**
'Something is washable if a washer can wash it'

e. Un **laveur** fait le **lavage** de quelque chose avec une **lavette**
f. Une **laveuse** fait le **lavage** de quelque chose avec une **lavette**
'A washer does the washing of something with a dishcloth'

g. Un **laveur lave** quelque chose dans un **lavoir** avec une **lavette**
h. Une **laveuse lave** quelque chose dans un **lavoir** avec une **lavette**
'A washer washes something in a wash house with a dishcloth'

6.3 Argumental level

The representation also provides the semantic role of each element with respect to the other members of the family. The argumental level associates the element of the family with their role in the argumental structure, which has been deducted from the category of relation where they are inscribed.

(15)

laver	predicate
lavage	pred. with support verb (pratiquer/faire)
laveur/laveuse	agent
lavoir/laverie	place
lavette	instrument
lavable	modifier

Relating *lavement,* it results to be difficult to place it in the same structure with the other elements of the subfamily because it poses a polisemy problem: the sense of *laver* in relation with *lavement* is not the same as *laver* when it is considered in relation with the other elements of the family. This is why it needs to be considered separately, since the only relation where it is involved is the one with *laver*:

(16)

laver	predicate
lavement	pred. with support verb (administrer/faire)

6.4 Catching paradigmatic generalizations

Our frame-like representation is also fit for the representation of the paradigmatic organization of the derivational lexicon. We tested the structure we built for *laver* on three other subfamilies: *observer* 'to observe', *imprimer* 'to print' and *nettoyer* 'to clean'. The three families we chose are articulated around verbs concerning human activities, like *laver.* In table 2 we present the other three subfamilies:

observer 'to observe'	observateur , 'observer(m.)'	observatrice 'observer' (f.)	observation , 'observation'	observable 'observable'	observatoire 'observatory'
imprimer 'to print'	imprimeur 'printer'(m.)	imprimeuse 'printer' (f.)	impression 'printing'	imprimable 'printable'	imprimerie 'copy shop'
nettoyer 'to clean'	nettoyeur 'cleaner' (m.)	nettoyeuse 'cleaner' (f.)	nettoyage 'cleaning'	nettoyable 'cleanable'	—

Table 2: (sub) families of *observer, imprimer* and *nettoyer*

The alignment in Table 2 can be extended to the relational level as in from tables 3 to table 10. The bottom line in each table provides an abstract definition where the lexemes are abstracted by the combination of the semantic role and the ontological type in square brackets.

Un **laveur**	**lave**	quelque chose
Un **nettoyeur**	**nettoie**	quelque chose
Un **observateur**	**observe**	quelque chose
Un **imprimeur**	**imprime**	quelque chose
Un **[agent; human m.]**	**[predicate; activity]**	quelque chose

Table 3: masculine human agent and activity

Une **laveuse**	**lave**	quelque chose
Une **nettoyeuse**	**nettoie**	quelque chose
Une **observatrice**	**observe**	quelque chose
Une **imprimeuse**	**imprime**	quelque chose
Une **[agent; human f.]**	**[predicate; activity]**	quelque chose

Table 4: feminine human agent and activity

On **lave**	quelque chose dans une	**laverie** **lavoir**
On **imprime**	quelque chose dans une	**imprimerie**
On **observe**	quelque chose dans un	**observatoire**
On **nettoye**	quelque chose dans un	**?**
On **[predicate;activity]**	quelque chose dans un/une	**[place; artifact]**

Table 5: activity and artifact

Quelque chose	est **lavable**	si on peut	la **laver**
Quelque chose	est **imprimable**	si on peut	l'**imprimer**
Quelque chose	est **observable**	si on peut	l'**observer**
Quelque chose	est **nettoyable**	si on peut	la **nettoyer**
Quelque chose	est [**modifier; attribute**]	si on peut	la/le/l' [**predicate; activity**]

Table 6: attribute and activity

The alignments in tables 3, 4 and 6 are complete, while in table 5 the family of *nettoyer* lacks a member denoting the place where the cleaning takes place. Sentences containing three elements could be aligned similarly:

Un **imprimeur**	**imprime**	quelque chose	dans une **imprimerie**
Un **observateur**	**observe**	quelque chose	dans un **observatoire**
Un **laveur**	**lave**	quelque chose	dans une **laverie**
Un **nettoyeur**	**nettoie**	quelque chose	dans une ?
Un [**agent; human m.**]	[**predicate; activity**]	quelque chose	dans un/une [**place; artifact**]

Table 7: human masculine agent, activity and artifact

Une **imprimeuse**	**imprime**	quelque chose	dans une **imprimerie**
Une **observatrice**	**observe**	quelque chose	dans un **observatoire**
Une **laveuse**	**lave**	quelque chose	dans une **laverie**
Une **nettoyeuse**	**nettoie**	quelque chose	dans une ?
Une [**agent; human f.**]	[**predicate; activity**]	quelque chose	dans un/une [**place; artifact**]

Table 8: human feminine agent, activity and artifact

Quelque chose est	**imprimable**	si un **imprimeur**	peut l'**imprimer**
Quelque chose est	**observable**	si un **observateur**	peut l'**observer**
Quelque chose est	**lavable**	si un **laveur**	peut la **laver**
Quelque chose est	**nettoyable**	si un **nettoyeur**	peut la **nettoyer**
Quelque chose	est [**modifier; potentiality**]	si un [**agent; human m.**]	peut la/l' [**predicate; activity**]

Table 9: Modifier, human masculine agent and activity

Quelque chose est	**imprimable**	si une **imprimeuse**	peut l'**imprimer**
Quelque chose est	**observable**	si une **observatrice**	peut l'**observer**
Quelque chose est	**lavable**	si une **laveuse**	peut la **laver**
Quelque chose est	**nettoyable**	si une **nettoyeuse**	peut la **nettoyer**
Quelque chose	est [**modifier; potentiality**]	si une [**agent; human f.**]	peut la/l' [**predicate; activity**]

Table 10: Modifier, human feminine agent and activity

As we can see, the alignment in Table 7 and Table 8 is partial due to the absence in the family of *nettoyer* of a lexeme denoting the location where the action takes place. In Table 9 and Table 10, on the other hand, the alignment works for the four families.

7   Conclusions

We showed that semantic frames used by *FrameNet* can be easily adapted to represent a derivational family and can also represent alignments of families and derivational paradigms. The next step consists in developing a program capable of building frame-like representations from lexical, lexicographic and distributional data.

Acknowledgements

This work benefited from the support of the project DEMONEXT ANR-17-CE23-0005 of the French National Research Agency (ANR).

References

Baker, C. F., Fillmore, C. J., and Lowe, J. B. (1998). The Berkeley Framenet project. In *Proceedings of the 17th international conference on Computational linguistics-Volume 1*, pages 86–90. Association for Computational Linguistics.

Bonami, O. and Strnadová, J. (2018). Paradigm structure and predictability in derivational morphology. *Morphology*, pages 1–31.

Fillmore, C. J. et al. (1976). Frame semantics and the nature of language. In *Annals of the New York Academy of Sciences: Conference on the origin and development of language and speech*, volume 280, pages 20–32.

Fillmore, C. J. et al. (2006). Frame semantics. *Cognitive linguistics: Basic readings*, pages 373–400.

Haspelmath, M. and Sims, A. (2013). *Understanding morphology*, pages 2–3. Routledge.

Hathout, N. (2009). Acquisition of morphological families and derivational series from a machine readable dictionary.

Hathout, N. and Namer, F. (2014). Démonette, a french derivational morpho-semantic network. *LiLT (Linguistic Issues in Language Technology)*, 11.

Hathout, N. and Namer, F. (2016). Giving lexical resources a second life: Démonette, a multi-sourced morpho-semantic network for french. In *Language Ressources and Evaluation Conference*.

Hathout, N., Namer, F., and Lignon, S. (2017). Adding morpho-phonological features to a french morphosemantic resource: the demonette derivational database. In *Workshop on Resources and Tools for Derivational Morphology (DeriMo)*.

Miller, G. A. (1995). Wordnet: a lexical database for english. *Communications of the ACM*, 38(11):39–41.

Miller, G. A., Beckwith, R., Fellbaum, C., Gross, D., and Miller, K. J. (1990). Introduction to wordnet: An on-line lexical database. *International journal of lexicography*, 3(4):235–244.

Ruppenhofer, J., Ellsworth, M., Schwarzer-Petruck, M., Johnson, C. R., and Scheffczyk, J. (2006). Framenet ii: Extended theory and practice.

Correlation between the gradability of Latin adjectives and the ability to form qualitative abstract nouns

Lucie Pultrová
Institute of Greek and Latin Studies
Faculty of Arts
Charles University (Prague)
Lucie.Pultrova@ff.cuni.cz

Abstract

Comparison is distinctly limited in scope among grammatical categories in that it is unable, for semantic reasons, to produce comparative and superlative forms for many representatives of the word class to which it applies as a category (adjectives and their derived adverbs). In Latin and other dead languages, it is non-trivial to decide with certainty whether an adjective is gradable or not: being non-native speakers, we cannot rely on linguistic intuition; nor can a definitive answer be reached by consulting the corpus of Latin texts (the fact that an item is not attested in the surviving corpus obviously does not mean that it did not exist in Latin). What needs to be found are properties of adjectives correlated with gradability/ non-gradability that are directly discernible at the level of written language. The present contribution gives one such property, showing that there is a strong correlation between gradability and the ability of an adjective to form abstract nouns.

1   Comparison: conceptual vs grammatical category

Comparison is a grammatical category that has for a long time practically escaped the attention of linguists studying Latin. Only relatively recently were detailed studies published on the phenomenon of comparison on a cognitive and functional basis,[1] investigating how two or more entities could be compared in a language, what patterns are used in these various ways of comparison in Latin, and what different meanings comparatives and superlatives may have. These studies clearly demonstrate – which is true in other languages as well – that it does not hold that comparison in Latin is always carried out using the forms of comparative and superlative, nor does it hold that comparatives and superlatives always perform the basic function of simple comparison of two or more entities. It follows that it is useful, even necessary, as with other grammatical categories, to differentiate between comparison on the one hand as a conceptual category that is expressed at the level of the whole proposition ("Paul is higher than John" = "John is not as high as Paul"), and on the other hand comparison as a grammatical/morphological category ("the formal modification of some predicative word – most often an adjective – representing a parameter of gradation or comparison"[2]). The present author is currently working on a monograph that examines the morphological category of Latin comparison. Put simply, she does not ask which means may be employed in Latin to express comparison, but how the forms of comparative and superlative are used. The present contribution deals with one question falling within the scope of this work.

2   Specific nature of category of comparison

The grammatical category of comparison is distinctly limited, not being able to produce the forms of comparative and superlative from all the representatives of the word class to which it applies as a category (i.e. adjectives and their derived adverbs). A certain degree of limitation is not exceptional in itself (e.g. in the category of number there are singularia tantum and pluralia tantum; in the category of verb voice, intransitive verbs, for instance, cannot form personal passive forms; etc.); however, comparison is restricted to an exceptional degree. For example, according to the *Czech National Corpus*,

---

[1] Bertocchi & Orlandini, 1996; Espinilla, Quetglas & Torrego, 2002; Cuzzolin, 2011.
[2] Cuzzolin & Lehmann, 2004: 1212.

in Czech – a language very similar to Classical Latin in its range of inflections – just 6% (!) of adjectives have degree forms, and only 3% have both degrees of comparison.[3]

A defining property of gradability is whether the adjective denotes a quality that can be measured, or, in other words, that can be expressed on a **scale**. Such adjectives are called **scalar** and only these (or, more precisely, only the scalar meanings of the individual adjectives – as a given adjective can have both a scalar and non-scalar meaning) are gradable.[4] In the modern classification of adjectives, scalarity is a fundamental property.

The fact that gradation may be relevant only for a small minority of adjectives raises the question of whether the term of grammatical category is still applicable. Where the borderline lies between being "already" a grammatical phenomenon or "still" a lexical/word-formative one is always a subjective matter to a certain extent, depending on the choice of criteria, or, better, on the weight ascribed to individual criteria.[5] Mere counting of the gradable elements of the class of adjectives suggests that comparison cannot be regarded as grammatical category. On the other hand, linguistic use (and common sense) sees comparison (it would probably be more correct to use the term gradability) as a basic adjectival grammatical category.[6] To address this seeming discrepancy, the concept of **centre** and **periphery** developed by members of the Prague Linguistic Circle[7] may be used, according to which no class is continuous: a class contains central elements, which exhibit all its characteristic features, and peripheral elements, which may lack some of these features. In this sense gradability is thus a defining characteristic of the class of adjectives: gradable adjectives stand at its centre, while the size of the periphery varies across languages. For example, Czech has an extremely large periphery, as it has, for instance, a very extensive derivation of adjectives of appurtenance (also from proper names), and even grammaticalized possessive adjectives of the type *otcův* 'father's'/ *matčin* 'mother's'. By contrast, English has a considerably smaller periphery compared to the centre: where Czech uses non-gradable adjectives, English prefers a noun in the genitive or a prepositional phrase. The fact that English is – for better or worse – the main language of reference in general linguistics may lead to formulations within the category of comparison that might be perceived as inaccurate by researchers interested primarily in other languages.[8]

3   Category of comparison in Latin

As concerns Latin, the periphery within the category of adjectives is presumed on theoretical grounds not to be as wide as in Czech (unlike Czech, Latin does not have grammaticalized possessive adjectives), but, on the other hand, this periphery is certainly more extensive than in English. Work with Latin linguistic material supports this view. Based on extensive excerption (described in more detail below in 3.1), estimates give that degree forms are attested in less than 14% of Latin adjectives while both degrees, comparative and superlative, are found in less than 7% of adjectives. Naturally, these figures obtained purely from literary texts, which moreover originate from an extremely large time span over a vast territory, cannot be taken as similarly statistically significant as figures obtained from modern corpora, immeasurably more extensive and containing both written and spoken texts; nevertheless, for Latin, this is as good as it gets, and even these figures, especially when looking at individual adjectives or adjectival types in more detail, clearly confirm the highly limited scope of this grammatical category in Latin.

---

[3] Cvrček et al., 2015: 249; www.korpus.cz.

[4] The scale may be of various types – see in particular Kennedy & Mc Nally, 2005.

[5] Another complication in our specific situation, however, is the problematic definition of the word class of adjectives itself, which – if at all defined in a language – is most often defined syntactically (as "modifiers of nouns"); thus there are practically always significant overlaps with other word classes (substantives, verbs, numerals, pronouns).

[6] E.g. Karlsson, 2000: 650: "One of the defining characteristics of adjectives in languages with appropriate inflection is the propensity to be gradable, in particular to have comparative and superlative forms."

[7] Especially Daneš, 1966; Neustupný, 1966.

[8] The quote given above in note 6 continues: "However, there are **several** stative or absolute adjectives normally lacking these forms…"

3.1 Employed Latin language corpus and its limitations

The linguistic material was gathered as follows: All the forms labelled as adjectives were excerpted from the *Oxford Latin Dictionary*, in total numbering almost exactly 10,000. For each of these adjectives (and adverbs derived therefrom, plus some isolated adverbs), an individual search was carried out in the database *Bibliotheca Teubneriana Latina III*[9] to find out whether the adjective is attested in synthetic comparative and/or superlative form, and also whether it is attested in periphrastic comparative and/or superlative form (in combination with the adverbs *magis* and *maxime*).

Despite the extensive scope of the excerpted material, its informative value is limited as it draws only on literary texts. On the other hand, such language material when dealing with the issue of comparison of adjectives carries a certain advantage when compared to modern languages, where it is basically always possible to "create" a form of comparative and superlative; this is, however, often at a price, as in modern languages a native speaker is able to invent an artificial context in which to use such a derivation. The Latin corpus is very comprehensive and varied in genre, and as such reflects authentic vocabulary on a large scale, while at the same time excludes similarly artificial derivations – it is thus in fact a relatively good source for this type of research.

Another significant limitation of statistics based on this corpus lies in the fact that the aggregate figures reported do not differentiate between a primary text and its citation – so e.g. Vergil's (*Aen.* I,199) *o passi graviora* occurs twelve times in the researched corpus due to its appearance in the texts of later commentators. Such cases were encountered relatively frequently, although rarely are the secondary citations so numerous.

3.2 Problems with defining scalarity in a dead language

In living languages, whether a given adjective (or rather its concrete meaning) is scalar may be determined by tests based on the ability of adjectives with a certain type of scale to be modified by only certain types of modifier.[10] Such tests draw on language data and always require the experience of a native speaker – whether this is the researcher him or herself, who introspectively poses a question as to the acceptability of a particular phrase, or another native speaker to whom the same question is posed. The native speaker then answers whether he or she considers grammatical, or at least acceptable, the comparative or superlative form of the given adjective in a particular context, and likewise for the connection of the given adjective with a particular modifier; the answers are used to determine if the adjective is scalar. Based on these results drawing on the assessment of primary data, the classification of scalar adjectives may be attempted.

Naturally, this procedure cannot be used when dealing with dead languages due to the absence of its key element – a native speaker. The method of a corpus probe is also problematic: despite its enormous scope when compared with other dead languages, the corpus of Latin texts has fundamental limitations (see 3.1 above) and the information that could be drawn therefrom is by no means comparable to that obtainable from modern corpora. This holds in particular for negatively formulated questions: put simply, the fact that an item is not attested in the surviving corpus does not mean that it did not exist in Latin when it was a living language. The fact that an adjective is not attested in the corpus in either degree form does not mean that the adjective is non-gradable. Moreover, not being native Latin speakers ourselves, to rely on our own language intuition in our understanding of the concrete meaning of an adjective can be very deceptive.

Work with extant Latin language material alone cannot by itself yield a cogent classification of scalar adjectives in Latin: such a classification needs to be based on already existing scalar classifications for modern languages, which can then be applied to concrete Latin adjectival types. In my work I have been using the adjective classification of Lehečková (2011) for Czech, a language very similar to Latin in its range of inflection and derivation. This classification is given schematically in the following table (explanatory notes and examples are drawn from those given by Lehečková):

---

[9] The search concerned only texts dating from the earliest records through to the 5th century AD, including Priscianus.

[10] E.g. proportional adverbs such as *half, completely* can be connected only with adjectives with a "closed scale", while common degree adverbs such as *very* only with the adjectives with an "open scale" (*completely full – very long*, but not *??very full – ??completely long*); see Kennedy & Mc Nally, 2005: 352; Kennedy, 2007; Rotstein & Winter, 2004; Yoon, 1996.

Adjectives					
non-restrictive	**restrictive**				
= adjectives that do not add to the intension (defining properties) of the noun they modify, having rather a deictic function, relating to a referential point given by or in the text, e.g. *today's, following, above-mentioned*	= adjectives that add to the intension (defining properties) of the noun they modify				
	absolute			**relative**[11]	
	relational	**scalar – complementary**[12]		**neutral**[13]	**scalar – polar**
	= adjectives that ascribe a property of a certain type to an object that distinguishes it from other objects having a different property of this type, e.g. for 'material' properties, *wooden/concrete floor*, or *wooden/metal table*	**maximal** e.g. *full, empty, clean*	**minimal** e.g. *dangerous, dirty*	e.g. *a 5-km-long way*	e.g. *long – short*

The various subtypes of adjective are not clearly demarcated. Non-restrictive and absolute relational adjectives are non-scalar; the other subtypes are scalar, with various specificities.

The present work with Latin material thus does not aim to develop its own classification but has an entirely practical objective: to offer guidelines to Latin users as to which adjective can be graded and which cannot (as personal linguistic intuition cannot be relied on in a second, non-native language). The main goal therefore (and that of the monograph in preparation mentioned in Section 1 above) is to **find elements that correlate with gradability/non-gradability** and that are **directly discernible at the level of written text** (e.g. specific suffixes or prefixes). The present contribution introduces one partial result: the correlation discovered between gradability and the ability of an adjective to form abstract nouns.

3.3 Correlation between gradability and the ability to form abstract nouns

In the language corpus described in Subsection 3.1 above, a correlation was identified between occurrence of gradable forms of adjectives and the existence of abstract nouns derived from these adjectives. Substantives with the following suffixes were excerpted:

-tudo (type *magnitudo* < *magnus*)
-tas (type *caritas* < *carus*)
-ia (type *clementia* < *clemens*)
-itia (type *iustitia* < *iustus*)

---

[11] A defining characteristic of relative adjectives is that they are – in contrast with absolute adjectives – context-dependent (*long hair* has a different length than *long nails*).

[12] Complementary scalar adjectives have a "closed scale", i.e. the quality they denote can reach an extreme point ("absolutely [of a kind]"). On the other hand, polar scalar adjectives have an "open scale": the quality they denote has no extreme point (nothing can be *??completely long* – always only *very long*); cf. note 10 above.

[13] The term "neutral" is not considered ideal even by Lehečková herself (2011: 91); the difference between "neutral" and "scalar-polar" adjectives lies in that the former, unlike the latter, are not evaluative.

The results are summarized in the following table:

suffix	number of abstract nouns with the given suffix that also have their base adjectives attested in the corpus	number of the corresponding base adjectives with an attested form of comparative and/or superlative	percentage
-itia	31	31	**100%**
-tudo	87	82	**94%**
-ia	168 (63 *-ia*, 105 *-ntia*)	136 (55 *-ia*, 81 *-ntia*)	**81%** **(87% *-ia*, 77% *-ntia*)**
-tas	434	334	**77%**

Compared with the proportion of adjectives in the whole corpus that have attested degree forms (less than 14% – see the introduction to Section 3 above), the proportion of adjectives able to form abstract nouns that have attested comparison is very high. The individual word-formative types will be discussed in more detail in the following subsections.

3.3.1 Suffix *-itia*

As can be seen from the table, abstract nouns derived by the suffix *-itia* are formed with no exception from adjectives that are attested to be gradable. In general, they are frequent adjectives, denoting psychological or physical qualities of people or things: *amicus, avarus, blandus, durus, ignotus, immundus, impudicus, impurus, inimicus, iniustus, iustus, laetus, lautus, lentus, maestus, mollis, mundus, nequam, niger, notus, piger, planus, pudicus, purus, saevus, scaber, segnis, spurcus, stultus, tristis, vafer.*

3.3.2 Suffix *-tudo*

In the researched corpus, there are in total 87 abstract nouns derived by the suffix *-tudo*. The correlation between the derivation of qualitative abstracts by the suffix *-tudo* and gradability of corresponding adjectives[14] is again quite considerable. Here also the adjectives are in general relatively frequent. Included among the abstract nouns in *-tudo* are nouns that are attested only once in a fragment from an Archaic author, e.g. *geminitudo, squalitudo, desertitudo* and others. Almost two thirds of abstract nouns in *-tudo* (56 in total) have competing counterparts in Classical Latin in the form of abstract nouns with other suffixes, the vast majority being those with suffix *-tas*; apparently, the suffix *-tudo* had lost its productivity in favour of the suffix *-tas*.

The five adjectives that form abstract nouns by the suffix *-tudo* while not having attested forms of comparison are the following:

perperus 'perverse': this adjective is attested only once in the whole corpus, and unreliably (Acc. *carm. frg.* 23), so no judgement as to its gradability or non-gradability may be reached;

canus 'white, whitened': in its basic meaning this is a restrictive absolute relational adjective, but in a transformed sense it has the meaning of 'old' (< 'white- or grey-haired'), i.e. relative/ scalar – polar; it

---

[14] I intentionally do not write "adjectives from which the abstract nouns are derived": from the formal point of view, it sometimes appears that the immediate founding word is not the adjective itself but a verb with the meaning of change of state (e.g. *consuetudo* < *consuesco*; *aritudo* < *aresco* [x *aridus*] etc.); the meaning of the abstract noun could then be understood as a result of this change of state.

is from this sense that the abstract noun is formed (*canitudo* 'greyness of hair'); presumably the adjective is gradable in this sense as well, but the number of occurrences of the adjective with this meaning is too low to be certain;

tabidus 'wasting away, melting away, decaying' and its abstract noun *tabitudo* 'emaciation' differ semantically from other members of the group: *tabitudo* does not denote a property but the result of an action, and, primarily, *tabidus* has, given the meaning of its root, an evidently "actual" character: it does not denote a permanent property; rather, it is synonymous with the participle *tabens* (cf. Subsection 3.3.3 below); as such, it cannot be graded;

· *lippus* 'having watery or inflamed eyes' and the abstract noun *lippitudo* 'inflammation or watering of the eyes' have a semantically non-standard mutual relation: the meaning of the abstract noun corresponds better to another meaning of the adjective, 'watery or inflamed (of the eyes themselves)', which is also attested, but with extremely few occurrences; the latter meaning of the given adjective is presumably gradable (whereas the more frequent, transferred possessive meaning is not);

lassus 'mentally tired' is an adjective with no instances of comparison in over 300 occurrences in the employed corpus. It must be confessed that why this adjective should be non-gradable, given its meaning, remains obscure.

3.3.3   Suffix *-ia*

This derivational type has two subtypes: abstract nouns derived from adjectives (participles) with the suffix *-nt-*, i.e. with the complex suffix *-ntia*, and abstract nouns from other types of adjectives.

-ntia

Adjectives with the suffix *-nt-* have the function of active imperfective participles, so functionally they are closer to verbs. Indeed, it is questionable whether they should be classed as adjectives in Latin at all, but if so then they must be non-restrictive adjectives. Nevertheless, many of these adjectives in certain contexts and depending on the type of the verb lose their verbal characteristics and may denote a permanent property.[15] For example, besides the basic participial meaning of 'that produces something' *efficiens* also has the (much less frequent in the corpus) adjectival (non-actual) meaning of 'capable of acting'. It is often very difficult to distinguish whether the *nt*-form functions as a participle or as a common adjective in a given sentence. This fact had two significant implications for our work with this type of adjective. First, in building the corpus for analysis it was found that in the *Oxford Latin Dictionary* (see 3.1 above) only some forms in *-nt-* have their own entry as an adjective, the others being only implicitly classed with the corresponding verbs. The criteria for deciding whether to give an independent entry are, to my knowledge, nowhere described, but it seems that an important reason for creating such an entry (that is, evidence of adjectival use of the given form) was the existence of attested graded forms. Only the adjectives in *-nt-* that have their own entry in the dictionary were excerpted into the basic file for our analysis; consequently, a considerable number of non-gradable adjectives were actually not included.[16] The second problem, pertaining directly to the research question addressed in this study, is that even the abstract nouns as such may accordingly have two meanings: one derived from an *nt*-form with a verbal meaning (participle), that is – depending on the meaning of the verb – "the act of -ing" or "being in a state of …"; the other derived from the same form with an adjectival meaning, that is, with the meaning of "the quality of being [of a kind]". The former example is thus not one of a qualitative abstract noun, but of an action noun.

---

[15] Cf. Pinkster, 2005: 61.

[16] As a result, the proportion of attested comparison for the group of adjectives in *-nt-* in the analysed corpus is 38.1%, which significantly exceeds the average proportion of 14% – see the introduction to Section 3 above. This is indeed a high proportion considering that many of the excerpted forms in *-nt-* have extremely low total frequency. (This also applies to various compounds created *ad hoc* such as *suaveolens* 'sweet-smelling', *semisonans* 'half-vocalized', etc.)

Of the total number of 105 substantives with the suffix *-ntia*, 24 corresponding adjectives[17] do not have attested comparison. However, 10 of these occur in the researched corpus with such low frequency that the fact that there are no attested instances of comparative or superlative does not amount to evidence of their non-gradability:[18] *blandiloquens* (1), *breviloquens* (1), *displicens* (6). *fragrans* (10), *graveolens* (7). *incogitans* (3), *inconsequens* (10), *suaviloquens* (6), *irreverens* (11), *desipiens* (15). In another adjective, *despiciens* 'contemptuous', we in fact have attested evidence of gradability thanks to a phrase containing the adverb *tam* 'to such a degree': *nemo umquam tam sui despiciens fuit* (Cic. *de orat.* 2,364).

Frequency is, however, also a significant factor for the majority of the 13 remaining adjectives; despite the fact that they occur relatively frequently, a significant proportion of these occurrences are with verbal/participial meaning, while the number of occurrences with adjectival meaning, that is, those that might potentially attest gradability, is as low as in the adjectives listed in the previous paragraph. This applies to the adjectives *consequens, efficiens, intellegens (-lig-),*[19] *invidens, loquens, repugnans, resonans.* The adjectives *absens* and *volens* and the nouns derived therefrom have only verbal meanings.

For the remaining four adjectives we can find various – more or less convincing – reasons why gradability is not attested:

indifferens is in its basic sense of 'neither good nor bad' evidently a non-gradable adjective; the substantive *indifferentia* is not a standard abstract noun, being used in specific linguistic contexts as a technical term, meaning either 'synonymity' or 'variableness of the quantity of a syllable';

praepotens 'superior to others in power': gradability is prevented by the prefix *prae-*, which itself carries the meaning of higher degree – adjectives with this prefix are generally non-gradable in Latin;[20] the abstract noun *praepotentia* 'superior or outstanding power' is used only once in Apuleius and testifies to a certain semantic evacuation of the prefix (*praepotentia* means practically the same as *potentia*);

prodigus 'wasteful, extravagant; lavish; unbridled' is an adjective that – should we rely on its translations into modern languages – gives no reason for its non-gradability; nor can it be due to its low frequency – there are over 150 attested instances of the adjective; an explanation may lie in an inaccurate understanding of the semantics of the adjective that has probably (as for other Latin adjectives with the same suffix that for synchronically unclear reasons do not have attested instances of graded forms) considerably more "verbal" character than we are able to perceive through modern languages (corresponding to a perfect participle in the original sense of the word); the substantive *prodigentia* 'extravagance, prodigality' is attested only in Tacitus – it is thus probably just an item of his idiolect;

varians is, similarly to the adjective *indifferens* above, an adjective that in its basic meaning 'of many different colours; of many different kinds' is evidently non-gradable; the abstract noun *variantia* has the meaning of 'diversity, variety', and is apparently derived from the adjective with an already slightly shifted meaning – presumably in this semantics the adjective should be gradable, but the number of occurrences in the researched corpus is too small (the total number of occurrences of the adjective in its all meanings is 43).

---

[17] For the substantives *beneficentia, magnificentia* and *prodigentia*, it is *beneficus, magnificus* and *prodigus* that are regarded as the "corresponding" adjectives; in Classical Latin, the forms in *-nt-* are not used in the positive; however, the comparatives and superlatives are derived from this particular stem: *magnificentior, magnificentissimus.*

[18] The number in brackets corresponds to the number of occurrences in the whole analysed corpus, not including secondary citations. What may be considered a "sufficient", or, on the other hand, "low" frequency when working with the Latin corpus is very subjective, however. For the purposes of my work on the monograph referred to in Section 1, a random sample of relatively frequent adjectives gave a mean ratio of the total frequency of the given adjective to the frequency of its attested degree forms, which is 10 : 1. If an adjective has ten attested occurrences or more in the corpus, there is a significantly better than even chance that one of these instances might be in the form of comparative or superlative, supposing that the adjective were gradable. However, as concerns the forms in *-nt-*, we must use a higher figure since the category of gradability is only relevant for a smaller proportion of them (namely those with a non-verbal meaning).

[19] The comparative *intelligentior* is quite common in later Latin texts; however, in Classical texts, the "non-actual" meaning 'endowed with intelligence' is still very rare in this adjective, with the actual form of 'discerning, having keen understanding' being much more common.

[20] See André, 1951; Pultrová (to appear).

The remaining abstract nouns in *-ia* are derived mostly from common adjectives, occurring frequently in the researched corpus. Only 8 abstract nouns of this subtype are derived from adjectives that do not have any attested comparative or superlative form: *copia, desidia, discordia, immodestia, iniuria, invidia, v(a)esania, vinolentia (-nul-)*. The already high percentage correlation between attested gradability and existence of the abstract noun is in fact even higher than that indicated in the table above, because another two adjectives (*deses* and *discors*) have their gradability attested via phrases with the degree adverb *tam* (similar to the adjective *despiciens* above). A further pair of adjectives are extremely infrequent (**cops*, gen. *copis* and *iniurus*). Only four adjectives remain: *immodestus* 'lacking of restraint, licentious' has only 17 occurrences in the whole corpus, and thus its frequency is rather marginal for us to be able to claim that gradability of the adjective not being attested means it is not gradable. The adjective *invidus* 'bearing ill will' belongs to the same word-formative type as the adjective *prodigus* – and the comment on this adjective above applies here as well. The adjective *vaesanus* 'acting incontrollably, frenzied, mad' is among those adjectives that are not graded by suffixation because high intensity is expressed by their prefix (here *v(a)e-*; cf. the adjective *praepotens* above).[21] The same explanation also holds for the adjective *vinolentus* 'immoderate in one's consumption of wine': here the word-formative affix (in this case the suffix *-lent-*) has itself the meaning of excessiveness, which would make the use of the comparative or superlative suffix redundant (it must be said, nevertheless, that some other adjectives with the same suffix have attested occurrences of comparison, e.g. *opulentus* or *corpulentus*; the semantics of the suffix was probably no longer entirely clear in Classical Latin).

3.3.4 Suffix *-tas*

The suffix *-tas* gradually became the main productive suffix for the formation of abstract nouns in Latin. Functionally, it corresponds to the suffix *-ost* in Czech, which can derive neologisms from practically any type of restrictive adjective (including adjectival pronouns and numerals, e.g. *jakost < jaký* 'of what kind', *dvojitost < dvojitý* 'double', etc.). A similar situation obtains in Latin. The suffix *-tas* often competes with other abstract suffixes (see *-tudo* above); there are attested nouns derived even from very rare adjectives (e.g. *brocchus* 'projecting (of teeth)', or *vacivus* 'unoccupied'); the suffix can also derive abstract nouns from adjectival pronouns and numerals (*qualitas < qualis* 'of what kind', in the Late period e.g. *triplicitas < triplex* 'triple', etc.) and even from substantives (*autumnitas < autumnus* 'autumn', *captivitas < captivus* 'one taken captive') or from the superlative forms of adjectives (*maximitas, supremitas* etc.). In light of this, it is almost surprising that the correlation between the existence of the abstract noun and gradability of the founding form is so high.

3.3.5 Conclusions

Compared with the proportion of adjectives in the whole corpus that have attested degree forms (less than 14% – see the introduction to Section 3 above), the proportion of adjectives able to form abstract nouns by the suffixes *-itia*, *-tudo* and *-ia* (including *-ntia*) that have attested comparison is extremely high. The existence of an abstract noun derived from a given adjective by the mentioned suffixes therefore serves as a strong indicator of its ability to be graded.

   This correlation between gradability of an adjective and existence of a corresponding abstract noun seems to be very strong even in the case of abstract nouns with the most productive suffix *-tas*. Thus, Latin users may even in this case presume that the attested occurrence of a given abstract noun signals with relatively high probability that the founding adjective will be gradable. This statement is, however, only a superficial description of what can be observed from the Latin corpus, and has no solid support in linguistic theory. Abstract nouns with the suffix *-tas* may be derived from restrictive adjectives of all types in Latin. It is highly improbable that the proportion of non-restrictive adjectives (that at the same time never occur with a restrictive meaning) should be so high as to influence the statistics to such an extent (to decrease the overall proportion of gradable adjectives from the 77% observed for adjectives with corresponding abstract noun in *-tas* toward the proportion of 14% observed for all adjectives).

---

[21] See Pultrová (to appear).

Evidently, the nature of the researched corpus itself plays a role; first, it is after all smaller by an order of magnitude than the large corpora of modern languages (even the most frequent Latin adjectives only reach figures that the *Czech National Corpus* would label as being, at best, of "lower-middle" frequency[22]); second, and more importantly, it only reflects literary language, and a considerably conservative one. Extremely infrequent words and neologisms are significantly less represented there in comparison with corpora that are richer in genre and contain both published and spoken texts.

This article was written as part of the grant project GAČR 17-11247S "Comparison of adjectives in Latin".

References

Jacques André. 1951. Les adjectifs et adverbes à valeur intensive en *per-* er *prae-*. *Revue des études latines* 29: 121–154.

Alessandra Bertocchi and Anna Orlandini. 1996. Quelques aspects de la comparaison en latin. *Indogermanische Forschungen* 101: 195–232.

Pierluigi Cuzzolin and Christian Lehmann. 2004. Comparison and gradation. In Geert Booij et al. (eds.). *Morphologie / Morphology. Ein internationales Handbuch zur Flexion und Wortbildung / An International Handbook on Inflection and Word-Formation, vol. 2*. De Gruyter, Berlin and New York, pages 1212–1220.

Pierluigi Cuzzolin. 2011. Comparatives and superlatives. In Philip Baldi and Pierluigi Cuzzolin (eds.). *New Perspectives on Historical Latin Syntax, Vol. 4: Complex Sentences, Grammaticalization, Typology*. Mouton de Gruyter, Berlin, pages 549–659.

Václav Cvrček et al. 2013. *Mluvnice současné češtiny I. Jak se píše a jak se mluví*. Karolinum, Praha.

František Daneš. 1966. The Relation of Centre and Periphery as a Language Universal. In *Travaux linguistiques de Prague 2 Les problèmes du centre et de la périphérie du système de la langue*. Academia, Praha, pages 9–21.

Empar Espinilla, Pere J. Quetglas and Esperanza Torrego (eds.). 2002. *La comparación en latín*. Universidad Autónoma de Madrid and Universidad de Barcelona, Madrid and Barcelona.

Fred Karlsson. 2000. Defectivity. In Geert Booij et al. (eds.). *Morphologie / Morphology. Ein internationales Handbuch zur Flexion und Wortbildung / An International Handbook on Inflection and Word-Formation, vol. 1*. De Gruyter, Berlin and New York, pages 647–654.

Christopher Kennedy and Louise McNally. 2005. Scale structure, degree modification and the semantics of gradable predicates. *Language* 81(2): 345–381.

Christopher Kennedy. 2007. Vagueness and grammar: The semantics of relative and absolute gradable adjectives. *Linguistics and Philosophy* 30(1): 1–45.

Dominika Kováříková, Lucie Chlumská and Václav Cvrček. 2012. What belongs in a dictionary? The Example of Negation in Czech. In Ruth Vatvedt Fjeld and Julie Matilde Torjusen (eds.). *Proceedings of the 15th Euralex International Congress*. University of Oslo, Oslo, pages 822–827.

Eva Lehečková. 2011. *Teličnost a skalárnost deadjektivních sloves v češtině*. Filozofická fakulta Univerzity Karlovy, Praha.

Jiří V. Neustupný. 1966. On the Analysis of Linguistic Vagueness. In *Travaux linguistiques de Prague 2 Les problèmes du centre et de la périphérie du système de la langue*. Academia, Praha, pages 39–51.

---

[22] E.g. *magnus* 'big' has a little over 12000 occurrences in the whole researched Latin corpus, *bonus* 'good' has fewer than 9000 occurrences, *longus* 'long' fewer than 5500, while e.g. the *Czech National Corpus* (cf. e.g. Kováříková, Chlumská & Cvrček, 2012) works with the following frequencies in adjectives (A = little frequent, E = highly frequent): A 250–1249, B 1250–6249, C 6250–31249, D 31250–156249, E 156250+.

Lucie Pultrová (to appear). Comparison of Compound Adjectives in Latin.

Carmen Rotstein and Yoad Winter. 2004. Total Adjectives vs. Partial Adjectives: Scale Structure and Higher-Order Modifiers. *Natural Language Semantics* 12: 259–288.

Youngeun Yoon. 1996. Total and partial predicates and the weak and strong intepretations. *Natural Language Semantics* 4: 217–236.

The Treatment of Word Formation
in the LiLa Knowledge Base of Linguistic Resources for Latin

Eleonora Litta, Marco Passarotti, Francesco Mambrini
CIRCSE Research Centre
Università Cattolica del Sacro Cuore
Largo Gemelli, 1 - 20123 Milan, Italy
{eleonoramaria.litta}{marco.passarotti}{francesco.mambrini}@unicatt.it

Abstract

The *LiLa* project consists in the creation of a Knowledge Base of linguistic resources for Latin based on the Linked Data framework and aimed at reaching interoperability between them. To this goal, LiLa integrates all types of annotation applied to a particular word/text into a common representation where all linguistic information conveyed by a specific linguistic resource becomes accessible. The recent inclusion in the Knowledge Base of information on word formation raised a number of theoretical and practical issues concerning its treatment and representation. This paper discusses such issues, presents how they were addressed in the project and describes a number of use-case scenarios that employ the information on word formation made available in the LiLa Knowledge Base.

1 Introduction

The increasing quantity, complexity and diversity of available linguistic resources has led, in recent times, to a growing interest in the sustainability and interoperability of (annotated) corpora, dictionaries, thesauri, lexica and Natural Language Processing (NLP) tools (Ide and Pustejovsky, 2010). This, initially, led to the creation of databases and infrastructures hosting linguistic resources, like CLARIN,[1] DARIAH,[2] META-SHARE[3] and EAGLE.[4] These initiatives collect resources and tools, which can be used and queried from a single web portal, but they do not provide real interconnection between them. In fact, in order to make linguistic resources interoperable, all types of annotations applied to a particular word/text should be integrated into a common representation that enables access to the linguistic information conveyed in a linguistic resource or produced by an NLP tool (Chiarcos, 2012, p. 162).

To meet this need, the *LiLa* project's objective (2018-2023)[5] is to create a Knowledge Base of linguistic resources for Latin based on the Linked Data framework,[6] i.e. a collection of several data sets described using the same vocabulary and linked together. The ultimate goal of the project is to exploit to the fullest the wealth of linguistic resources and NLP tools for Latin developed so far, and to bridge the gap between raw language data, NLP and knowledge description (Declerck et al., 2012, p. 111).

The LiLa Knowledge Base is highly lexically-based: one of its core components is an extensive list of Latin lemmas extracted from the morphological analyser for Latin Lemlat. The portion of the lexical basis of Lemlat concerning Classical and Late Latin (43,432 lemmas) was recently enhanced with information on word formation taken from the Word Formation Latin lexicon (WFL) (Litta, 2018), which was also included in the Knowledge Base. This has raised a number of theoretical and practical issues concerning the treatment and representation of word formation in LiLa. This paper discusses such issues, presents how they were addressed in the project and describes a number of use-case scenarios that make use of the information on word formation made available in the LiLa Knowledge Base.

---

[1]http://www.clarin.eu
[2]http://www.dariah.eu
[3]http://www.meta-share.org/
[4]http://www.eagle-network.eu
[5]https://lila-erc.eu/
[6]See Tim Berners-Lee's note at https://www.w3.org/DesignIssues/LinkedData.html.

Proceedings of the 2nd Int. Workshop on Resources and Tools for Derivational Morphology (DeriMo 2019), pages 35–43,
Prague, Czechia, 19-20 September 2019.

2 The LiLa Knowledge Base

In order to achieve interoperability between distributed resources and tools, LiLa adopts a set of Semantic Web and Linked Data standards and practices. These include ontologies that describe linguistic annotation (OLiA, Chiarcos and Sukhareva, 2015), corpus annotation (NLP Interchange Format (NIF), Hellmann et al., 2013; CoNLL-RDF, Chiarcos and Fäth, 2017) and lexical resources (Lemon, Buitelaar et al., 2011; Ontolex[7]). Furthermore, following Bird and Liberman (2001), the Resource Description Framework (RDF) (Lassila et al., 1998) is used to encode graph-based data structures to represent linguistic annotations in terms of triples: (1) a predicate-property (a relation; in graph terms: a labeled edge) that connects (2) a subject (a resource; in graph terms: a labeled node) with (3) its object (another resource, or a literal, e.g. a string). The SPARQL Protocol and RDF Query Language (SPARQL) is used to query the data recorded in the form of RDF triples (Prud'Hommeaux et al., 2008).[8]

The highly lexically-based nature of the LiLa Knowledge Base results from a simple, fundamental assumption: textual resources are made of (occurrences of) words, lexical resources describe properties of words, and NLP tools process words. Particularly, the lemma is considered the ideal interconnection between lexical resources (such as dictionaries, thesauri and lexica), annotated corpora and NLP tools that lemmatise their input text. Lemmas are canonical forms of words that are used by dictionaries to cite lexical entries, and are produced by lemmatisers to analyse tokens in corpora. For this reason, the core of the LiLa Knowledge Base is represented by the collection of Latin lemmas taken from the morphological analyser Lemlat[9] (Passarotti et al., 2017), which has proven to cover more than 98% of the textual occurrences of the word forms recorded in the comprehensive *Thesaurus formarum totius latinitatis* (TFTL, Tombeur, 1998), which is based on a corpus of texts ranging from the beginnings of Latin literature to the present, for a total of more than 60 million words (Cecchini et al., 2018). Interoperability can be achieved by linking all entries in lexical resources and corpus tokens that refer to the same lemma, thus allowing a good balance between feasibility and granularity.

Figure 1 shows a simplified representation of the fundamental architecture of LiLa, highlighting the relations between the main components and the (meta)data providers of the Knowledge Base. The components of the Knowledge Base and their relations are formalised as classes of objects in an ontology. There are two nodes representing as many kinds of linguistic resources providing data and metadata: a) **Textual Resources**: they provide texts, which are made of **Tokens** (class: *Word*, as defined by the NIF vocabulary), i.e. occurrences of word forms (class: *Form*, as defined by Ontolex)[10]; b) **Lexical Resources**: they describe lexical items, which can include references to lemmas, e.g. in a bilingual dictionary, or to word forms, e.g. in a collection of forms like TFTL. A **Lemma** (class: *Lemma*, subclass of *Form*)) is an (inflected) **Form** conventionally chosen as the citation form for a lexical item. Both tokens and forms/lemmas are assigned **Morphological Features**, like part-of-speech (PoS), inflexional category and gender. Finally, **NLP tools** such as tokenisers, PoS taggers and morphological analysers can process respectively textual resources, tokens and forms.

Using the Lemma node as a pivot, it is thus possible to connect resources and make them interact, for instance by searching in different corpora all the occurrences of the forms of a lemma featuring some specific lexical properties (provided by one or more lexical resource).

3 The Word Formation Latin Lexicon

The WFL lexicon is a resource that deals with word formation in Classical and Late Latin. The lexicon is based on a set of word formation rules (WFRs) represented as directed one-to-many input-output relations between lemmas. The lexicon was devised according to the Item-and-Arrangement (I&A) model of morphological description (Hockett, 1954): lemmas are either non-derived lexical morphemes, or a concatenation of a base in combination with affixes. This theoretical model was chosen because it emphasises the semantic significance of affixal elements, and because it had been previously adopted by

---

[7]https://www.w3.org/community/ontolex/

[8]A prototype of the LiLa triplestore is available at https://lila-erc.eu/data/.

[9]https://github.com/CIRCSE/LEMLAT3

[10]The degree of overlapping between tokens and forms depend on the criteria for tokenisation applied. Given the morphosyntactic properties of Latin, in LiLa this overlapping is complete.

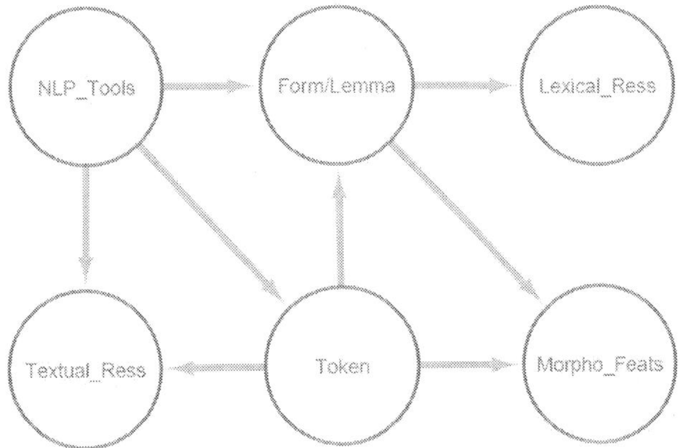

Figure 1: The fundamental architecture of LiLa.

other resources treating derivation, such as the morphological dictionaries Word Manager (Domenig and ten Hacken, 1992).

WFL is characterised by a step-by-step morphotactic approach: each word formation process is treated individually as the application of one single rule. For instance, the adjective *classiarius* 'of the fleet' is recorded in WFL as derived from the noun *classis* 'class, great division' via a WFR that creates denominal adjectives with the suffix *-ari*. In WFL, simple conversion (i.e. change of PoS without further affixation) is treated as a separate WFR, like in the case of the noun *classicum* 'trumpet-call' derived from the adjective *classicus* 'belonging to the highest class of citizens/connected with the fleet/with the trumpet call'. However, when considering formations involving both the attachment of an affix and a shift in PoS (as, for example, *classis>classiarius*), these are handled in one step. Each output lemma can only have one input lemma, unless the output lemma qualifies as a compound. This results in a hierarchical structure, whereby one or more lemmas derive from one ancestor lemma. A set of lemmas derived from one common ancestor is defined as a "word formation family". In the web application for querying the WFL lexicon, this hierarchical structure is represented in a directed graph resembling a tree.[11] In the graph of a word formation family, nodes are occupied by lemmas, and edges are labelled with a description of the WFR used to derive the output lemma from the input one. For instance, Figure 2 shows the derivation graph for the word formation family whose ancestor (or "root") lemma is *classis*.

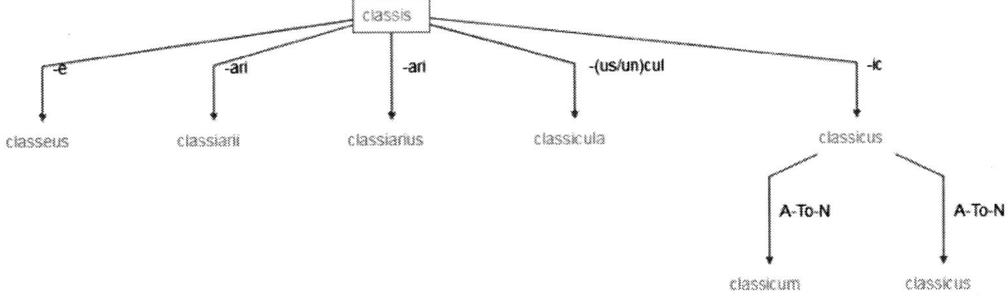

Figure 2: Derivation graph for the word formation family of *classis* in WFL.

However, portraying word formation processes via directed graphs has raised some significant theoretical issues, especially in cases where the derivational relation is ambiguous or unsuitable to be represented by a single step-by-step process, as shown in Budassi and Litta (2017). In such cases, WFL resorts to a series of tactics to work around the problem. When considering, to give an example, the relation between the verb *amo* 'to love', the noun *amicus* 'friend', and the adjective amicus 'friend', did the word formation process work like *amo > amicus* A > *amicus* N, or like *amo > amicus* N > *amicus* A? In cases like this, in which there has been a conversion from noun to adjective or the reverse, there is a lot of space for interpretation on which direction the change has happened from-to, and which between noun or adjective generated the children lemmas: *Oxford Latin Dictionary* (OLD) (Glare, 1982) is usually employed in the compilation of WFL to verify the provenance of lemmas, and reports how *amo > amicus* A > *amicus* N is the correct process. Even so, in other occasions it has been necessary to take some independent choices: for instance, OLD states that diminutive noun *amiculus* 'a pet friend' derives from the adjective *amicus*; we, however, chose to make it derive from noun *amicus* as it seems more probable that a diminutive noun was created to diminish a noun rather than an adjective. Another method used in WFL to work around non-linear derivations is the creation of "fictional" lemmas that act as placeholders between attested words in order to justify extra "mechanical" steps. The existence of these fictional lemmas has however proven to be less than ideal. User feedback has reported confusion and puzzlement at the existence of the fictional element in the derivational tree. Moreover, when browsing the data, the existence of fictional lemmas needs to be factored in. For instance, if looking for all lemmas created with the suffix *-bil* in WFL, 598 lemmas are given as a result.[12] In WFL, 103 of these are fictional lemmas (17% of the total number of lemmas derived using the *-bil* suffix), most of which were created to connect lemmas such as adverb *imperabiliter* 'authoritatively' to their "next of kin", verb *impero* 'to demand / to order'. Because in WFL it is not possible to connect two lemmas using two suffixes at the same time (*-bil* and *-ter*), adjective **imperabilis* was created as a further step in the word formation process. The presence of fictional lemmas in the WFL dataset means that when making general considerations on the distribution of the *-bil* suffix in Classical and Late Latin, for instance, one should keep in mind that a good portion of what is extracted from WFL needs to be discarded.

4 Word Formation in *LiLa*

The recent emergence of interest in the application of Word and Paradigm (W&P) models to derivational morphology led to the exploration of their potential in describing those processes that do not fit into a linear hierarchical structure. In particular, the theoretical framework of the word-(and sign)-based model known as Construction Morphology (CxM) (Booij, 2010), has been crucial for including the WFL data into the LiLa Knowledge Base.[13] CxM revolves around the central notion of "constructions", conventionalised pairings of form and meaning (Booij, 2010, p. 6). For example, the English noun *walker* is analysed in its internal structure as $[[\text{walk}]_V \text{ er}]_N \longleftrightarrow [\text{someone who walk}_V]_N$. Constructions may be hierarchically organised and abstracted into "schemas". The following schema, for instance, describes a generalisation of the construction of all words displaying the same morphological structure as *walker*, like for instance *buyer*, *player* and *reader*: $[[\text{x}]_{Vi} \text{er}]_{Nj} \longleftrightarrow [\text{someone who SEM}_{Vi}]_{Nj}$.[14]

CxM schemas are word-based and declarative, which means that they describe static generalisations, as opposed to explaining the procedure of change from one PoS to another like WFRs do (e.g. V-to-N *-er*), and are purely output-oriented. This is particularly fit for the needs of LiLa, as words are described into their formative elements, which can be organised into (connected) classes of objects in an ontology.

In particular, in the ontology the LiLa Knowledge Base is based on, three classes of objects are used for the treatment of derivational morphology: (1) Lemmas, (2) Affixes, divided into Prefixes and Suffixes, and (3) Bases. Bases are currently not assigned a further description, and play the role of connectors of the lemmas belonging to the same word formation family. Like any object in LiLa, Affixes and Bases are assigned a unique identifier. Each Affix is labelled with a citation form chosen to represent it in the Knowledge Base, while lemmas are connected to their Written Representation(s).

---

[12]These are in Latin adjectives that have generally instrumental (e.g. *terribilis* 'by whom/which one is terrified') and/or passive and potential meaning (e.g. *amabilis* 'which/who can be loved') (Kircher-Durand, 1991 and Litta, 2019).

[13]For a full description of the theoretical justification of why W&P approaches such as CxM can be advantageous in describing word formation in Latin see Litta and Budassi (Forthcoming).

[14]Subscript like *V*, *N*, *i* and *j* are traditionally used as placeholders for morphological (e.g. *V* and *N*) and semantic (e.g. *i* and *j*) features that are referred to elsewhere

These three classes of objects are connected to each other via labelled edges. A Lemma node is linked (a) to the Affix nodes that are part of its construction through the relationship `hasPrefix` or `hasSuffix` and (b) to its Base (or Bases, in the case of compounds) through the relationship `hasBase`. Lemmas are never related to each other, so as not to take assumptions on the direction of the formative process. Figure

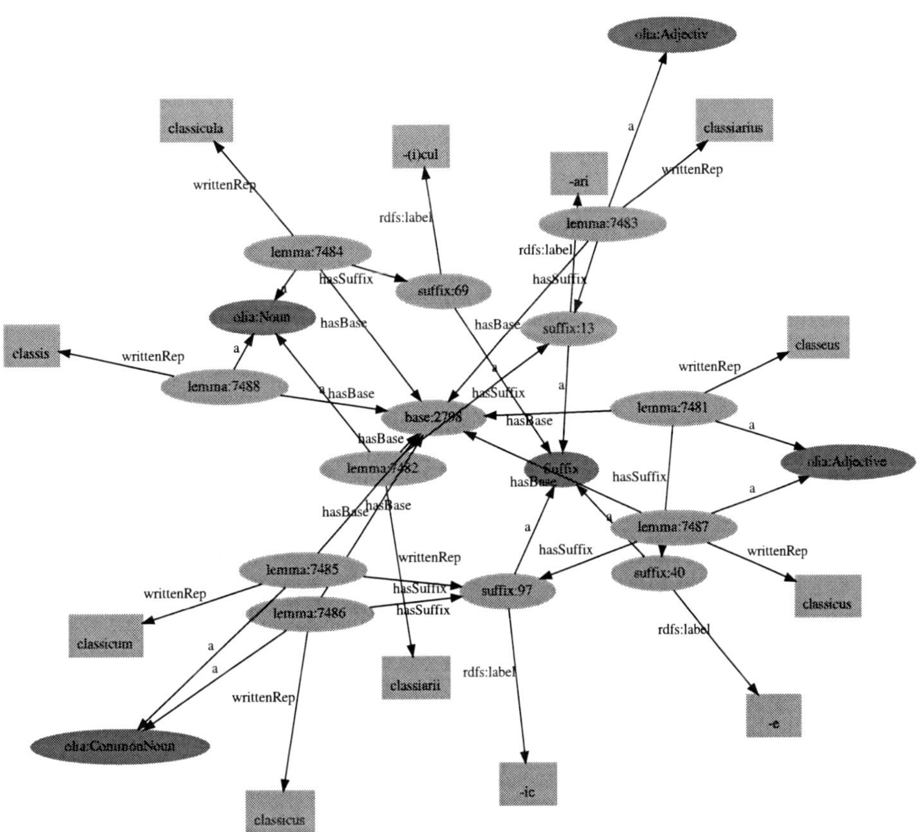

Figure 3: The word formation familiy of *classis* in LiLa.

3 shows the word formation family of *classis* as it is represented in LiLa. Nodes for Lemma objects are assigned a unique identifier and are connected to (a) their Written Representation, (b) their PoS, (c) a Base and (d) [optional] an Affix. For instance, lemma:7483 has Written Representation 'classiarius', PoS adjective (see the '(is-)a' edge connecting to the OLiA class olia:Adjective), suffix:13 (with Written representation 'ari') and base:2798. This Base node has 8 ingoing edges, one for each of the lemmas belonging to the word formation family *classis* belongs to. Conversion is not marked: lemmas such as *classicus* adjective and *classicum* noun are simply related to their Base and to the Suffix node *-ic*.

5   Use-case Scenarios

5.1   Inside Derivational Data

As it stands, querying the LiLa Knowledge Base can support a number of investigations on word formation that were not so comprehensively and instantly feasible before.

One of the most basic queries is the retrieval of all lemmas linked to the same lexical base (i.e. all the members of a word formation family) via the `hasBase` object property. The query starts by finding a given lemma, then identifies the lexical base linked to it, and finally lists all the other lemmas connected to the same base. Starting from the adjective *formalis* 'of a form, formal', 67 lemmas are retrieved,[15] These can be grouped by PoS: 32 adjectives (including e.g. *serpentiformis* 'shaped like a snake' and *uniformis* 'uniform'), 25 nouns (e.g. *forma* 'shape', *formella* 'mould' and *informator* 'one who shapes'), 9 verbs (e.g. *informo* 'to shape', 'to inform' and *reformo* 'to transform'), and 1 adverb (*ambiformiter* 'with double meaning').

Similar queries can be performed using affixes as starting points. These can be useful, as an example, when considering that the same affixes have a tendency to be frequently associated in complex words. The LiLa Knowledge Base allows accurate empirical evidence on which among affixes are more often found together in the same lemma. A query that performs this operation traverses all the lemmas in the LiLa Knowledge Base, counts all couplets of prefixes and/or suffixes, and finally reports statistics on those that are most frequently associated.

For example: with 121 instances, the most frequently associated prefixes in the LiLa lemma collection are *con-* and *in-* (with meaning of negation).[16] These two affixes are preponderantly found together in adjectives (96), such as *incommutabilis* 'unchangeable', less frequently nouns (23, e.g. *inconsequentia* 'lack of consistency') and adverbs (2, *incommote* 'immovably/firmly' and *incorribiliter* 'incorrigibly'). The association of (negative) *in-* prefix and *ex-* is however less frequent (79 lemmas); examples are for instance adjective *inefficax* 'unproductive' and noun *inexperientia* 'inexperience'.

As for suffixes, the most frequent association is that of *-(i)t* and *-(t)io(n)*, which are found in combination in 214 nouns such as *dissertatio* 'dissertation' and *excogitatio* 'a thinking out'. The second most attested combination (153 lemmas) involves again *-(i)t* and the suffix *-(t)or*, the latter mainly typical of agent or instrumental nouns. This association occurs in nouns like *dictator* 'dictator' and the adjective *gestatorius* 'that serves for carrying'.

The two most productive associations between a prefix and a suffix in LiLa are those between the negative *in-* prefix and the suffix *-bil* (296 lemmas, such as adjective *insuperabilis* 'that cannot be passed'), and between the prefix *con-* and the suffix *-(t)io(n)*, with 290 lemmas, which are mostly nouns like *contemplatio* 'viewing/contemplation' and *reconciliatio* 're-establishing'.

5.2 Outside Derivational Data

The data on word formation stored in the LiLa Knowledge Base can also be used to perform corpus-based queries. Users can use the link between lemmatised texts and the lemmas of the LiLa collection to maximum advantage to explore which are the most frequently occurring derivational morphemes in the textual resources connected so far in LiLa. These are three Latin treebanks, namely (1) the *Index Thomisticus* Treebank (IT-TB) (Passarotti, 2011), based on works written in the XIIIth century by Thomas Aquinas (approximately 400k nodes), (2) the PROIEL corpus (Haug and Jøhndal, 2008), which includes the entire New Testament in Latin (the so called *Vulgata* by Jerome) along with other prose texts of the Classical and Late Antique period and (3) the Late Latin Charter Treebank (Korkiakangas and Passarotti, 2011) (LLCT; around 250k nodes), a syntactically annotated corpus of original VIIIth-IXth century charters from Central Italy. Both the IT-TB and the PROIEL treebanks were queried in their Universal Dependencies (UD) version (Nivre et al., 2016).[17]

For instance, if we are looking for statistics on the incidence of verbs formed with prefixes *de-* and *ex-* in Latin texts, we can design a query to observe the distribution of the forms of such verbs in the corpora linked to the LiLa Knowledge Base. The results are shown in Table 1, where we report both the number of occurrences of any given verb formed with the two prefixes (Tokens), and of the different verbs attested (Lemmas).

The LiLa Knowledge Base can also be used to answer such questions as: what are the most frequent affixes in Latin texts? For instance, the use of prefixes and suffixes in the lexicon of the PROIEL corpus, the most balanced Latin treebank in terms of textual genres, can be observed with a SPARQL query that retrieves all tokens and all affixes linked with a LiLa lemma. The results are reported in Table 2. It can

---

[15]The starting word *formalis* is included in the count.

[16]In Latin there are two prefixes *in-*, respectively with negative and entering meaning.

[17]http://universaldependencies.org/

| | de- | | ex- | |
Corpus	Tokens	Lemmas	Tokens	Lemmas
IT-TB (UD)	1,274	59	1,326	76
PROIEL (UD)	1,011	128	1,328	152
LLCT	209	28	155	16

Table 1: Occurrences of verbs formed with the prefixes *de-* and *ex-* in the corpora linked to LiLa.

Affix	Type	Lemmas	Tokens
-(t)io(n)	Suffix	393	2,157
con-	Prefix	344	3,297
ad-	Suffix	201	2,514
e(x)-	Prefix	197	2,713
-i	Suffix	194	2,052
de-	Prefix	182	1,294
in (entering)-	Prefix	178	1,559
-(i)t	Suffix	158	1,275
-tas/tat	Suffix	157	1,582
re-	Prefix	151	1,858

Table 2: The 10 affixes most frequently associated with a token in the PROIEL corpus.

be noted that, while tokens of words derived with the suffix *-(t)io(n)* rank only in the fourth place and are considerably outnumbered by tokens formed with the prefix *con-*, the lemmas displaying the suffix *-(t)io(n)* outnumber all the others. Such distribution reflects the greater productivity of this suffix as recorded in WFL: 2,686 lemmas formed with *-(t)io(n)* vs. 748 with *con-*.

6 Conclusions

In this paper, we have described the treatment of word formation in the LiLa Knowledge Base, which links together distributed linguistic resources for Latin.

The information about derivational morphology recorded in the list of Latin lemmas of LiLa was taken from the WFL lexicon, which was built on the portion for Classical and Late Latin of the Lemlat's lexical basis. However, since LiLa is not meant to be limited to a specific era of Latin only, extending the coverage of WFL to the Medieval Latin lemmas included in Lemlat (around 86,000) represents a major next step in the coming years. Although probabilistic models can be used in the first phase of this task (like, for instance, the one described by Sumalvico, 2017), much manual work of disambiguation of the results, as well as to retrieve both false positives and negatives is expected.

Another potential development of the description of word formation in the LiLa Knowledge Base would be to assign some kind of linguistic information to the Base nodes, which are currently just empty connectors of lemmas belonging to the same word formation family. One possible solution could be to assign to each Base a Written Representation consisting of a string describing the lexical "element" that lies behind each lemma in the word formation family (e.g. DIC- for *dico* 'to say', or *dictio* 'a saying'). This procedure is however complicated by the fact that different bases can be used in the same word formation family: for example *fer-*, *tul-* and *lat-* can all be found as bases in the word formation family the verb *fero* 'to bring' belongs to.

Acknowledgements

This project has received funding from the European Research Council (ERC) under the European Union's Horizon 2020 research and innovation programme - Grant Agreement No 769994.

References

Steven Bird and Mark Liberman. 2001. A formal framework for linguistic annotation. *Speech communication* 33(1-2):23–60.

Geert Booij. 2010. Construction morphology. *Language and linguistics compass* 4(7):543–555.

Marco Budassi and Eleonora Litta. 2017. In Trouble with the Rules. Theoretical Issues Raised by the Insertion of -sc- Verbs into Word Formation Latin. In *Proceedings of the Workshop on Resources and Tools for Derivational Morphology (DeriMo)*. Educatt, pages 15–26.

Paul Buitelaar, Philipp Cimiano, John McCrae, Elena Montiel-Ponsoda, and Thierry Declerck. 2011. Ontology lexicalisation: The lemon perspective. In *WS 2 Workshop Extended Abstracts, 9th International Conference on Terminology and Artificial Intelligence*. pages 33–36.

Flavio Massimiliano Cecchini, Marco Passarotti, Paolo Ruffolo, Marinella Testori, Lia Draetta, Martina Fieromonte, Annarita Liano, Costanza Marini, and Giovanni Piantanida. 2018. Enhancing the Latin Morphological Analyser LEMLAT with a Medieval Latin Glossary. In Elena Cabrio, Alessandro Mazzei, and Fabio Tamburini, editors, *Proceedings of the Fifth Italian Conference on Computational Linguistics (CLiC-it 2018). 10-12 December 2018, Torino*. aAccademia university press, pages 87–92.

Christian Chiarcos. 2012. Interoperability of corpora and annotations. In *Linked Data in Linguistics*, Springer, pages 161–179.

Christian Chiarcos and Christian Fäth. 2017. CoNLL-RDF: Linked Corpora Done in an NLP-Friendly Way. In Jorge Gracia, Francis Bond, John P. McCrae, Paul Buitelaar, Christian Chiarcos, and Sebastian Hellmann, editors, *Language, Data, and Knowledge*. Springer International Publishing, Cham, pages 74–88. https://link.springer.com/content/pdf/10.1007%2F978-3-319-59888-8_6.pdf.

Christian Chiarcos and Maria Sukhareva. 2015. OLiA - Ontologies of Linguistic Annotation. *Semantic Web Journal* 6(4):379–386. http://www.semantic-web-journal.net/content/olia-%E2%80%93-ontologies-linguistic-annotation.

Thierry Declerck, Piroska Lendvai, Karlheinz Mörth, Gerhard Budin, and Tamás Váradi. 2012. Towards linked language data for digital humanities. In *Linked Data in Linguistics*, Springer, pages 109–116.

Mark Domenig and Pius ten Hacken. 1992. *Word Manager: A system for morphological dictionaries*, volume 1. Georg Olms Verlag AG, Hildesheim.

Peter GW Glare. 1982. *Oxford Latin dictionary*. Clarendon Press. Oxford University Press, Oxford, UK.

Dag TT Haug and Marius Jøhndal. 2008. Creating a parallel treebank of the old Indo-European Bible translations. In *Proceedings of the Second Workshop on Language Technology for Cultural Heritage Data (LaTeCH 2008)*. European Language Resources Association (ELRA), Marrakesh, Morocco, pages 27–34.

Sebastian Hellmann, Jens Lehmann, Sören Auer, and Martin Brümmer. 2013. Integrating NLP using Linked Data. In *12th International Semantic Web Conference, Sydney, Australia, October 21-25, 2013*. https://svn.aksw.org/papers/2013/ISWC_NIF/public.pdf.

Charles F. Hockett. 1954. Two Models of Grammatical Description. *Words* 10:210–231.

Nancy Ide and James Pustejovsky. 2010. What does interoperability mean, anyway. *Toward an Operational* .

Chantal Kircher-Durand. 1991. Syntax, morphology and semantics in the structuring of the Latin lexicon, as illustrated in the -lis derivatives. In Robert Coleman, editor, *New Studies in Latin Linguistics, Proceedings of the 4th International Colloquium on Latin Linguistics, Cambridge, April 1987*. John Benjamins, Cambridge.

Timo Korkiakangas and Marco Passarotti. 2011. Challenges in annotating medieval Latin charters. *Journal for Language Technology and Computational Linguistics* 26(2):103–114.

Ora Lassila, Ralph R. Swick, World Wide, and Web Consortium. 1998. Resource Description Framework (RDF) Model and Syntax Specification.

Eleonora Litta. 2018. Morphology Beyond Inflection. Building a Word Formation-Based Lexicon for Latin. In Paola Cotticelli-Kurras and Federico Giusfredi, editors, *Formal Representation and the Digital Humanities*. Cambridge Scholars Publishing, Newcastle upon Tyne, pages 97–114.

Eleonora Litta. 2019. On the Use of Latin -bilis Adjectives across Time. *Quaderni Borromaici. Saggi studi proposte* 6:149–62.

Eleonora Litta and Marco Budassi. Forthcoming. What we talk about when we talk about paradigms. In Jesús Fernández-Domínguez, Alexandra Bagasheva, and Cristina Lara-Clares, editors, *Paradigmatic relations in derivational morphology*.

Joakim Nivre, Marie-Catherine de Marneffe, Filip Ginter, Yoav Goldberg, Jan Hajič, Christopher Manning, Ryan McDonald, Slav Petrov, Sampo Pyysalo, Natalia Silveira, Reut Tsarfaty, and Daniel Zeman. 2016. Universal Dependencies v1: A Multilingual Treebank Collection. In *Proceedings of the Tenth International Conference on Language Resources and Evaluation (LREC 2016)*. European Language Resources Association (ELRA), Portorož, Slovenia, pages 1659–1666.

Marco Passarotti. 2011. Language resources. The state of the art of Latin and the *Index Thomisticus* treebank project. In Marie-Sol Ortola, editor, *Corpus anciens et Bases de données*. Presses universitaires de Nancy, Nancy, France, number 2 in ALIENTO. Échanges sapientiels en Méditerranée, pages 301–320.

Marco Passarotti, Marco Budassi, Eleonora Litta, and Paolo Ruffolo. 2017. The Lemlat 3.0 Package for Morphological Analysis of Latin. In *Proceedings of the NoDaLiDa 2017 Workshop on Processing Historical Language*. Linköping University Electronic Press, 133, pages 24–31.

Eric Prud'Hommeaux, Andy Seaborne, et al. 2008. Sparql query language for rdf. w3c. *Internet: https://www.w3.org/TR/rdf-sparql-query/[Accessed on February 27th, 2019]* .

Maciej Sumalvico. 2017. Unsupervised Learning of Morphology with Graph Sampling. In *Proceedings of the International Conference on Recent Advances in Natural Language Processing (RANLP 2017)*. Varna, Bulgaria.

Paul Tombeur. 1998. *Thesaurus formarum totius latinitatis a Plauto usque ad saeculum XXum*. Brepols, Turnhout, Belgium.

Combining Data-Intense and Compute-Intense Methods
for Fine-Grained Morphological Analyses

Petra Steiner
Friedrich-Schiller-Universität Jena
Jena, Germany
`petra.steiner@uni-jena.de`

Abstract

This article describes a hybrid approach for German derivational and compositional morphology. Its first module is based on retrieval from morphological databases. The second module builds on the results of a word segmenter and uses a context-based approach by exploiting 1.8 million texts from Wikipedia for the disambiguation of multiple morphological splits. Insights from Quantitative Linguistics help countering two sparse-data problems. The results can become more fine-grained during each cycle of computation and be added to the lexical input data with or without supervision. The evaluation on an inflight magazine shows a good coverage and an accuracy of 93% for the deep-level analyses.

1 Introduction

German is a language with highly productive and complex processes of word formation. Moreover, spelling conventions do not permit spaces as indicators for boundaries of constituents as in (1). Therefore, the automatic segmentation and analysis of the resulting word forms are challenging.

(1)   Arbeitsaufwand 'work effort, expenditure of labor'

Often, many combinatorially possible analyses exist, though usually only one of them has a conventionalized meaning (see Figure 1). For instance, for *Aufwand* 'expense, expenditure', word segmentation tools can yield the wrong split. In this case, there is a linking element within the word form which could be wrongly interpreted as part of a morph.[1] Here, the wrong alignment leads to a result containing *Sauf* 'to drink$_{animal}$, to booze' and *Wand* 'wall' as erroneously segmented morphs.

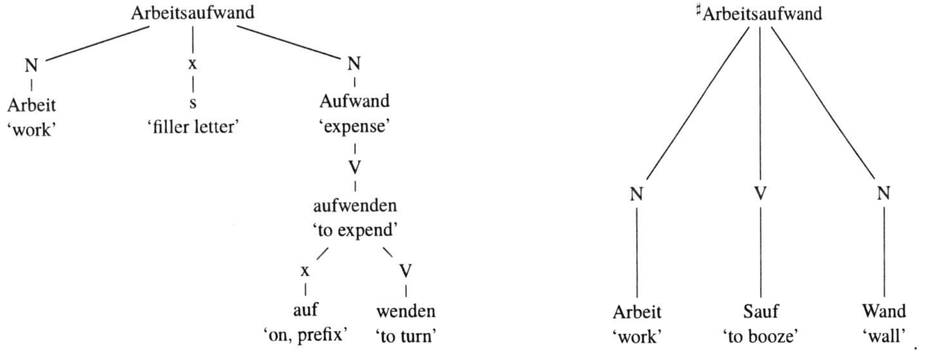

Figure 1: Ambiguous analysis of *Arbeitsaufwand* 'expenditure of labor'

---

[1]By some approaches, linking elements are considered as a special kind of morphemes and called *Fugenmorpheme*. We like to avoid such classifications and use the labels *filler letter(s)* or *interfix*.

Proceedings of the 2nd Int. Workshop on Resources and Tools for Derivational Morphology (DeriMo 2019), pages 45–54,
Prague, Czechia, 19-20 September 2019.

German compounds can consist of derivatives and derivatives can have compounds as their constituents. In (1), *Aufwand* is the result of a conversion process from *aufwenden* 'to expend, to spend', which again consists of a prefix and a verb stem. Many orthographical words are highly ambiguous. Therefore, automatic segmentation with many possible analyses for one orthographical form is a standard problem for German word formation.

In this paper, we use a hybrid approach for finding the correct splits of words and augmenting a morphological database. In Section 2, we provide an overview of related work in word segmentation and word parsing for German with a focus on structural analysis. Section 3 describes the combination of data-intense procedures for the morphological analyses and supervised database enhancements with compute-intense methods by exploiting a Wikipedia corpus. We also derive some quantitative heuristics to cope with sparse data problems. Section 4 shows an evaluation of the analyses of ambiguous word forms from the corpus of an inflight journal. Section 5 summarizes the main points of our results, and finally Section 6 gives a short outlook on future work.

2   Related Work

The first developments in morphological segmentation tools for German started in the early Nineties. Most of them are based on finite state transducers, for instance Gertwol (Haapalainen and Majorin, 1995), Morphy (Lezius, 1996), and later SMOR (Schmid et al., 2004) and TAGH (Geyken and Hanneforth, 2006). These morphological segmenters for complex German words often include dozens of flat word splittings for derivatives and compounds. There are different ways to resolve such kind of ambiguity, most of which are applied merely to compounds and yield flat segmentations of the immediate constituent level:

Cap (2014) and Koehn and Knight (2003) use ranking scores, such as the geometric mean, for the different morphological analyses and then choose the segmentation with the highest ranking. Sugisaki and Tuggener (2018) use a probabilistic model for composition activity of the constituents of noun compounds. They exploit the frequencies of large corpora.

Another approach consists in exploitation the sequence of letters, e.g. by pattern matching with tokens (Henrich and Hinrichs, 2011, 422) or lemmas (Weller-Di Marco, 2017). Ziering and van der Plas (2016) use normalization methods which are combined with ranking by the geometric mean. Ma et al. (2016) apply Conditional Random Fields modeling for letter sequences.

Recent approaches exploit semantic information for the ranking of compound splittings, such as look-ups of similar terms inside a distributional thesaurus such as Riedl and Biemann (2016). Their ranking score is a modification of the geometric mean. Ziering et al. (2016) use the cosine as a measure for semantic similarity between compounds and their hypothetical constituents and combine these similarity values by computing the geometric means and other scores for each produced split. The scores are then used as weights to be multiplied by the scores of former splits. Their investigation considers left-branching compounds consisting of three lexemes by using distributional semantic modelling. If the head is too ambiguous to correlate strongly with the first part, this often fails. Here, the test data of the left-branching compounds is preselected.

Few approaches take steps into the direction of hierarchical word segmentation: Ziering and van der Plas (2016) develop a splitter which makes use of normalization methods and can be used recursively by re-analyzing the results of splits. Schmid (2005) tests the disambiguation of morphological structures by a head-lexicalized probabilistic context-free grammar. The input are flat segmentations from SMOR. The baseline of 45.3% for the accuracy is obtained by randomly selecting an analysis from the least complex results. The parser is trained by using the Inside-Outside algorithm on different models e.g. frequencies of tokens vs. types, and lexicalized vs. unlexicalized training and combinations of these during the iteration process. The best results reach 68%. Besides this, the paper systematically describes the pitfalls of automatic morphological segmentation for immediate constituents and morphs. Some of these cases will be reconsidered when discussing the test data in Section 4. Another advance with a probabilistic context free grammar for full morphological parsing was undertaken by Würzner and Hanneforth (2013), however, it is restricted to derivational adjectives.

Most these approaches build upon corpus data. Only Henrich and Hinrichs (2011) enrich the output of morphological segmentation with information from the annotated compounds of GermaNet. This can in a further step yield hierarchical structures. Steiner and Ruppenhofer (2018) and Steiner (2017) build on this idea to derive complex morphological structures from lexical resources. In the following section, we will describe how we use the combined morphological information of GermaNet and CELEX as the foundation for a hybrid analyzing tool.

3   Combining Contextual Retrieval with Data-intense Methods

We will combine the look-up in a morphological database with a morphological segmenter and a contextual evaluation process. Figure 2 presents an overview of the procedure. It shows two databases of morphological trees: the German morphological trees database and a incremental database for all newly found morphological analyses (new splits). Furthermore, it comprises a set of monomorphemic lexemes.

If the database retrieval fails, the word splitting and weighting of alternative morphological structures is started. The output of a segmentation tool is analyzed by a contextual method by exploiting 1.8 million texts. If this fails, frequencies counts of a very large corpus is the next strategy. Some effects of typical frequency distributions are compensated by adequate weights. At the end of each word analysis, all subparts of the word are being searched within the database and the newsplit set. In case that entries for these subparts exist, their analyses can integrated into the results. The deeper analysis can then substitute the former one or is added as a new entry. These possible changes are represented by the dashed lines between the check block and the lexical databases.

3.1   Data-intense Methods for Morphological Analysis

We use the German morphological trees database built by the tools of Steiner (2017). It combines the analyses of the German part of the CELEX database (Baayen et al., 1995) and the compound analyses from the GermaNet database (Henrich and Hinrichs, 2011). (2) shows the entry for (1) *Arbeitsaufwand*. It comprises information on compounding from GermaNet and derivation from CELEX, for instance the constituent *Aufwand* 'expenditure' is analyzed as a derivation from the verb *aufwenden* 'to expend'. Non-terminal constituents are marked by asterisks.

(2)   Arbeitsaufwand (*Arbeit* arbeiten)|s|(*Aufwand* (*aufwenden* auf|wenden))

Figure 2 shows two databases of morphological trees: the German morphological trees database comprising 101,588 entries of complex lexemes, and an incremental database for all newly found morphological analyses. Furthermore, it comprises a set of monomorphemic lexemes, starting with 6,339 entries from the refurbished German CELEX database.

The hybrid word analyzer starts with a basic look-up. If this search can retrieve the respective tree or simplex form for the word, all of its subparts are being looked up within the lexical databases. These subanalyses are being integrated and old entries within the lexical databases are being substituted for the new ones. No further analyses are necessary.

3.2   Word Splitting and Contextual Retrieval

If neither an entry within the tree lexicons nor within the list of monomorphemes can be found, we use the output from SMOR as start for the further processing. We adjusted the SMOR output to our needs by the add-on Moremorph as it is described in Steiner and Rapp (in press). The flat structures include filler letters and tags of free and bound morphemes as in (3) for *Chefredakteurin* 'editor-in-chief$_{female}$'. The *l:s* notation shows lexical and surface characters of the two-level morphology which SMOR is based on. Eight of the ten analyses comprise false analyses, such as $^{\sharp}$(Chef|reden|Akte|Urin) '(Chief|to talk|file|urine)', all are analyzed as nouns (<NN>). We previously adjusted and enriched SMOR's lexicons and rules to our needs (Steiner and Rapp, in press). Under these premises and if inflectional information is cut off, the flat segmentation yields approximately two structures per word form. If case and number features were included, the number of analyses was about thrice as large (Schmid, 2005).

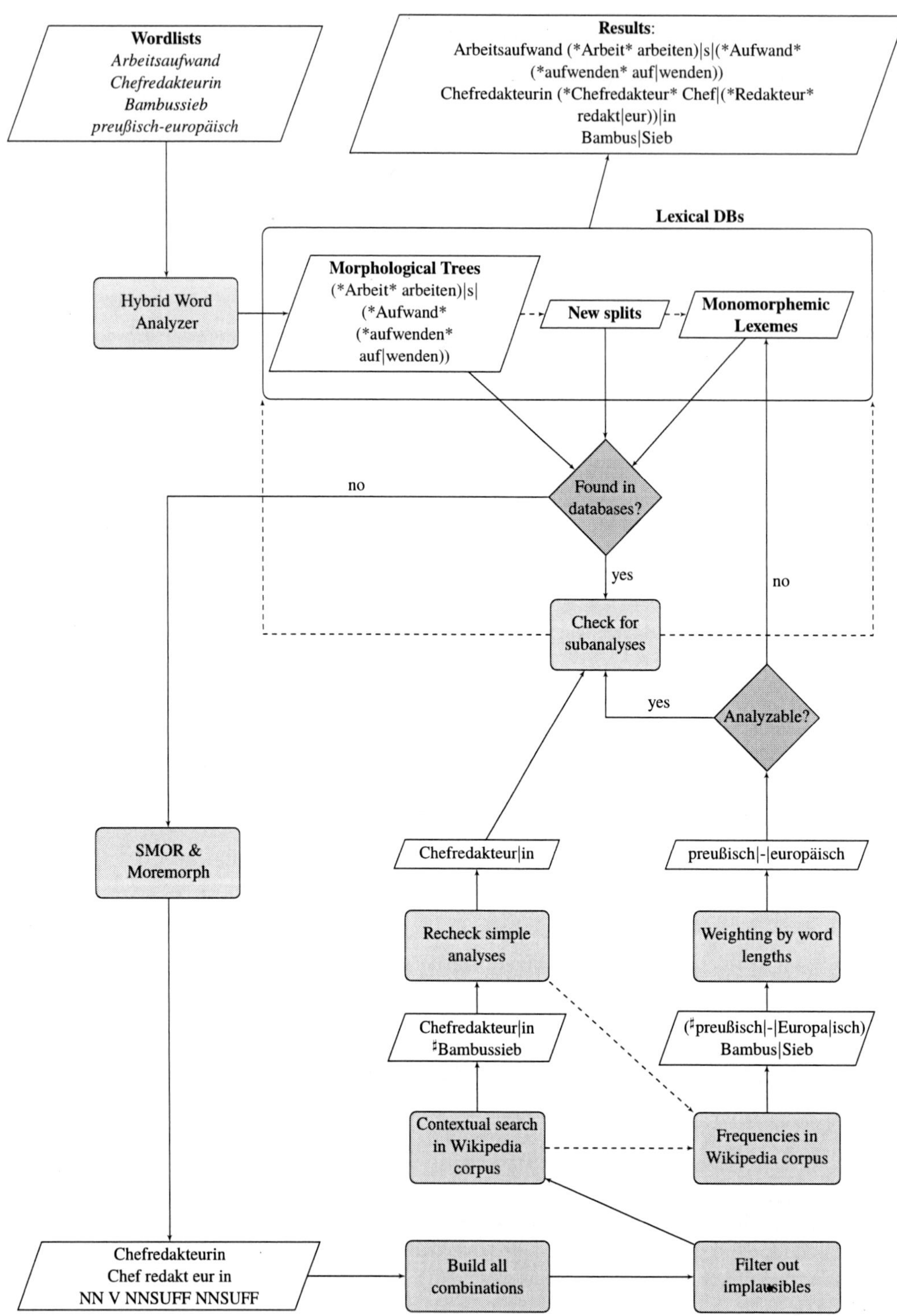

Figure 2: Hybrid word analysis: Morphological trees database, word segmenter, and two different evaluation procedures as alternative methods for word splitting

For each of these flat analyses, 2^{n-1} combinations of the immediate constituents exist, some of which are implausible, e.g. a constituent consisting just of a suffix. For the first flat analysis in (3), three splits are combinatorially possible and linguistically plausible (4). (4-a) describes a derivation of *Chefredakteur* 'editor-in-chief$_{masc}$' and the suffix *in*. But also, a composition of *Chef* and *Redakteurin* 'editor$_{female}$' is possible as in (4-b). Finally, (4-c) describes the erroneous analysis as a monomorphemic lexeme. Only the first combination shows the correct morphological structure.

<pre>
(3) Chefredakteurin   Chef R:redakteur in   NN NN NNSUFF   <NN>
     Chefredakteurin   Chef rede:<>n:<> A:akte U:urin   NN V NNSUFF NN NN   <NN>
     Chefredakteurin   Chef rede:<>n:<> A:akteur in   NN V NNSUFF NN NNSUFF   <NN>
     Chefredakteurin   Chef rede:<>n:<> A:akt e U:urin   NN V NNSUFF NN FL NN   <NN>
     Chefredakteurin   Chef rede:<>n:<> akt eur in   NN V NNSUFF V NNSUFF NNSUFF   <NN>
     Chefredakteurin   Chef rede:<>n:<> A:akte U:urin   NN V NN NN   <NN>
     Chefredakteurin   Chef rede:<>n:<> A:akteur in   NN V NN NNSUFF   <NN>
     Chefredakteurin   Chef rede:<>n:<> A:akt e U:urin   NN V NN FL NN   <NN>
     Chefredakteurin   Chef rede:<>n:<> akt eur in   NN V V NNSUFF NNSUFF   <NN>
     Chefredakteurin   Chef redakt eur in   NN V NNSUFF NNSUFF   <NN>
</pre>

(4) a. [[NN,NN],[NNSUFF]]   Chefredakteur|in
     b. ♯[[NN],[NN, NNSUFF]]   Chef|redakteurin
     c. ♯[[NN, NN, NNSUFF]]   Chefredakteurin

For all such flat analyses, all plausible combinations of strings and tags for the level of the immediate constituents are built, which results in large sets of hypothetical constituent sequences.

For splits of unknown compounds, we presuppose that each immediate constituent should be found within the same close textual environment at least somewhere inside a large corpus. For derivatives, this holds only for hypothetical constituents which are free morphs or lexemes. In both cases, the sum of frequencies of the constituents in texts should be much lower for erroneous splits than the frequencies for correct segmentations.

Therefore, the free morphs and lexemes of these constituent sets are searched within their contexts. Here, we define contexts as the texts of a corpus in which the respective analyzed word form occurs. The 1.8 million articles of the annotated German Wikipedia Korpus of 2015 (Margaretha and Lüngen, 2014)[2] totals to 18.71 million word-form types. This provides a sample which is large enough for getting sufficiently many hits. The corpus was tokenized by a modified version of the tool from Dipper (2016) and lemmatized by the TreeTagger (Schmid, 1999). Text indices were built both for the tokenized and lemmatized forms. For each text, all frequencies of its lemmas and tokens are stored. For each text containing the input word form, the frequencies of its hypothetical constituents are retrieved.

For every word form W_{wf}, building and filtering the combinations of hypothetical immediate constituents produces a set of morphological splits. Each such morphological split $sp_{wf,s}$ consists of a sequence of hypothetical constituents $c_{wf,s,1}, c_{wf,s,2} \cdots c_{wf,s,n}$.

$$sp_{wf,s} = \{c_{wf,s,1}, c_{wf,s,2}, \ldots, c_{wf,s,n}\} \qquad (1)$$

All texts comprising the word form W_{wf} are retrieved from the text indices. For each split and for every text T_t which contains the word form W_{wf}, the document frequencies ($df_1 \ldots df_m$) of the free hypothetical immediate constituents ($c_{wf,s,1} \ldots c_{wf,s,n}$) are being retrieved and summarized. This yields a text frequency score ($S_{wf,s,t}$) for each text and split of n constituents.

$$S_{wf,s,t} = \sum_{c=1}^{n} df_i \qquad (2)$$

For every text, the highest text frequency score $Best_{wf,t}$ from all hypothetical analyses is chosen.

$$Best_{wf,t} = \max_{1,m} S_{wf,s,t} \qquad (3)$$

---

[2] see http://www1.ids-mannheim.de/kl/projekte/korpora/verfuegbarkeit.html

Of all morphological analyses for W_{wf}, the one with the largest $Best_{wf,t}$ score is processed for the storage. (Equation 4).

$$BestSplitScore_{wf,t} = \max_{1,n} Best_{wf,t} \qquad (4)$$

If no text contains W_{wf}, the score is 0. A missing hypothetical constituent inside a text containing W_{wf} leads to a document frequency of 0 for this constituent, which in principle can be compensated by the frequencies of the other constituents of the split sequence.

Bound morphemes are not considered for the BestSplitScores. As they are often ambiguous with function words, this avoids wrong segmentations such as (5-a) for *Abfertigung* 'check-in, dispatching' and leads to a preference to analyses as in (5-b) which then can be further expanded to the complex structure in (5-c).

(5)   a.   ♯Ab|Fertigung 'prefix, off|manufacture'
        b.   abfertigen|ung 'to check-in|suffix'
        c.   (*abfertigen* ab|(*fertigen* fertig|en))|ung

3.2.1 Morphological Segmentation based on Corpus Frequencies

If no text contains the word form W_{wf}, the corpus itself is considered as a textual environment in the widest sense. For example, the copulative adjective compound *preußisch-europäisch* 'Prussian-European' (6) is not in the Wikipedia text index, though its hypothetical constituents *preußisch* 'Prussian$_{adj}$', *Preuße* 'Prussian$_{n}$', *Europa* 'Europe' and *europäisch* 'European$_{adj}$' are.

(6)	preußisch-europäisch	P:preuße:<> isch - E:europa:ä isch	NN ADJSUFF HYPHEN NN ADJSUFF	<ADJ>
	preußisch-europäisch	preußisch - E:europa:ä isch	ADJ HYPHEN NN ADJSUFF	<ADJ>

For all free morphemes and lexemes of each split, the sums of corpus frequencies are calculated. The hypothetical analysis with the highest value is chosen, and the morphological analysis with this score is processed for the storage. As a final back-off strategy, a default value of 0.1 is assigned to constituents which are unfound in the large corpus.

3.3 Reducing Sparse Data Effects

The derivation of hierarchical word structures from sequences of hypothetical constituents produces three types of error: These are: too few partitions, too many partitions, or a correct number but wrong subsets. In the first case, immediate constituents are less frequent than their constructions, in the second, hypothetical immediate constituents are more frequent than their constructions. The third error can be considered as a combination of the two previous ones.

3.3.1 Missing Constituents

The frequency of immediate constituents can be lower than the frequency of their word form. For example, the correct analysis for *Bambussieb* 'bamboo screen' is in (7-a). (7-b) shows the erroneous analysis of a compound as a monomorphemic lexeme. The overall text frequency of *Bambussieb* in the corpus is 3. None of these texts contains both constituents, and the frequencies of the compound outnumber the counts of the constituent *Sieb* 'sieve, screen' within these texts. This leads to a preference for the unsplit combination. However, this kind of analysis is desired or at least acceptable for real monomorphic and opaque word forms as in (7-c). Here, the SMOR split is false (7-c), however the look-up cannot obtain the word forms and hypothetical constituents of the erroneous analysis (7-d) within the same text, and the unsplit form is chosen.

(7)   a.   [[NN],[NN]]   Bambus|Sieb
        b.   ♯[[NN, NN]]   Bambussieb
        c.   ♯[[NN], [NN]]   ♯da|rinnen '(there|trickle)'
        d.   [[NN, NN]]   darinnen

Investigations on the lengths of German morphemes show that German simplex lexemes rarely possess more than 7 phonemes (98.41%) (Menzerath, 1954; Gerlach, 1982). The number of graphemes is proportional and slightly larger (Krott, 1996). Therefore, all word forms with more than 8 characters can be considered as candidates for polymorphemic analyses. For these, it is checked if a. BestScores were found only for splits comprising just one constituent but b. hypothetical splits with more than one constituent do exist. If these conditions hold, the word form undergoes a double check by the analysis based on the Wikipedia corpus frequencies. In Figure 2, this is indicated by the dashed line from the Recheck box.

3.3.2 Frequency Distributions of Constituents

The frequency-based weighting has a bias towards constructions with small constituents. While bound morphs which are often ambiguous with function words do not contribute to the scores (see 3.2), the problem is obvious for small frequent word forms as in (8).

(8)   a. $^\sharp$Figur|Kombi|Nation 'figure|combi (short form of combination)|nation'

          b.   Figur|Kombination 'figure|combination'

          c.   Figur|(*Kombination* kombin|ation)

The relation between length and frequency of German morphs and lexemes was investigated by Köhler (1986) and Krott (2004). Both observed oscillating functions for morph and lexeme frequency depending on length. As the functional dependency is mutual and influenced by other factors such as the age of words and lexicon size, fitting typical distributions such as the mixed negative binomial distribution yields bad results and has no convincing linguistic interpretation. We found the same effects for the lexeme lengths and frequencies of our test corpus (see 4) and decided to use the frequencies of word length classes as inverse weights for the scores. For each constituent with a length of l characters, the frequency of its word length class L_l is used as an inverse proportional factor for the document frequencies (5). The weighted best scores are defined as in 3.2.

$$WeightedS_{wf,s,t} = \sum_{c=1}^{n} \frac{df_i}{freq(L_{l(c)})} \tag{5}$$

3.4 Substitution of Analyses

For all found best splits, the analyses for every immediate constituents are being searched in the databases and integrated into the analysis. Figure 2 shows an example for *Chefredakteurin* 'chief editor (female)'. The contextual search leads to the split *Chefredakteur|in* which can be refined by the analysis of *Chefredakteur* 'chief editor (male)'. These morphological splits are added to the new splits database.

4   Evaluation

The test data was extracted from *Korpus Magazin Lufthansa Bordbuch (MLD)* which is part of the DeReKo-2016-I (Institut für Deutsche Sprache, 2016) corpus.[3] We tokenized and lemmatized the texts by the TreeTagger (Schmid, 1999).[4] The resulting data comprises 276 texts with 260,114 tokens, 38,337 word-form types, and 27,902 lemma types. 15,622 of these lemma types are inside the databases of trees or monomorphemic words. This is a coverage of 55.99% with an accuracy of nearly 100% due to the quality of the CELEX and GermaNet data.

The remaining 44.01% of all lemma types were processed by SMOR and Moremorph with a coverage of 100%. We took the counts of the word length classes from the set of lemmatized tokens of the MLD corpus. Unknown words, e.g. numbers, are analyzed as simplex words. We took a sample of 1,006 word forms by extracting every 27th line of the produced output. For this evaluation, we distinguish a correct analysis for all levels, no or missing splits on the level of the ICs, flat or partially flat analyses, and erroneous segmentations.

---

[3] See Kupietz et al. (2010) and http://www1.ids-mannheim.de/kl/projekte/korpora/archiv/mld.html for further information.
[4] See Steiner and Rapp (in press) for details.

Typical examples for analyses without any splits are word forms which are on a scale between adjectives and participle forms (9-a). Other forms occur more often than their constituents within a relatively small amount of contexts (9-b). Flat analyses are a typical outcome for words with sequences of short hypothetical immediate constituents (9-c). Sometimes, they are questionable but mostly close to a senseful interpretation on the surface morph-level. We found one erroneous split which was transferred from GermaNet, wrongly analyzed as endocentric compound instead of a syntagmatic construction (9-d). Besides this, wrong analyses are usually based on frequencies of homographs as in (9-e).

(9)　　a.　folgend 'following', gewandt 'turned$_v$, skillful$_{adj}$'
　　　　b.　Papierticket 'paper ticket', Metallkäfig 'metal cage', Tierärztin 'vet$_{fem}$'
　　　　c.　Ab|Flug|Gate '(prefix, away|flight|Gate), departure gate', Roll|vor|Gang '$^\sharp$?(to roll|prefix, before|gait), rolling procedure',
　　　　d.　$^\sharp$?(Land|Nahme) '(land|"take"), settlement'
　　　　e.　$^\sharp$(Parlament|(*arisch* ar|isch)) '(parliament|(*Aryan* Ar|ian), parliamentary'
　　　　f.　rollen|(*Vorgang* (*vorgehen* vor|gehen)) 'to roll|(*procedure* (*to proceed* pro|ceed))'

The recheck analyses word forms which were otherwise annotated as consisting of one constituent. Therefore the chance for wrong complex analyses grows. For instance, due to a preference for small constituents, *Metallkäfig* receives the split $^\sharp$(Met|All|Käfig) '(mead|space|cage), metal cage'. However, the word-length weighting method changes this to the correct split, same as for *Rollvorgang* (9-c), (9-f). Table (9) presents a concise summary of the evaluation.

Table 1: Results of hybrid word analyzing

	correct analy- sis (all levels)	no analysis	(partially) flat analysis	wrong analysis
DBs	≈ 55.99%			
DBs + Context + Corpus Look-up	87.77%	7.45%	3.48%	1.29%
+ Recheck	92.44%	2.68%	2.88%	1.99%
+ Recheck + Weighting	93.34%	2.58%	2.78%	1.29%

For all procedures, we found 18 or less wrongly analyzed word forms inside the sample of a thousand words. This shows a good quality of the analysis. Preferences do neither exist for right-branching Schmid (2005) nor for left-branching, but rather for flat structures. 5,696 new entries were added to the monomorphemic lexemes and 8,448 to the new splits. Those analyses can be added to the knowledgment base with or without human supervision.

5　Summary

We presented a hybrid approach for deep-level morphological analysis. On the one hand, it is based on databases of previous work which we recycled and combined to a new form. On the other hand, flat structures from a morphological segmentation tool served as a starting point. All plausible combinations of the immediate constituents were evaluated by look-ups in textual environments of a large corpus or inside the set of all types as a back-off strategy. Biases towards small constituents with high frequencies on the one side and unsplit words on the other were tackled by insights from investigations in quantitative linguistics. The combination of the methods lead to an accuracy of 93% for complex structures and 98.7% for acceptable output.

6　Future Work

For improvement, there are two directions: using larger corpora, to possibly obtain a better fit of the wordlength-frequency relationship. On the other hand, inhomogeneous data can blur models. Therefore, analyzing words text by text could help to achieve larger contextual dependency and to find morphological structures fitting to the direct environment. This would result in different structures for orthographical words according to their contexts.

Acknowledgments

Work for this publication was partially supported by the German Research Foundation (DFG) under grant RU 1873/2-1. I especially thank Reinhard Rapp for the joint work, and Helmut Schmid for developing SMOR, for making it freely available, and for his cooperation and advice for making changes in the lexicons and transition rules.

References

Harald Baayen, Richard Piepenbrock, and Léon Gulikers. 1995. The CELEX lexical database (CD-ROM).

Fabienne Cap. 2014. *Morphological processing of compounds for statistical machine translation*. Ph.D. thesis, Universität Stuttgart. https://doi.org/10.18419/opus-3474.

Stefanie Dipper. 2016. Tokenizer for German. https://www.linguistics.rub.de/ˉdipper/resources/tokenizer.html.

Rainer Gerlach. 1982. Zur Überprüfung des Menzerathschen Gesetzes im Bereich der Morphologie. In W. Lehfeldt and U. Strauss, editors, *Glottometrika 4*, Brockmeyer, Quantitative Linguistics 14, pages 95–102.

Alexander Geyken and Thomas Hanneforth. 2006. TAGH: A Complete Morphology for German based on Weighted Finite State Automata. In *FSMNLP 2005, Helsinki, Finland, September 1-2, 2005. Revised Papers*, Springer, Berlin/Heidelberg, volume 4002 of *LNCS*, pages 55–66. https://doi.org/10.1007/11780885_7.

Mariikka Haapalainen and Ari Majorin. 1995. GERTWOL und morphologische Disambiguierung für das Deutsche. http://www2.lingsoft.fi/doc/gercg/NODALIDA-poster.html.

Verena Henrich and Erhard Hinrichs. 2011. Determining Immediate Constituents of Compounds in GermaNet. In *Proceedings of the International Conference Recent Advances in Natural Language Processing, Hissar, Bulgaria, 2011*. Association for Computational Linguistics, pages 420–426. http://www.aclweb.org/anthology/R11-1058.

Institut für Deutsche Sprache. 2016. Deutsches Referenzkorpus / Archiv der Korpora geschriebener Gegenwartssprache 2016-I (Release from 31.03.2016). www.ids-mannheim.de/DeReKo.

Philipp Koehn and Kevin Knight. 2003. Empirical Methods for Compound Splitting. In *Proceedings of the 10th Conference of the European Chapter of the Association for Computational Linguistics, April 12-17, 2003, Budapest, Hungary*. Association for Computational Linguistics, volume 1, pages 187–193. https://doi.org/10.3115/1067807.1067833.

Reinhard Köhler. 1986. *Zur linguistischen Synergetik: Struktur und Dynamik der Lexik*. Quantitative Linguistics 31. Studienverlag Dr. N. Brockmeyer, Bochum.

Andrea Krott. 1996. Some remarks on the relation between word length and morpheme length. *Journal of Quantitative Linguistics* 3(1):29–37. https://doi.org/10.1080/09296179608590061.

Andrea Krott. 2004. Ein funktionalanalytisches Modell der Wortbildung [A functional analytical model of word formation]. In Reinhard Köhler, editor, *Korpuslinguistische Untersuchungen zur Quantitativen und Systemtheoretischen Linguistik [Corpus-linguistic Investigations of Quantitative and System-theoretical Linguistics]*, Elektronische Hochschulschriften an der Universität Trier, Trier, pages 75–126. http://ubt.opus.hbz-nrw.de/volltexte/2004/279/pdf/04_krott.pdf.

Marc Kupietz, Cyril Belica, Holger Keibel, and Andreas Witt. 2010. The German reference corpus DeReKo: A primordial sample for linguistic research. In *Proceedings of the International Conference on Language Resources and Evaluation, LREC 2010, 17-23 May 2010, Valletta, Malta*. European Language Resources Association (ELRA), pages 1848–1854. http://www.lrec-conf.org/proceedings/lrec2010/pdf/414_Paper.pdf.

Wolfgang Lezius. 1996. Morphologiesystem Morphy. In R. Hausser, editor, *Linguistische Verifikation. Dokumentation zur ersten Morpholympics 1994*. Niemeyer, Tübingen, pages 25–35. http://www.ims.uni-stuttgart.de/projekte/corplex/paper/lezius/molympic.pdf.

Jianqiang Ma, Verena Henrich, and Erhard Hinrichs. 2016. Letter Sequence Labeling for Compound Splitting. In *Proceedings of the 14th SIGMORPHON Workshop on Computational Research in Phonetics, Phonology, and Morphology, August 16, 2016, Berlin, Germany*. Association for Computational Linguistics, pages 76–81. https://doi.org/10.18653/v1/W16-2012.

Eliza Margaretha and Harald Lüngen. 2014. Building linguistic corpora from wikipedia articles and discussions. *Journal of Language Technology and Computational Linguistics. Special issue on building and annotating corpora of computer-mediated communication. Issues and challenges at the interface between computational and corpus linguistics* 29(2):59 – 82. http://nbn-resolving.de/urn:nbn:de:bsz:mh39-33306, http://www.jlcl.org/2014_Heft2/3MargarethaLuengen.pdf.

Paul Menzerath. 1954. *Die Architektonik des deutschen Wortschatzes*. Phonetische Studien. Dümmler, Bonn ; Hannover ; Stuttgart.

Martin Riedl and Chris Biemann. 2016. Unsupervised Compound Splitting With Distributional Semantics Rivals Supervised Methods. In *Proceedings of the Conference of the North American Chapter of the Association for Computational Linguistics: Human Language Technologie, June 12-17, 2016, San Diego, California, USA*. Association for Computational Linguistics, pages 617–622. https://doi.org/10.18653/v1/N16-1075.

Helmut Schmid. 1999. Improvements in Part-of-Speech Tagging with an Application to German. In Susan Armstrong, Kenneth Church, Pierre Isabelle, Sandra Manzi, Evelyne Tzoukermann, and David Yarowsky, editors, *Natural Language Processing Using Very Large Corpora*, Springer Netherlands, Dordrecht, pages 13–25. https://doi.org/10.1007/978-94-017-2390-9_2.

Helmut Schmid. 2005. Disambiguation of Morphological Structure using a PCFG. In *Proceedings of Human Language Technology Conference and Conference on Empirical Methods in Natural Language Processing, 6-8 October, 2005, Vancouver, British Columbia, Canada*. Association for Computational Linguistics, pages 515–522. https://www.aclweb.org/anthology/H05-1065.

Helmut Schmid, Arne Fitschen, and Ulrich Heid. 2004. SMOR: A German Computational Morphology Covering Derivation, Composition and Inflection. In *Proceedings of the Fourth International Conference on Language Resources and Evaluation, LREC 2004, May 26-28, 2004, Lisbon, Portugal*. European Language Resources Association (ELRA). http://www.aclweb.org/anthology/L04-1275.

Petra Steiner. 2017. Merging the Trees - Building a Morphological Treebank for German from Two Resources. In *Proceedings of the 16th International Workshop on Treebanks and Linguistic Theories, January 23-24, 2018, Prague, Czech Republic*. pages 146–160. https://aclweb.org/anthology/W17-7619.

Petra Steiner and Reinhard Rapp. in press. Building and Exploiting Lexical Databases for Morphological Parsing. In *Proceedings of The International Conference on Contemporary Issues in Data Science, March 5-8, 2019, Zanjan, Iran*. Springer, Lecture Notes in Computer Science.

Petra Steiner and Josef Ruppenhofer. 2018. Building a Morphological Treebank for German from a Linguistic Database. In Nicoletta Calzolari, Khalid Choukri, Christopher Cieri, Thierry Declerck, Sara Goggi, Koiti Hasida, Hitoshi Isahara, Bente Maegaard, Joseph Mariani, Hélène Mazo, Asuncion Moreno, Jan Odijk, Stelios Piperidis, and Takenobu Tokunaga, editors, *Proceedings of the Eleventh International Conference on Language Resources and Evaluation (LREC 2018), Miyazaki, Japan*. European Language Resources Association (ELRA). https://www.aclweb.org/anthology/L18-1613.

Kyoko Sugisaki and Don Tuggener. 2018. German Compound Splitting Using the Compound Productivity of Morphemes. In *14th Conference on Natural Language Processing - KONVENS 2018*. Austrian Academy of Sciences Press, pages 141–147. https://www.oeaw.ac.at/fileadmin/subsites/academiaecorpora/PDF/konvens18_16.pdf.

Marion Weller-Di Marco. 2017. Simple Compound Splitting for German. In *Proceedings of the 13th Workshop on Multiword Expressions (MWE 2017), Valencia, Spain*. Association for Computational Linguistics, pages 161–166. https://doi.org/10.18653/v1/W17-1722.

Kay-Michael Würzner and Thomas Hanneforth. 2013. Parsing morphologically complex words. In *Proceedings of the 11th International Conference on Finite State Methods and Natural Language Processing, FSMNLP 2013, St. Andrews, Scotland, UK, July 15-17, 2013*. pages 39–43. http://aclweb.org/anthology/W/W13/W13-1807.pdf.

Patrick Ziering, Stefan Müller, and Lonneke van der Plas. 2016. Top a Splitter: Using Distributional Semantics for Improving Compound Splitting. In *Proceedings of the 12th Workshop on Multiword Expressions, 11 August, 2016, Berlin, Germany*. Association for Computational Linguistics, pages 50–55. https://doi.org/10.18653/v1/W16-1807.

Patrick Ziering and Lonneke van der Plas. 2016. Towards Unsupervised and Language-independent Compound Splitting using Inflectional Morphological Transformations. In *Proceedings of the 2016 Conference of the North American Chapter of the Association for Computational Linguistics: Human Language Technologies, San Diego, California, USA, June 12-17, 2016*. Association for Computational Linguistics, pages 644–653. https://www.aclweb.org/anthology/N16-1078.

The Tagged Corpus (SYN2010[1]) as a Help and a Pitfall in the Word-formation Research

Klára Osolsobě

Ústav českého jazyka FF MU

Arna Nováka 1, 602 000 Brno, Czech Republic

osolsobe@phil.muni.cz

Abstract

Today, language corpora are the primary source of linguistic observation. The purpose of this paper is to illustrate some of the problems associated with word-formation research based upon morphologically tagged synchronous corpora. Three problems emerged during work on the linguistic handbook *Dictionary of affixes used in Czech – Slovník afixů užívaných v češtině* (Šimandl et al, 2016): a) tokenization, b) lack of the morphological dictionary, and c) POS tagging. This paper describes the solutions utilized by the authors of the dictionary in response to the above listed problems. These solutions, used in SAUČ, simplistic as they may seem, resulted in particular suggestions for improvement of the automatic morphological analysis of Czech, conducted as a part of the NovaMorf project (Osolsobě et al. 2017).

1. Introduction

The *Dictionary of Affixes used in Czech* (hereinafter referred to as SAUČ) is a new manual, which as well as the printed version issued by the Karolinum publishing house, is also available in a free electronic version (http://www.slovnikafixu.cz/). The entries are the product of thirteen contributory authors which reflect in minor variations due to authors' individual writing styles.

The dictionary is sorted alphabetically by the first letter of the particular affix (the header of the entry located on the left – prefix, in the middle – associated affix, on the right – suffix). A brief morphological characterization of the words formed by the respective affix (information about the inflection and alternations) follows. The text section summarizes information about the structural meanings / word classes corresponding to the analysed affix, the individual meanings being numbered. Respective entries referring to native and loaned affixes include, a so-called, "frequency report".[2] Both parts are based on the analysis of data accessible through the SYN2010 language corpus. In the textual part, the authors also relied on a variety of sources (native speakers intuition or opinion, other corpora, internet).

The SAUC preface further states: "When we use this dictionary, we can concentrate upon the affix system depending on their frequency or productivity."

When examining affixes, the lexeme, as a unit of the language system (*langue*), is analysed. Therefore, the lemmatised and POS tagged corpus would seem to be helpful; however the lemmatisation and POS tagging are the result of automatic morphological analysis and therefore it is of importance that SAUČ' users have knowledge of automatic morphological analysis. We shall demonstrate, using specific examples taken from the SAUČ, how the results of automatic tagging become pitfalls for corpus based linguistic research (part 2.). In conclusion, (part 3.) of the article, will demonstrate the benefits of working with data for further development of automatic morphological analysis tools, specifically within the NovaMorf project.

---

[1] Corpus SYN2010 is a synchronous representative corpus of contemporary written Czech containing 100 million text words. For more information, see http://wiki.korpus.cz/doku.php/cnk:syn2010.

[2] Part of entry differentiated by a font type. At the beginning there is corpus query, by which the corpus data had been obtained, the number of hits and their relevance. A section "20 most frequent lemmas" (for sparsely documented affixes, all lemmas are listed) follows. For each lemma reference is made to the meaning (corresponds to numbered meanings in the text above) and the number of occurrences (frequency) of the lemma in the analysed corpus.

2. Three steps of the automatic analysis[3]

Automatic morphological analysis generally involves three steps, namely, tokenization, the assignment of linguistic interpretations in the form of a lemma[4] and a tag[5], and disambiguation (if the word form analysed is both word and / or morphologically ambiguous / homonymous, and therefore the interpretations assigned are greater in number based on the dictionary).

All three of these steps are done by the engine automatically and have an impact on the final form of the morphological interpretation (lemma and POS / tag), and hence on all linguistic research based on the corpus. In the following sections, we will show how the use of the results of the automatic analysis has affected the work on the SAUČ.

2. 1 Pitfall No 1: The tokenization[6]

The tokenization is the process of demarcating and possibly classifying sections of a string of input characters. The resulting tokens are then passed on to some other form of processing. The process can be considered a sub-task of automatic morphological analysis. In corpus linguistics, a number of difficulties related to the reduction of the word form to a graphically defined unit (a string of defined alphabet characters separated from both sides by separators) are dealt with as a part of Multiword Expressions (MWE)[7] processing.

The affixes described in SAUČ are usually graphically a part of a single lexeme. Unlike German, there are no separable prefixes – *'trennbare Präfixe'* in Czech, but there are some cases that are somewhat analogous. Some Czech adverbs originate from prepositional phrases of names (nouns: *na konec → nakonec – ultimately*), nominal forms of adjectives: *do cela → docela – quite, z blízka → zblízka – close*, pronouns: *po tom → potom – then, přede vším → především – above all*, or numerals: *za prvé → zaprvé, z prvu → zprvu – first*). The creation of the compound adverb (*adverbiální spřežka*) is typically gradual. The completion of the process of the adverbialization is not only the graphical realization of a compound adverb as one graphical unit, but it is no more possible to insert another word form between the preposition and the nominal form. Usually the two ways of writing (two graphical units / one graphical unit) coexist.[8] The formation of these types of adverbs could be considered as associated affixation, in which the original preposition takes the role of the new prefix and the original ending takes the role of the new suffix. However for the POS tagging the preposition that is not graphically united with some newly created adverb is an independent unit tagged as a preposition and its nominal part is very often not identified (A lot of nominal parts of compound adverbs are no more used, and therefore the lemmas are not included in the dictionary of respective morphological analyser cf. Žižková, 2017.).

An example is the entry *na- -o* (http://www.slovnikafixu.cz/heslar/na-%20o).

The text states: "Typically, an adverb is characterized by dual writing, cf. *na černo / načerno* (*black, blackly*), *na hrubo / nahrubo* (*coarse, coarsely*), *na měkko/ naměkko* (*soft, softly*). The first way of writing is here essential. Whereas only "written together variants" are included in the frequency

---

report." The same way is also followed in analogous entries (e. g. *do- -a* http://www.slovnikafixu.cz/heslar/do-%20-a). Yet this way can be considered questionable with regard to both frequency and productivity research. The results of the frequency report do not show the frequency of the adverbs formed by the fusion of the preposition and the nominal form (often the name is not documented as a separate word outside the collocation with the corresponding preposition), but only the frequency of one of the graphical variants (in addition, only variants stored in the automatic analyser dictionary, see below).

The second example covers the entries describing such affixes that form verbs by prefix and reflexive particle *se/si*, e. g. *myslet* → *zamyslet se* (*think* → *reflect* as an intransitive verb). Let's have a look at the entry *za- se* (http://www.slovnikafixu.cz/heslar/za-%20se). We read in the text: "The statistical report was created by manual editing, with limited data accuracy guarantees."

What's going on? The free word order in Czech allows that the reflexive particle *se/si* can be separated by several word forms from its corresponding verb. The proper place of the particle *se/si* from the verb to the left side is not limited (it is driven by the principles of sentence stress). The proper place of the particle *se* from the verb to the right side is at the maximum on the third position (between the verb and *se* only some short words – clitics can be inserted). But the manual selection of each word order variant would be very time-consuming and probably inaccurate . We considered, for the sake of frequency report, the two most frequent word order variants (variants with the particle *se* immediately before / after the verb). It is, admittedly, a simplistic approach.

2. 2 Pitfall No 2: Assigning lemma + tag interpretation based on the morphological dictionary[9]

The second step of the automatic morphological analysis is to assign all interpretations based on the dictionary of the automatic morphological analyser. The lemmatization results depend on the scope and content of the respective dictionary. Although the dictionary is extensive and growing, the number of hapax[10] expressions in any new text is constantly variable. The productivity measuring is dictionary-dependent.

Now we can return to the case of compound adverbs mentioned above. In the dictionary only some (presumably codified) compound adverbs are stored. If we repeat the query **lemma="na.*o"** (http://www.slovnikafixu.cz/heslar/na-%20o) with the omission of the morphological tag specification, we obtain more relevant lemmas (e. g. adverbs as *natěsno – tight* or *tightly, nakratičko – short* or *shortly, naneurčito – vague*) that will not appear in the frequency report. These are words of low frequency, but they correspond to the model of such type of compound adverbs in Czech and show its productivity. The productivity picture based on the results of automatic analysis is inaccurate.

Is it possible to overcome the limitations of a dictionary? At this point we can focus on the entry *-oš* (http://www.slovnikafixu.cz/heslar/-o%C5%A1).

It is clear from the queries[11] that not only data based on the results of POS tagging were taken into account. For an entry that describes an affix, with which expressive words (hypocoristic proper names as *Miloš, Leoš, Antoš*)[12] are derived, this is an appropriate strategy. The examples given to illustrate the second query would indicate, that if we were not doing so, productivity would be significantly skewed.

---

[9] https://www.czechency.org/slovnik/ANOTACE

[10] https://www.czechency.org/slovnik/HAPAX

[11] Query [lemma=".*oš" & tag="NN[MI].*"] gives 125 lemmas, 69 are relevant. Query [lemma="(.*oš)|(.*oš[eiů])|(.*ošich)|(.*ošům) & tag="X.*"] gives 282 words, 36 relevant lemmas.

[12] The dictionary was built particularly for analysing written language. In the dictionary of automatic morphological analyser the expressive vocabulary (e. g. hypocoristic proper names) is rather neglected.

2. 3 Pitfall No 3: The disambiguation[13]

The last step of automatic morphological analysis is disambiguation (the process of identifying which interpretation of a word is used in context). Its results depend on the method of disambiguation. The biggest problem here is homonymy[14] (cf. Petkevič, 2015). In the case of word-formation, the problem of homonymy affects cases of part of speech transition, polyfunctional affixes, and overgeneration of formal query. Corpus analysis results are „disambiguation-addicted".

The problem of homonymy illustrates the entry *-cí* (http://www.slovnikafixu.cz/heslar/-c%C3%AD). We read in the text: "… adjectives formed by suffix *-cí* are in many cases nominalised – they have the meaning of (3) agentive names".

In the frequency report, this meaning (the meaning number (3)) is not differentiated by the number of occurrences of nominalised usage. The reasons behind this decision are as follows: 1) in the dictionary of the automatic analyser the nominalised adjectives are stored rather unsystematically. Except for some frequent lexemes (e. g. *vedoucí – leading* or *leader, kolemjdoucí – passing* or *passenger*, etc.), most lemmas have only one (adjective) POS interpretation (cf. Richterová, 2017, Žižková, 2019). 2) The potency of adjectives to transform into nouns is almost unlimited, and moreover, the boundaries can't be defined only in terms of the dictionary, since in many cases we have to deal with contextual ellipses. 3) The disambiguation (see Figure 1) is far from satisfactory (the hints on lines number 3, 5, 8, 10 are disambiguated wrongly).

Figure 1

1	člověk (nebo někdo , kdo jako člověk vypadá)	cestující/cestující/AGFP4-----A-----	s Nadiankou mnohem podezřelejší . Auto zastavilo mezi poli zarostlými
2	ho zamění za celodenní permanentku . Službu může využit každý	cestující/cestující/NNMS1-----A----	, který se zdržuje na Slovensku a zjisti , že
3	Na Dálném východě je kontrola jízdenek zdlouhavá záležitost , protože	cestující/cestující/AGIP1-----A----	mají lístky poschovávané na těch nejpodivnějších místech . Kim předložil
4	nesmi být příliš . Zřízeni vizové povinnosti pro české občany	cestující/cestující/AGMP4-----A----	do Kanady zásadně utlumi příliv Romů s nadějí klepajících na
5	"! Zatraceně ! "" Doktor podal zabalené nemluvné jednomu z"	cestujících/cestující/AGMP2-----A----	, pak se začal posouvat směrem k dusící se ženě
6	kličku , hlasové ovládání , televizi v hlavových opěrkách pro	cestující/cestující/AGMP4-----A----	na zadních sedadlech a další vymoženosti . V každém případě
7	, a ustoupil od dveří , aby udělal místo druhému	cestujícímu/cestující/NNMS3-----A----	, který právě vystupoval z limuziny . Malone ztuhl .
8	letenky by závisela na celkové váze jak zavazadla , tak	cestujícího/cestující/AGMS2-----A----	. Podle mluvčího americké Letecké asociace (ATA) Davida
9	aut . Aby nedělní změny nevyvolaly chaos , doporučuji dopravci	cestujícím/cestující/NNMP3-----A----	spoléhat se hlavně na takzvané páteřní linky . V oblasti
10	faktorů hodnocených v analýze scénářů . V případě požáru jsou	cestující/cestující/AGMP1-----A----	v tunelu vystaveni účinkům tepla a toxickým a dráždivým plynům

The problem of overgeneration is illustrated by the lines below the frequency report referring to the lemmas, which doesn't correspond to the words created by the affix. For example in the entry *sou- -í* (http://www.slovnikafixu.cz/heslar/sou-%20-%C3%AD) 28 lemmas (e. g. *soustředění – concentration, soužití – coexistence, soutěžení – competition, soužení – suffering/problem, sousedství – neighborhood, soukromí – privacy*) were excluded. We would like to finish with a (politically incorrect) language joke based on overgenerated segmentation: "*Několik soch je **sou-soš-í**, několik žen je **sou=žen=í/s-ouž-en-í***" ("*Several sculptures create a sculptural group, several women create a problem.*").

3. Conclusion

Our goal was to show that the authors of the *Dictionary of affixes used in Czech* were very well aware of the limits of working with the results of automatic part of speech tagging. We added detailed commentaries concerning simplistic solutions for the dictionary readers. All data (unless otherwise indicated) referring to the corpus are taken from the reference corpus (SYN2010) and the method of data mining is sufficiently described at the beginning of the frequency report (the corpus query). Therefore, every dictionary user can repeat the query with the same reference corpus or with different data (other corpora). The SAUČ as a whole meets the requirements for empirical testability of the presented results as required by the corpus linguistics. Despite the above-mentioned simplistic solutions, it is not disputed that without using the results of automatic tagging, any way of creating the *Dictionary of affixes used in Czech* would be a) incomparably more time-consuming, b) more expensive and c) in its result less objective.

---

[13] https://www.czechency.org/slovnik/DISAMBIGUACE%20/%20DESAMBIGUACE
[14] https://www.czechency.org/slovnik/HOMONYMIE

Nevertheless the problems which emerged during work on the *Dictionary of affixes used in Czech* become a starting point for research oriented towards improving automatic morphological tagging (see more Žižková, 2017, 2019). A detailed morphological description of word forms based on the data gained during the work on SAUČ is reflected in the *NovaMorf* project (Osolsobě et al. 2017).

Acknowledgement

This work was supported by the project MUNI/A/1061/2018 Čeština v jednotě synchronie a diachronie – 2019.

References

Hajič, J., Hlaváčová, J. 2016. *MorfFlex CZ*, LINDAT/CLARIN digital library at Institute of Formal and Applied Linguistics, Charles University in Prague. http://hdl.handle.net/11858/00-097C-0000-0015-A780-9.

Karlík, P. – Nekula, M. – Pleskalová, J. 2016. *Nový encyklopedický slovník češtiny*. Nakladatelství Lidové noviny, Praha. https://www.czechency.org/slovnik/.

Křen, M. – Bartoň, T. – Cvrček, V. – Hnátková, M. – Jelínek, T. – Kocek, J. – Novotná, R. – Petkevič, V. – Procházka, P. – Schmiedtová, V. – Skoumalová, H. *SYN2010: žánrově vyvážený korpus psané češtiny*. Ústav Českého národního korpusu FF UK, Praha 2010. http://www.korpus.cz.

Osolsobě, K. – Hlaváčová,J. – Petkevič, V. – Šimandl, J. – Svášek, M. 2017. Nová automatická morfologická analýza češtiny. *Naše řeč* 100 (4): 225-234.

Petkevič, V. 2015. *Morfologická homonymie v současné češtině*. Nakladatelství Lidové noviny, Praha.

Pravdová, M. – Svobodová, I. 2014. *Akademická příručka českého jazyka*. Academia, Praha. http://prirucka.ujc.cas.cz/.

Richterová, O. 2017. *Od slovesa ke jménu a předložkám Departicipiální formy v češtině: forma, funkce, konkurence. From Verbs to Nouns and Prepositions. Departicipial Forms in Czech: Form, Function, Complementarity*. Ph.D. Thesis. FF UK, Praha.

Šimandl, J. (ed.). 2016. *Slovník afixů užívaných v češtině*. Karolinum, Praha. http://www.slovnikafixu.cz/index.

Žižková, H. 2017. Compound Adverbs as an Issue in Machine Analysis of Czech Language. *Jazykovedný časopis* 68 (2): 396-403.

Žižková, H. 2019. *Slovnědruhové přechody jako problém automatické morfologické analýzy. Part of speech transitions as a problem of automatic morphological analysis*. Ph.D. Thesis. FF MU, Brno.

Attempting to separate inflection and derivation
using vector space representations

Rudolf Rosa   **Zdeněk Žabokrtský**
Charles University, Faculty of Mathematics and Physics,
Institute of Formal and Applied Linguistics
Malostranské náměstí 25, 118 00 Prague 1, Czech Republic
{rosa,zabokrtsky}@ufal.mff.cuni.cz

Abstract

We investigate to what extent inflection can be automatically separated from derivation, just based on the word forms. We expect pairs of inflected forms of the same lemma to be closer to each other than pairs of inflected forms of two different lemmas (still derived from a same root, though), given a proper distance measure. We estimate distances of word forms using edit distance, which represents character-based similarity, and word embedding similarity, which serves as a proxy to meaning similarity. Specifically, we explore Levenshtein and Jaro-Winkler edit distances, and cosine similarity of FastText word embeddings. We evaluate the separability of inflection and derivation on a sample from DeriNet, a database of word formation relations in Czech. We investigate the word distance measures directly, as well as embedded in a clustering setup. Best results are achieved by using a combination of Jaro-Winkler edit distance and word embedding cosine similarity, outperforming each of the individual measures. Further analysis shows that the method works better for some classes of inflections and derivations than for others, revealing some limitations of the method, but also supporting the idea of replacing a binary inflection-derivation dichotomy with a continous scale.

1   Motivation

The distinction between inflection and derivation is a traditional linguistic dichotomy, with a range of criteria to tell them apart (Stump, 1998; Haspelmath and Sims, 2013). However, the criteria are typically not easily testable in an automated way; rather, they are designed for a manual investigation carried out by a linguist.

In this work, we attempt to distinguish inflection from derivation automatically, based solely on the word forms, without using any annotated resources and any human decision-making. For each pair of morphologically related word forms, we want to automatically decide whether they are inflected forms (inflections, for short) of the same lemma, or not. We specifically focus on the lexical meaning change criterion by Stump (1998), as listed by Bonami and Paperno (2018): "if two morphologically related words have distinct lexical meaning, they must be related by derivation".

Obviously, if there is a lemmatizer available for the language under study (or a corpus annotated with lemmas which can be used to train the lemmatizer), the task could be trivially solved by lemmatizing the two word forms and checking whether the lemmas are identical or distinct. However, we are not interested in such a solution, as the necessary resources are only available for a small number of languages. The vast majority of the world's languages are under-resourced, lacking such datasets or tools, which gravely limits any research on such languages. The ability to perform the inflection-derivation distinction automatically, assuming only the availability of a plain text corpus of the language, would thus be of great value. Admittedly, for many languages, no plain text corpus of a considerable size is available; in such cases, we are out of luck. Nevertheless, medium-size plain text corpora exist for hundreds of languages – Wikipedia[1] covers 300 languages (Rosa, 2018), JW300 (Agić and Vulić, 2019) features texts

---

[1]https://www.wikipedia.org/

from Watchtower[2] for 300 languages (around 100k sentences each), and the text of the whole or a part of the Bible is available for as many as 1,400 languages (Mayer and Cysouw, 2014).

Still, in this work, our goal is not (yet) practical, i.e. devising a tool applicable to under-resourced languages, but rather exploratory, investigating the mere feasibility of such an approach. Therefore, we only use a single resource-rich language for the investigation, so that we can reliably analyze the performance of our approach, for which we need annotated datasets.

Moreover, as an outlook to future work, we are also interested in empirically exploring the boundary between derivation and inflection, which is notoriously vague. We hope that empirical computational methods could provide some solid ground in this respect, revealing to which extent the boundary can be observed, and possibly even providing empirical means of estimating the inflectionality and derivationality of individual phenomena, e.g. in the form of a scalar value.

Thus, while we hope the presented work to have some practical applications, our primary motivation is sheer curiosity. Can we automatically distinguish inflection from derivation, without using annotated data? How clear does the boundary seem to be? Can we estimate the position of a morphological operation on the inflection-derivation scale? Which operations, traditionally annotated as derivations, seem to behave more like inflections, and vice versa? This work is just a starting point on our journey to empirically explore such questions. Nevertheless, it already allows us to peek at what really seems to be going on in language (Czech language, at this stage) in terms of inflection and derivation.

2   Related Work

In morphology, derivation and inflection are traditionally distinguished. The former one deals with creating word forms from the same lexeme, while the latter one captures processes for the creation of new lexemes. Like with many other linguistic dichotomies, there is a critical debate about the existence of a real divide between inflection and derivation, ranging from approaches trying to define precise operational criteria to distinguish the two, through those that assume rather a gradual scale, to those that reject this opposition as such. The arguments used in the debate were summarized e.g. by Booij (2006) and by ten Hacken (2014).[3]

Originally, the criteria for distinguishing inflection from derivation were formulated mostly using high-level linguistic notions (for instance, inflected forms of lexemes are supposed to preserve lexical meaning), which makes it difficult to evaluate in an objective way. More recently (roughly in the last two decades), there are attempts to find the boundary using also psycholinguistic or even brain-imaging methods, see e.g. (Julínková, 2012) and (Bozic and Marslen-Wilson, 2010), respectively. Typically, the experimental results are mixed, indicating that some such assumed opposition partially correlates with measurements, but without offering any clear-cut divide either. In addition, all such experiments are naturally hard to scale to bigger data and/or more languages.

In our study, we take the existence of a crisp inflection-derivation boundary as an assumption, and we try to get close to the boundary in a fully unsupervised way, using only unlabelled corpus data.

For evaluation purposes, we accept the boundary as technically defined in existing morphological NLP resources for Czech. More specifically, we use MorfFlex CZ (Hajič and Hlaváčová, 2016) to bind inflected word forms with their lemmas (more exactly, we use only corpus-attested word forms), and the word-formation database DeriNet (Ševčíková and Žabokrtský, 2014), in which relations between derivationally related lexemes are represented in the form of rooted trees (one tree per a derivational family).

To the best of our knowledge, the only work to investigate a similar question is the recent research of Bonami and Paperno (2018). Similar to us, the authors are interested in a way to turn the human-centered criteria of distinguishing inflection from derivation into something empirically testable. The authors investigated the semantic regularity criterion ("inflection is semantically more regular than derivation"),

---

[2]https://www.jw.org/
[3]The debate seems not much heated for the Czech language nowadays, however, there are linguistic phenomena in Czech which are considered inflection by some scholars and derivation by others. For instance, the category of comparative is handled as inflection in modern NLP tools for Czech, but was considered word formation e.g. by Trávníček (1951).

while we selected the lexical meaning change criterion in this work (distinct lexical meanings indicate derivation).

Both Bonami and Paperno (2018) and us are interested in the meanings of the individual words, and both works make the usual choice of using word embeddings as a proxy to word meanings. As the criterion that we test is simpler, our method is also simpler: we directly measure the difference of word embeddings to estimate the distance of meanings. To estimate the *regularity* of meaning change, Bonami and Paperno (2018) take a further step of estimating an embedding vector shift corresponding to a particular morphological operation, and observe that the vector shift tends to be more regular for inflectional operations than for derivational operations.

A partially related work is that of Musil et al. (2019), showing that there is some regularity in the vector shift corresponding to individual derivational operations. However, the authors do not contrast this with inflectional operations. We utilize their work to provide categories of derivational operations, which are not yet annotated in DeriNet and have to be estimated heuristically.

While the methods used by us and previously mentioned authors are rather simple, we are unaware of any other substantial research in this direction. There is research on unsupervised morphology induction, represented by the well-known Morfessor system of Creutz and Lagus (2007), the interesting ParaMor system (Monson et al., 2008) which attempts to find inflectional paradigms, as well as the earlier minimum description length-based system of Goldsmith (2001). While some ideas behind these systems are related to our interests and may potentially be useful to us, their goal is to perform morphological segmentation, which is a related but different task. Another related area is stemming (Lovins, 1968; Porter, 2001), which can be thought of as simple lemmatization. However, stemmers tend to be too coarse, often assigning the same stem to both inflections and derivations. Moreover, they are typically rule-based and thus language-specific, which is not in line with our goals.

3 Approach

Our central hypothesis is that word forms that are inflections of the same lemma tend to be *more similar* than inflections of different lemmas. To measure the similarity of word forms, we investigate two somewhat orthogonal simple approaches.

Our first method is to use string edit distances, which measure how much the word forms differ on the character level. In our work, we use the Jaro-Winkler (JW) edit distance (Winkler, 1990) and the Levenshtein edit distance (Levenshtein, 1966).

As the second method, we propose to measure similarity of word embeddings (Mikolov et al., 2013; Grave et al., 2018). It has been shown that cosine similarity of word embeddings tends to capture various kinds of word similarities, including morphological, syntactic, and semantic similarities, and can be thought of as a proxy to meaning similarity.

We then apply the methods to sets of corpus-attested words belonging to one derivational family, i.e. a set of words that are, according to a database of word formation relations, all derived from a common root, together with their inflections extracted from a lemmatized corpus. Some words in the set are thus inflections of a common lemma, while others are inflections of different lemmas derived from a common root. We evaluate the accuracy with which the methods separate inflections from derivations, both independently for each pair of word forms as well as in an unsupervised clustering setup.

4 Word form distance measures

4.1 String similarity

For string similarity, we use the Levenshtein (LD) edit distance (Levenshtein, 1966) and the Jaro-Winkler (JW) edit distance (Winkler, 1990).

A potential advantage of JW over LD is that it gives more importance to the beginnings of the strings than to their ends. We find this to be advantageous, as most of the inflection usually happens at the end of the word, i.e. suffixing is more common than prefixing. Specifically, as shown by Table 1, adapted from the WALS database by Dryer and Haspelmath (2013), half of the studied languages showing a non-trivial amount of inflectional morphology are predominantly suffixing, and further 15% show a preference for suffixing; moreover, nearly all Eurasian languages, which one is most likely to encounter in practice, fall into this category. For the languages with no clear prefixing-suffixing preference (18% of studied inflectional languages), we expect LD to be more appropriate than JW; however, these are mostly low-resource indigenous languages found in central Africa and the Americas, not frequently encountered in practice.[4]

Value	Languages	% of all	% of inflectional
Little or no inflectional morphology	141	15%	–
Predominantly suffixing	406	42%	49%
Moderate preference for suffixing	123	13%	15%
Approximately equal amounts of suffixing and prefixing	147	15%	18%
Moderate preference for prefixing	94	10%	11%
Predominantly prefixing	58	6%	7%

Table 1: Values of Map 26A, Prefixing vs. Suffixing in Inflectional Morphology, showing the number and proportion of languages with various prefixing/suffixing preferences. Adapted from WALS (Dryer and Haspelmath, 2013).

Moreover, JW is in the $[0, 1]$ range, making it easily comparable and combinable, while LD returns a natural number of edit operations. For practical reasons, we transform LD into the $[0, 1]$ range by dividing it with the total length of the pair of word forms:[5]

$$LD_{rel}(w1, w2) = \frac{LD_{abs}(w1, w2)}{|w1| + |w2|} \tag{1}$$

While the edit distances treat all distinct characters as equally distant, some types of changes to the word form tend to be more common during inflection, and thus should presumably have a lower weight in the distance measure. To compute the edit distance of a pair of strings, we thus optionally average their edit distance with edit distance of their *simplified variants*; the simplification consists of lowercasing, transliteration to ASCII using the Unidecode library,[6] and deletion of non-initial vowels (a e i o u y).

4.2   Word embedding similarity

We use the cosine similarity of pretrained FastText word embeddings (Grave et al., 2018), downloaded from the FastText website.[7] Compared to the classical Word2vec (Mikolov et al., 2013), FastText embeddings have the benefit of employing subword embeddings. This means that they seamlessly handle out-of-vocabulary word forms, and also that they implicitly capture string similarity to some extent.[8]

The cosine similarity is computed as the inner product of the normalized FastText vectors of the pair of word forms; for practical reasons, we also shift it from the $[-1, 1]$ interval to the $[0, 1]$ interval, and reverse it to turn the similarity measure into a distance measure:

$$COS(w1, w2) = \frac{1 - vec(w1) \cdot vec(w2)}{2 \cdot |vec(w1)| \cdot |vec(w2)|} \tag{2}$$

4.3   Combined distance measure

We also combine the edit distance with the embedding distance via multiplication of the similarities.[9] As will be shown later, JW achieves better results than LD; therefore, we only use JW in the combination:

$$CD(w1, w2) = 1 - (1 - JW(w1, w2)) \cdot (1 - COS(w1, w2)) \tag{3}$$

---

[4]When dealing with a language with a preference for prefixing inflectional morphology (18% of studied inflectional languages), one can simply reverse the word forms before applying JW.

[5]Another option would be to divide the distance only by the length of the longer word. In our case, we chose a normalization that implicitly incorporates length similarity of the words.

[6]https://pypi.org/project/Unidecode/

[7]https://fasttext.cc/

[8]In brief preliminary experiments, FastText achieved significantly better results than Word2vec.

[9]The multiplication works like a logical "and": close word forms should be *similar* both string-wise *and* in meaning.

5 Evaluation

5.1 Evaluation methods

For the main evaluation, we use two methods, both evaluating to which extent the distance measures are able to separate inflections of the same lemma from inflections of different lemmas on a set of words belonging to a common derivational family.

5.1.1 Pairwise evaluation

In the pairwise evaluation method, we find a distance threshold that optimally separates inflection pairs from non-inflection pairs. We define W_{infl} as the set of all pairs of word forms that are inflections of the same lemma, and W_T as the set of all pairs of word forms whose distance is lower than a threshold T:

$$W_{infl} = \{w1, w2 | lemma(w_1) = lemma(w_2)\}; W_T = \{w1, w2 | dist(w_1, w_2) < T\} \tag{4}$$

We then compute the precision, recall, and F1 score of inflection pairs closer than T:

$$P_T = \frac{|W_{infl} \cap W_T|}{|W_T|}; R_T = \frac{|W_{infl} \cap W_T|}{|W_{infl}|}; F_T = \frac{2 \cdot P_T \cdot R_T}{P_T + R_T} \tag{5}$$

And finally, we find a threshold T that maximizes the F_T score:

$$F_{pairwise} = argmax_{T \in [0,1]} F_T \tag{6}$$

The resulting F1 score is a kind of an upper bound accuracy for the method, as the optimal separating threshold is selected in an oracle manner.

5.1.2 Clustering-based evaluation

We also perform a clustering of the word forms, and then evaluate the resulting clusters. We apply agglomerative clustering[10] from Scikit-learn (Pedregosa et al., 2011) with average linkage. The algorithm starts by assigning each word form to a separate cluster. In each step, it then merges the pair of clusters with the lowest average distance of their elements. We stop the algorithm once the number of clusters reaches the oracle number of lemmas in the derivational family.

We then evaluate the clustering in a similar way as in the pairwise method, with the objective that inflections should fall into common clusters and non-inflections should fall into different clusters. We define W_{infl} as in (4), and W_{clust} as the set of all pairs of word forms that fell into the same cluster:

$$W_{clust} = \{w1, w2 | clust(w_1) = clust(w_2)\} \tag{7}$$

We then compute the precision, recall, and F1 score of inflection pairs clustered together:

$$P_{clust} = \frac{|W_{infl} \cap W_{clust}|}{|W_{clust}|}; R_{clust} = \frac{|W_{infl} \cap W_{clust}|}{|W_{infl}|}; F_{clust} = \frac{2 \cdot P_{clust} \cdot R_{clust}}{P_{clust} + R_{clust}} \tag{8}$$

5.2 Experiment setting

We extract derivational families from DeriNet v1.7 (Žabokrtský et al., 2016),[11] a database of Czech word formation relations. As the database only contains word lemmas, we enrich the extracted lemma sets with inflections of the lemmas found in the Czech National Corpus, subcorpus SYN v4 (Křen et al., 2016), a large corpus of Czech lemmatized automatically using morphological analyzer MorfFlex CZ (Hajič and Hlaváčová, 2016).[12] We lowercase all the word forms.

---

[10]`https://scikit-learn.org/stable/modules/clustering.html#hierarchical-clustering`
[11]`http://ufal.mff.cuni.cz/derinet`
[12]MorfFlex CZ (Hajič and Hlaváčová, 2016) offers complete inflectional paradigms, which leads to generating many extremely rare or even unused word forms. Thus we prefer to use only corpus-attested word forms in our study.

Distance	Embeddings (COS)	Levenshtein (LD)		Jaro-Winkler (JW)		Combination (CD)	
Simplified	–	no	yes	no	yes	no	yes
Pairwise	35.13%	37.71%	38.49%	38.73%	38.47%	41.27%	41.86%
Clustering	30.36%	31.75%	32.04%	34.39%	34.75%	36.44%	37.13%

Table 2: F1 scores of inflection identification using pairwise or clustering-based evaluation, with various word form distance measures. Edit distances optionally additionally use simplified word forms.

For the evaluation presented here, we randomly sampled 42 out of the 561 derivational families which contain at least 50 lemmas.[13,14] The derivational families range from 51 to 751 lemmas, totalling 4,514 lemmas, which are expanded through the corpus to 69,743 word forms.

We perform both the pairwise evaluation and the clustering-based evaluation on each of the derivational families separately, and report macro-averages[15] of F1 scores.

5.3 Results

The results in Table 2 show that the proposed method can separate inflection from derivation to some extent, reaching F1 scores around 40%.

This number is somewhat hard to interpret, as there is no clear baseline to compare it to. On one hand, current supervised lemmatizers typically reach accuracies well over 90%, but in a quite different setting. On the other hand, inflection pairs form only around 2% of our dataset, as the vast majority of the word form pairs are various inflections of rather distant derivations, so a trivial random baseline would achieve a score around 2%. The proposed distance measures thus manage to separate a small set of close inflections and derivations from a large set consisting of most of the non-inflections and some of the inflections.

Interestingly, both the edit distances and the embedding distance achieve accuracies in a similar range (with the embedding distance being slightly weaker), despite the methods being quite different.[16] Their combination then achieves even better results in both evaluation measures.

The JW distance achieves slightly better performance than LD, presumably due to the fact that it gives more weight to prefixes than suffixes, while inflection mostly happens at the suffix, as was already discussed. We can also see that the word form simplification generally slightly improves the results.

6 Further analysis

To get a better understanding on how the suggested distance measures perform on the task, we perform several further pairwise analyses.

In the main evaluation, we used pairs of all word forms belonging to the same derivational family. In such a setting, most pairs consist of rather distant word forms, which are clearly non-inflectional and thus rather boring. Therefore, we now focus only on the closest pairs of word forms, linked by a single inflectional or derivational operation:

- lemmas linked by a derivational edge; e.g. "dýchat" (breathe) – "dýchatelný" (breathable)
- forms of one lemma, differing only in one feature;[17] e.g. "písně" ($song_{sg,gen}$) – "písní" ($songs_{pl,gen}$)
- forms of two lemmas linked by a derivational edge, not differing in any morphological feature; e.g. "barvám" ($colours_{pl,dat}$) – "barvičkám" ($crayons_{pl,dat}$)

---

[13]While this may bias the research, we found that small derivational families, when filtered against corpus-attested forms, typically provide too small and sparse data for a meaningful analysis of derivational relations.

[14]Specifically, we use the following derivational roots: barva, báseň, bavit, bílý, bloknout, bloudit, budovat, bydlet, část, cena, cesta, chránit, dýchat, hádat, hospodář, hrát, hvězda, kód, kouř, křest, kult, malovat, norma, pět, politika, prach, produkt, program, rada, rodit, rovný, spět, střelit, tělo, typ, um, vědět, vinout, vládat, voda, zeď, žena.

[15]As the number of word form pairs grows quadratically with the number of word forms, we need to prevent a few largest derivational families from dominating the results.

[16]It is worth noting that FastText operates on character n-grams as well as full words, thus implicitly also capturing some string-based similarity.

[17]If a feature is set for only one of the forms (e.g. gender which is marked on verbs in the past tense but not in the present tense), we treat it as not differing; thus e.g. a change of verb tense is treated as a change in the tense feature only.

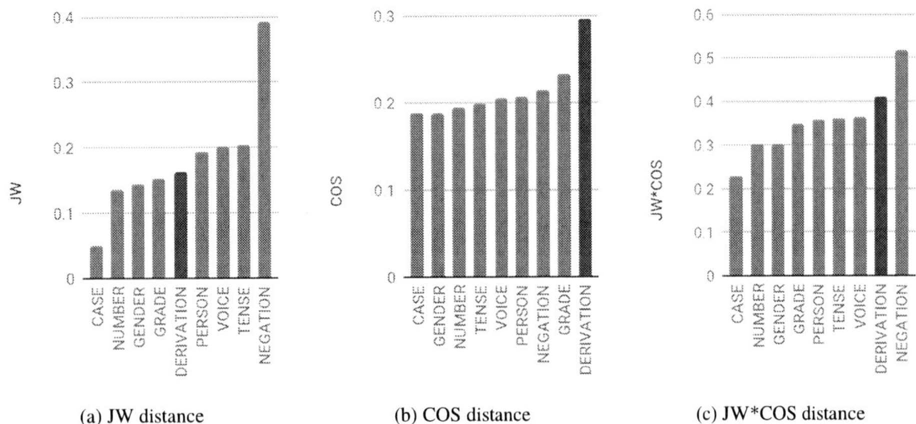

(a) JW distance   (b) COS distance   (c) JW*COS distance

Figure 1: Count-weighted average distances based on inflection type (or derivation).

Even then, although we are filtering the data for only corpus-attested forms, the corpus is large enough to contain many weird uncommon word forms, which we are not particularly interested in analyzing, as we rather want to see how the distance measures perform in typical situations. Therefore, we perform a token-based rather than type-based evaluation, simulating repeated evaluation of each word form based on its count in the corpus; as we are performing pairwise evaluation, we simply take the product of the counts of the individual word forms for the pair count.

6.1 Inflections

Figure 1 shows the count-weighted average distances of inflections that differ in the individual morphological features; average distance of derivations is also shown.

JW distance (Figure 1a) is very high for negation; this is expected since it modifies the beginning of the word (using the 'ne-' prefix), to which JW is particularly sensitive. The average JW distance for case inflection is very low; this is due to the token-based evaluation, as most frequent cases typically differ only in one or two word-final characters. We also note that the JW distance for grade inflection is surprisingly low, given the fact that superlatives in Czech are formed by prefixation ('nej-'); however, comparatives are much more common in the corpus (in type-based evaluation, grade inflection would rank much higher). JW clearly does not separate derivation from inflection well, as derivations exhibit a medium JW distance on average. Obviously, JW is also quite unsuitable for irregular inflections and suppletives, such as "jde" – "šel" (goes – went).

Figure 1b shows that COS distance of word embeddings separates inflection from derivation very well. Otherwise, highest COS distances are observed for negation and grade inflections, which are morphological operations on the boundary between inflection and derivation. While word embeddings are known to often perform poorly at distinguishing synonyms from antonyms, we did not observe this issue.

In the combined distance measure (Figure 1c), derivation remains quite well separated from inflection, apart from the boundary operation of negation. In all measures, the same three operations show the lowest distances: inflection for case, number, and gender.[18] These are quite typical pure inflections, extremely productive, governed by clear rules, mostly determined by syntactic rules and agreement, with a small and regular effect on the meaning of the inflected words.

---

[18] A morphological change of gender is considered to be an inflectional operation in Czech on verbs and adjectives, where it is governed by agreement, but not on nouns.

6.2 Derivations

In Figure 1, we grouped all derivational operations together, as the version of DeriNet we used does not contain any labels of derivational edges. However, with the help of the heuristic labelling by Musil et al. (2019), we performed a manual inspection of the results and gathered a number of observations.

We observed very low distances in all measures for the change from a perfective verb to its imperfective counterpart. While traditionally treated as derivation in Czech, this is a very regular and productive suffixation, and the change in meaning is also quite small and regular, and could thus be also treated as inflection. Interestingly, this is only partially true for the inverse of forming a perfective from a naturally imperfective verb, where a range of prefixes can be used, and there are often multiple options in use with varying meanings. This is correspondingly manifested by large JW distances of the forms, but COS distances remain low (although higher than for the perfectivisation).

Other low-distance operations that we observed are the transition from an adjective to an adverb (low JW, medium COS), formation of a diminuitive noun (low JW and COS), and formation of a possessive adjective from a noun (medium to low JW and COS), all of which are highly regular and productive, associated with a regular small change of meaning. All of these can be regarded as somewhere between a derivation and an inflection, motivating the idea of using a continous inflection-derivation scale rather than a strict binary categorization.

Derivations that radically change the part of speech, such as a transition between a verb and a noun, typically have higher COS distances, as the shift of the meaning is usually large; JW distances are medium to high, as there is often a large change of the suffix, sometimes accompanied by changes in the root. This is in line with these being quite prototypical derivations.

We observed a rather high contrast of a medium to low JW but a high COS distance for the change of a masculine noun to its feminine variant. This is typically performed by a small semi-regular suffix change, but considerably changes the meaning, albeit in a very regular way.

7 Conclusion

In this work, we attempted to automatically distinguish inflection from derivation without learning from annotated data, mainly based on the assumption that derivations tend to shift the meaning more than inflections. We tried several word distance measures, based both on the characters in the word forms, as well as distributional vector space representations of the word forms. We found a multiplication of Jaro-Winkler distance with cosine distance of FastText word embeddings to achieve the best results.

We used two evaluation setups, either directly separating the word form pairs based on the optimal distance threshold found in an oracle way, or clustering the word forms with an agglomerative clustering algorithm.

We conducted experiments on a subset of a Czech word formation database, observing F1 accuracy of inflection separation around 40%. Further analysis of the results showed that different classes of inflections and derivations are typically associated with different word form distances. To some extent, this corresponds to the inflectionality of some derivations and the derivationality of some inflections; however, to some extent, this is simply an artifact of the properties of the methods.

In future, we would like to employ multiple inflection-derivation distinction criteria described in the literature to improve the methods. From a research point of view, we are interested in arriving at an empirical measure of inflectionality versus derivationality of morphological operations, as this seems to be a more adequate view than a strict binary separation of inflection from derivation.

We also intend to extend this method to a wider range of languages. Our preliminary experiments on a set of 23 languages (Rosa and Žabokrtský, 2019) indicate that this should be feasible, obtaining some promising results for 20 of the languages (Arabic, Estonian, and 18 Indo-European languages).

We make all our code available on GitHub.[19]

---

[19]https://github.com/ptakopysk/lemata

Acknowledgments

This work was supported by the grants No. GA19-14534S and GA18-02196S of the Czech Science Foundation and the project No. DG16P02B048 of the Ministry of Culture of the Czech Republic. It has been using language resources developed, stored, and distributed by the LINDAT/CLARIAH CZ project (LM2015071, LM2018101).

References

Željko Agić and Ivan Vulić. 2019. JW300: A wide-coverage parallel corpus for low-resource languages. In *Proceedings of the 57th Annual Meeting of the Association for Computational Linguistics*. Association for Computational Linguistics, Florence, Italy, pages 3204–3210. https://www.aclweb.org/anthology/P19-1310.

Olivier Bonami and Denis Paperno. 2018. Inflection vs. derivation in a distributional vector space. *Lingue e linguaggio* 17(2):173–196.

Geert Booij. 2006. Inflection and derivation. In Keith Brown, editor, *Encyclopedia of Language and Linguistics, Second Edition*, Elsevier, pages 654–661.

Mirjana Bozic and William Marslen-Wilson. 2010. Neurocognitive contexts for morphological complexity: Dissociating inflection and derivation. *Language and Linguistics Compass* 4(11):1063–1073.

Mathias Creutz and Krista Lagus. 2007. Unsupervised models for morpheme segmentation and morphology learning. *ACM Transactions on Speech and Language Processing (TSLP)* 4(1):3.

Matthew S. Dryer and Martin Haspelmath, editors. 2013. *WALS Online*. Max Planck Institute for Evolutionary Anthropology, Leipzig. http://wals.info/.

John Goldsmith. 2001. Unsupervised learning of the morphology of a natural language. *Computational Linguistics* 27(2):153–198. https://doi.org/10.1162/089120101750300490.

Edouard Grave, Piotr Bojanowski, Prakhar Gupta, Armand Joulin, and Tomas Mikolov. 2018. Learning word vectors for 157 languages. In *Proceedings of the International Conference on Language Resources and Evaluation (LREC 2018)*.

Jan Hajič and Jaroslava Hlaváčová. 2016. MorfFlex CZ 160310. LINDAT/CLARIN digital library at the Institute of Formal and Applied Linguistics (ÚFAL), Faculty of Mathematics and Physics, Charles University. http://hdl.handle.net/11234/1-1673.

Martin Haspelmath and Andrea Sims. 2013. *Understanding morphology*. Routledge.

Radka Julínková. 2012. „*Split Morphology Hypothesis*" *na materiálu češtiny*. Master's thesis, Univerzita Palackého v Olomouci, Filozofická fakulta.

Michal Křen, Václav Cvrček, Tomáš Čapka, Anna Čermáková, Milena Hnátková, Lucie Chlumská, Tomáš Jelínek, Dominika Kováříková, Vladimír Petkevič, Pavel Procházka, Hana Skoumalová, Michal Škrabal, Petr Truneček, Pavel Vondřička, and Adrian Zasina. 2016. SYN v4: large corpus of written Czech. LINDAT/CLARIN digital library at the Institute of Formal and Applied Linguistics (ÚFAL), Faculty of Mathematics and Physics, Charles University. http://hdl.handle.net/11234/1-1846.

Vladimir Iosifovich Levenshtein. 1966. Binary codes capable of correcting deletions, insertions, and reversals. In *Soviet physics doklady*. volume 10, pages 707–710.

Julie Beth Lovins. 1968. Development of a stemming algorithm. *Mech. Translat. & Comp. Linguistics* 11(1-2):22–31.

Thomas Mayer and Michael Cysouw. 2014. Creating a massively parallel Bible corpus. In *Proceedings of the Ninth International Conference on Language Resources and Evaluation (LREC-2014)*. European Languages Resources Association (ELRA), Reykjavik, Iceland, pages 3158–3163. http://www.lrec-conf.org/proceedings/lrec2014/pdf/220_Paper.pdf.

Tomas Mikolov, Ilya Sutskever, Kai Chen, Greg S Corrado, and Jeff Dean. 2013. Distributed representations of words and phrases and their compositionality. In *Advances in neural information processing systems*. pages 3111–3119.

Christian Monson, Jaime Carbonell, Alon Lavie, and Lori Levin. 2008. Paramor: Finding paradigms across morphology. In Carol Peters, Valentin Jijkoun, Thomas Mandl, Henning Müller, Douglas W. Oard, Anselmo Peñas, Vivien Petras, and Diana Santos, editors, *Advances in Multilingual and Multimodal Information Retrieval*. Springer Berlin Heidelberg, Berlin, Heidelberg, pages 900–907.

Tomáš Musil, Jonáš Vidra, and David Mareček. 2019. Derivational morphological relations in word embeddings. In *Proceedings of the 2019 ACL Workshop BlackboxNLP: Analyzing and Interpreting Neural Networks for NLP*. Association for Computational Linguistics, Florence, Italy, pages 173–180. https://www.aclweb.org/anthology/W19-4818.

F. Pedregosa, G. Varoquaux, A. Gramfort, V. Michel, B. Thirion, O. Grisel, M. Blondel, P. Prettenhofer, R. Weiss, V. Dubourg, J. Vanderplas, A. Passos, D. Cournapeau, M. Brucher, M. Perrot, and E. Duchesnay. 2011. Scikit-learn: Machine learning in Python. *Journal of Machine Learning Research* 12:2825–2830.

Martin F Porter. 2001. Snowball: A language for stemming algorithms.

Rudolf Rosa. 2018. Plaintext Wikipedia dump 2018. LINDAT/CLARIN digital library at the Institute of Formal and Applied Linguistics (ÚFAL), Faculty of Mathematics and Physics, Charles University. http://hdl.handle.net/11234/1-2735.

Rudolf Rosa and Zdeněk Žabokrtský. 2019. Unsupervised lemmatization as embeddings-based word clustering. *CoRR* abs/1908.08528. http://arxiv.org/abs/1908.08528.

Gregory T Stump. 1998. Inflection. In Andrew Spencer and Arnold M. Zwicky, editors, *The Handbook of Morphology*, London: Blackwell, pages 13–43.

Pius ten Hacken. 2014. Delineating derivation and inflection. In *The Oxford handbook of derivational morphology*, Oxford University Press.

František Trávníček. 1951. *Mluvnice spisovné češtiny*, volume 1. Slovanské nakl.

Magda Ševčíková and Zdeněk Žabokrtský. 2014. Word-Formation Network for Czech. In *Proceedings of the 9th International Conference on Language Resources and Evaluation*. ELRA, Reykjavik, Iceland, pages 1087–1093.

William E. Winkler. 1990. String comparator metrics and enhanced decision rules in the Fellegi-Sunter model of record linkage. In *Proceedings of the Section on Survey Research Methods (American Statistical Association)*. pages 354–359. http://www.amstat.org/sections/srms/Proceedings/papers/1990_056.pdf.

Zdeněk Žabokrtský, Magda Ševčíková, Milan Straka, Jonáš Vidra, and Adéla Limburská. 2016. Merging data resources for inflectional and derivational morphology in Czech. In *Proceedings of the Tenth International Conference on Language Resources and Evaluation (LREC 2016)*. pages 1307–1314.

Redesign of the Croatian derivational lexicon

Matea Filko
Faculty of Humanities
and Social Sciences
University of Zagreb
`matea.filko@ffzg.hr`

Krešimir Šojat
Faculty of Humanities
and Social Sciences
University of Zagreb
`ksojat@ffzg.hr`

Vanja Štefanec
Faculty of Humanities
and Social Sciences
University of Zagreb
`vstefane@ffzg.hr`

Abstract

This paper deals with the redesign of the Croatian derivational lexicon – CroDeriV. In its first online version the lexicon consisted solely of verbs analyzed for morphemes. In further steps of its development, lexemes of other POS (adjectives, nouns) are analyzed, both in terms of their morphological structure and word-formation patterns, and imported into the lexicon. Dealing with new POS as well as the annotation of word-formation patterns among lexemes required the modification of the database structure. In this paper we present a restructured version of the database, adapted to include other POS and to explicitly mark word-formation patterns. These procedures enable precise and refined queries based on various parameters through the online search interface.

1 Introduction

Although the development of language resources dealing with word-formation has begun almost twenty years ago, derivational resources nowadays exist for a relatively limited number of languages (CatVar (Habash and Dorr, 2003) for English; Démonette (Hathout and Namer, 2014) for French; DeriNet (Žabokrtský et al., 2016; Ševčíková and Žabokrtský, 2014) and Derivancze (Pala and Šmerk, 2015) for Czech; Word Formation Latin (Passarotti and Mambrini, 2012; Litta et al., 2016) for Latin; DerIvaTario (Talamo et al., 2016) for Italian; DErivBase (Bajestan et al., 2017; Zeller et al., 2013) for German and DErivBase.HR (Šnajder, 2014) for Croatian). These resources predominantly focus on the annotation of word-formation processes within and across derivational families, i.e. among lexemes with the same root. The majority of them does not take into account the morphemics, in other words, they do not mark the complete morphological structure of lexemes. Procedures applied in their development range from automatic or semi-automatic to completely manual.

Croatian is a Slavic language with rich morphological processes. High-quality language resources dealing with the morphological structure and derivational relations of Croatian lexemes are needed in numerous NLP tasks and they are valuable for various theoretical research. In this paper, we present the development and enrichment of the existing version of the Croatian derivational lexicon – CroDeriV (Šojat et al., 2013).[1] Procedures applied in the building of this lexicon significantly differ from those listed above: 1) the previous version of the lexicon contained only verbs[2]; 2) the focus was on a thorough analysis of the morphological structure of lexemes, whereas word-formation processes among them were not explicitly marked. In the second phase of its development, its structure has been expanded with words of other POS and the representation of derivational relations between stems and derivatives has been introduced. Consequently, the online interface has been adapted to offer a wider range of possible queries.

The paper is structured as follows: in Section 2 we present the current structure of the derivational lexicon and possible queries via online interface; in Section 3 we discuss how the analysis of verbal derivational families used so far can be applied to adjectives and nouns; Section 4 presents the new structure of the database and new query parameters. Section 5 brings concluding remarks and the outline of future work.

---

[1] The search interface of the current version of the lexicon is available at `croderiv.ffzg.hr`.

[2] Cf. (Šojat et al., 2012) for the motivation to include only verbs in the first phase of the lexicon development.

2 Croatian derivational lexicon v. 1.0

In its first version, the derivational lexicon consisted of ca 14.500 verbs collected from two large Croatian corpora (Croatian National Corpus (Tadić, 2009), and Croatian web corpus hrWaC (Ljubešić and Klubička, 2014)) and free online dictionaries. All verbal lemmas, i.e. their infinitive forms, were segmented into morphemes and verbs sharing the same root were grouped into derivational families. As in other Slavic languages, aspect is an inherent category of Croatian verbs (Marković, 2012, 183). Each verb was therefore additionally marked as perfective, imperfective or bi-aspectual.[3]

The morphological segmentation was divided into two steps: 1) automatic segmentation via rules based on lists of various derivational affixes; 2) manual checking of the results which was necessary due to extensive homography and allomorphy of affixes and roots. Thus, all the homographic forms were manually disambiguated and all the allomorphs were linked to single representative morphemes. This line of processing resulted in a two-layer annotation consisting of a surface and a deep layer.

At the surface, all allomorphs were identified and marked for their type. Possible types of morphemes recognized in Croatian lexemes are prefixes, roots, derivational suffixes, inflectional suffixes and interfixes for compounds. The surface form of the verb *ispuniti* 'to fulfill, to fill out' can be represented as follows:

is-pun-i-ti

is = prefix; *pun* = root; *i* = derivational (thematic) suffix; *ti* = inflectional (infinitive) suffix,

whereas the verb *odobrovoljiti* 'to cheer up' was segmented as follows:

o-dobr-o-volj-i-ti

o = prefix; *dobr* = root2; *o* = interfix; *volj* = root1; *i* = derivational suffix; *ti* = inflectional (infinitive) suffix.

At the deep layer, the prefixal allomorph *is* was connected to its representative morph *iz*. The representative morph is the one from which other allomorphs can be established with the least number of morpho-phonological rules. This kind of analysis enables queries over roots and all derivatives within derivational families, but also over specific affixes or even their combinations (prefixal, suffixal and both) used in various derivational families.[4] The CroDeriV database is available online and it has already been widely used for research and teaching purposes. As indicated, this version of the derivational lexicon is limited in two ways: 1) it is restricted to only one POS; 2) derivational relations between lexemes are not represented. In the following sections, we discuss how the database originally structured for the full analysis of Croatian verbal morphology was modified and expanded.

3 Croatian derivational lexicon v. 2.0

The expansion of the derivational lexicon followed the principles set in previous phases. First, nominal and adjectival lemmas were collected from corpora and online dictionaries of Croatian. In order to obtain a representative sample for further analysis and processing, we chose approx. 6.000 nouns and 1.000 adjectives according to their frequency indicated by the Croatian frequency dictionary (Moguš et al., 1999) and frequency lists generated by corpus management system NoSketchEngine for both representative corpora (Croatian National Corpus and Croatian web corpus hrWaC).[5] Both motivated and unmotivated lexemes were included in our analysis. They were added to the lexicon, in order to capture the word-formational path from the base, unmotivated lexeme, to the final, motivated lexeme. However, named entities were excluded from the lists, since they are not formed via productive word-formation patterns in Croatian (Babić, 2002, 16).

---

[3] Verbal aspectual pairs are considered separate lemmas in Croatian. Therefore, the so-called thematic suffixes, as *-i-* in *is-pun-i-ti* (see the example in this section), are classified as derivational suffixes (Marković, 2012, 188). Apart from derivation of aspectual pairs, these suffixes are also used to form verbs from other parts of speech, e.g. adjectives or nouns (*pun* 'full' – *pun-i-ti* 'to fill, imperfective' – *is-pun-i-ti* 'to fulfill, perfective'; *rad* 'work' – *rad-i-ti* 'to work, imperfective' – *za-rad-i-ti* 'to earn, perfective'), which is another proof of their derivational status.

[4] The extensive statistics on roots, affixes and their combinations in Croatian is presented in (Šojat et al., 2013).

[5] The procedure of collection and analysis of adjectives is thoroughly described in (Filko and Šojat, 2017). The number of approx. 6.000 nouns was obtained by merging the lists of 5.000 most frequent nouns from the above-mentioned sources.

The next steps consisted of 1) the manual segmentation of lexemes into morphemes, and 2) the analysis of their morphological structure. Our main objective was to establish general rules pertaining to their morphological structure and relevant word-formation processes, both POS-maintaining and POS-changing. The aim of the whole procedure is to enable a rule-based procedure for automatic morphological segmentation to be applied to the rest of the compiled data.[6]

As opposed to verbs, predominantly formed via prefixation or highly-regular suffixation from other verbs (Šojat et al., 2012), nouns and adjectives are mostly formed by means of suffixation. Babić (2002) lists 526 nominal and 160 adjectival suffixes out of the total of 771 suffixes used in Croatian. Although these data are useful in many aspects, the productivity of certain affixes is not provided. Productivity here refers to the number of co-occurrences of an affix and various stems as recorded in data, i.e. the number of different lexemes formed via particular derivational affix. Preliminary research clearly shows that a relatively small subset of suffixes compared to the numbers listed above is used for nominal and adjectival derivation (in our sample, at least). The results will be used for the creation of rules for morphological segmentation in the analysis of the remaining data.

Generally, the morphological segmentation is based on the two-layered approach previously applied to verbs: at the surface layer all possible morphs are identified and marked for their type; at the deep layer allomorphs are connected to the single representative morph, e.g. the noun *učiteljica* 'female teacher' was segmented as follows:

uč-i-telj-ic-a

uč = root; *i*, *telj*, *ic* = derivational suffixes; *a* = inflectional suffix,

whereas the adjective *izlječiv* 'curable' was segmented and processed as follows:

iz-lječ-iv-Ø

iz = prefix; *lječ* = root; *iv* = derivational suffix; *Ø* = inflectional suffix, and the allomorph *lječ* is at the deep layer connected to the representative root morph *lijek*.

The morphological structure of lexemes regardless of their part of speech consists of the following types of morphemes: prefixes, roots, interfixes, and derivational and inflectional suffixes. Each morpheme type can occur more than once in the morphological structure.

In the next step, derivational relations among selected lexemes were annotated. After the lexemes were morphologically segmented and all the allomorphs were linked to representative morphemes, the stem, and the word-formation pattern was determined for each lexeme in the database. Lexemes are POS-tagged and motivated lexemes are derivationally linked to their base lexeme. The derivational connection is established only if there are simultaneous phonological and semantic relations between the base and the derived lexeme (Babić, 2002, 25). In other words, no derivational connection exists 1) between suppletive allomorphs, 2) between two lexemes with diachronically remotely connected meanings. However, if the derivational connection is synchronically transparent, the derivational link is established, inspite of the significant shift in meaning from the base word to the derived lexeme (e.g. *čeznuti* 'to long for' *iščeznuti* 'to vanish'). In that case, the affix sense is marked as idiosyncratic.

The new version of the database thus provides the information on the following word-formational properties:

- word-formation pattern: ***učiteljica*** < *učitelj* + *ica* [suffixation]; ***izlječiv*** < *izliječiti* + *iv* [suffixation]

- allomorph of the stem – stem: *učitelj – učitelj*; *izlječ – izliječ*

- allomorph of the affix – affix: *ica – ica*; *iv – iv*

- affix sense: agent, feminine; possibility

- POS of the stem: N; V.[7]

---

[6] A more straightforward rule-based procedure based on a simple set of rules for the detection and segmentation of single nominal suffixes was applied in (Šojat et al., 2014). However, the main goal of this procedure was to detect words of the same derivational family, not to analyze their morphological structure.

[7] This representation is in line with Babić (2002, 16), probably the most extensive and thorough book on word-formation for a Slavic language, where it is stated that derivational representation should at least show 1) word-formational units (affixes); 2) word-formational stems; 3) types of word-formation processes; 4) meanings of derived words.

The word-formation patterns and affixal senses as presented in our lexicon are explained in more detail in the following subsections.

3.1 Word-formation patterns

We take into account word-formation processes in Croatian that are recorded and described in relevant reference literature:

1. **suffixation:**

   - *pjev(ati)* 'to sing' + *-ač* > *pjevač* 'singer'
   - *glas* 'voice' + *-ati* [8] > *glasati* 'to vote'
   - *učitelj* 'teacher' + *-ev* > *učiteljev* 'teacher's'

2. **prefixation:**

   - *za-* + *pjev(ati)* 'to sing' > *zapjevati* 'to start singing'
   - *do-* + *predsjednik* 'president' > *dopredsjednik* 'vicepresident'
   - *pred-* + *školski* 'school, ADJ' > *predškolski* 'preschool'

3. **simultaneous suffixation and prefixation:**

   - *o-* + *svoj* 'one's own' + *-iti* > *osvojiti* 'to conquer, to win'
   - *bez-* + *sadržaj* 'content' + *-an* > *besadržajan* 'pointless, content-free'

4. **compounding:**

   - *vjer(a)* 'trust' + *-o-* + *dostojan* 'worthy' > *vjerodostojan* 'trustworthy'
   - *zlo* 'evil' + *upotrijebiti* 'to use' > *zloupotrijebiti* 'to misuse, to abuse'
   - *polu* 'half' + *mjesečni* 'monthly' > *polumjesečni* 'semimonthly'

5. **simultaneous compounding and suffixation:**

   - *vod(a)* + *-o-* + *staj(ati)* 'to stand' > *vodostaj* 'water level'
   - *vanjsk(a)* 'external' + *-o-* + *trgovin(a)* 'trade' + *-ski* > *vanjskotrgovinski* 'external trade, ADJ'

6. **simultaneous prefixation and compounding:**

   - *o-* + *zlo* 'evil' + *glasiti* 'to say' > *ozloglasiti* 'to discredit, to bring into disrepute'

7. **back-formation:**

   - *izlaz(iti)* 'to exit' > *izlaz* 'exit'

8. **conversion or zero-derivation:**

   - *mlada* 'young, feminine, ADJ' > *mlada* 'bride, N'

9. **ablaut:**

   - *plesti = plet + (Ø) + (ti)* 'to twine' > *plot* 'fence'.

The word-formation pattern at the same time indicates the type of the word-formation process. In determining the word-formation pattern, we take into account only the last step in the formation of the particular lexeme. For example, the verb *ispunjavati* 'to fulfill, imperfective' is derivationally related to the verb *puniti* 'to fill, imperfective' via indirect derivational connection. However, it is directly formed from the verb *ispuniti* 'to fulfill, perfective'. Therefore, we mark only this last derivational step in the word-formation pattern:

---

[8] In traditional approaches, thematic suffix and infinitive ending are considered as one word-formational element consisting of two morphemes.

ispun(iti) 'to fulfill, perfective' + *-javati* > *ispunjavati* 'to fulfill, imperfective' [suffixation].

The remote derivational link is available via word-formation pattern of the verb *ispuniti* 'to fulfill, perfective':

is- + *puniti* 'to fill, imperfective' > *ispuniti* 'to fullfil, perfective' [prefixation].

In some cases, it is hard to determine the word-formation pattern due to several plausible possibilities, especially when dealing with suffixation. In these cases, we follow the criteria established in Babić (2002, 38–41):

- if one of the competing solutions increases the overall number of derivational units in Croatian, the other solution should be selected as the more appropriate one;

- if one of the competitive solutions can be applied to the wide range of motivated lexemes, and others cannot, the first solution should be selected as the more appropriate one.

3.2 Affixal senses

Affixes are in our database structured as polysemous units, which is in line with recent approaches to affixal meanings (Babić (2002, 38), Lehrer (2003), Lieber (2004, 11), Lieber (2009, 41), Aronoff and Fudeman (2011, 140–141)). In relation to other constituents of the word-formation pattern, one of the affixal meanings is realized in the final motivated lexeme. For example, verbal prefix *nad-* can have two meanings. It can express:

1. **location** (subtype: *over*), e.g. *letjeti* 'to fly' > *nadletjeti* 'to fly over'

2. **quantity** (subtype: *exceeding*), e.g. *rasti* 'to grow' > *nadrasti* 'to outgrow'.

The detailed typology of possible meanings of verbal prefixes in Croatian is explained in Šojat et al. (2012), whereas possible meanings of the most productive adjectival suffixes are discussed in Filko and Šojat (2017). The inventory of possible affixal meanings for Croatian nouns is designed according to descriptions in Croatian grammar and reference books. Affixes and their meanings are treated differently in Croatian literature. Whereas some grammar books (e.g .(Babić, 2002)) list affixes alphabetically and note their possible meanings, the others (e.g. Silić and Pranjković (2005) and Barić et al. (1995)) list possible meanings of motivated words (e.g. diminutives, locations, instruments, male agents, female agents, animals, etc.) and indicate which affixes can be used for the creation of these meanings. This, in other words, means that suffixes are grouped according to at least one of their meanings. We combined the information from these sources and modified the final polysemous structure of affixes if needed according to the lexemes in our database. The above-mentioned nominal suffix *-ica* can express at least the following meanings[9]:

1. **agent, female**, e.g. *učitelj* 'teacher, male' > *učiteljica* 'teacher, female'

2. **person, both sexes**, e.g. *izbjegao* 'exiled' > *izbjeglica* 'refugee'

3. **animal, female**, e.g. *golub* 'pigeon, male' > *golubica* 'pigeon, female'

4. **diminutive**, e.g. *pjesma* 'song' > *pjesmica* 'ditty, rhyme'

5. **thing**, e.g. *sanjar* 'dreamer, male' > *sanjarica* 'dream book'

6. **drink**, e.g. *med* 'honey' > *medica* 'honey liqueur'

7. **plant**, e.g. *otrovan* 'poisonous' > *otrovnica* 'poisonous plant, mushroom (and venomous snake)'

8. **location**, e.g. *okolo* 'around' > *okolica* 'surrounding'

9. **temporal mark**, e.g. *godišnji* 'yearly' > *godišnjica* 'anniversary'

---

[9] These are the meanings annotated so far in our material. For a more extensive account, including idiosyncratic meanings, cf. Babić (2002, 183–189)

10. **disease**, e.g. *vruć* 'hot' > *vrućica* 'fever'

11. **literary type**, e.g. *slovo* 'letter' > *poslovica* 'saying'

12. **linguistic term – type of word/sentence**, e.g. izveden 'derived, ADJ' > izvedenica 'derived lexeme'

13. **number of men involved**, e.g. *dvoje* 'two, of different gender' > *dvojica* 'two, of male gender'

14. **anatomical part**, e.g. *jagoda* 'strawberry' > *jagodica* 'cheekbone, fingertip'

In the following section, we present the redesign of the database based on the analysis of the initial set of nouns and adjectives in terms of their morphological structure and word-formation properties.

4   Redesign of the database

In its first publicly available version, the CroDeriV database was structured according to the generalized morphological structure of Croatian verbs, consisting of four slots for prefixes (P), two slots for stems (L), one slot for an interfix between two stems (I), three slots for derivational suffixes (S) and one slot for the inflectional suffix (END). This structure is sufficient to accommodate all Croatian verbs[10]:

   (P4) (P3) (P2) (P1) (L2) (I) **L1** (S3) **S2 S1 END**.

Online queries are possible across several categories: P2, P1, L1, S2, S1, lemma, and their combinations. Additionally, information about the root is shown by the mouse hover over the stem, and the information about the aspect and reflexivity of verbs is shown by clicking on the Details button. Apart from listing all verbs with the same root, i.e. from the same derivational families, other derivational data among lexemes are not presented. In order to include lexemes of other POS and to show derivational relations among them, the database and online search interface had to be modified. We discuss these modifications in the following subsections.

4.1   Expanding to other POS

The generalized morphological structure of Croatian lexemes differs according to their part of speech. The generalized structure is a theoretical construct that serves to represent the maximum number of slots for morphemes and their combinations across various POS (as presented above for verbs). Generally, the maximum number of prefixes recorded in Croatian lexemes is four, the maximum number of roots is six, and the maximum number of suffixes is seven (Marković, 2013).[11] The first version of the database was structured according to the generalized structure provided for verbs. However, this structure cannot be applied to nouns and adjectives due to the complexity of their suffixal parts. In this stage of work, we have to address issues as: 1) how to present the morphological structure of lexemes in terms of roots, derivational and inflectional morphemes in a consistent manner, regardless of their POS; 2) how to present which lexemes belong to the same derivational families, i.e. have identical lexical morphemes; 3) how to present derivational processes applied between stems and derivatives within families as well as affixes or their combinations thereby used. In order to accommodate the lemmas of different POS, the overall structure of the database was re-organized in a POS-independent manner. Therefore, additional suffixal slots (up to seven) are provided to accommodate the morphologically most complex nouns and adjectives.

Various queries over the database are based on the surface form of the lemma analyzed for morphemes.[12] The type of each segmented morpheme (prefix, root, suffix, interfix) is marked. Additional information pertains to the **part of speech** of the entry and specific grammatical categories. For example, **aspect** and **reflexivity** for verbs, **gender** for nouns and adjectives and **definiteness** for adjectives.

---

[10] Brackets denote that the segment is optional.

[11] In our material, we recorded up to four prefixes for verbal lemmas, as well as three roots and five suffixes (four derivational + one inflectional) for adjectival lemmas.

[12] Although the surface form of the lemma will be presented, only the queries via morphemes and their combinations, not allomorphs, will be enabled.

4.2 Word-formation relations and word-formation patterns

Apart from the complete morphological structure of lemmas and their grammatical categories, the new version of the Croatian derivational lexicon will include information on their word-formation properties. As indicated in Section 3, we manually marked 1) word-formation patterns, 2) allomorphs and morphs of stems, 3) allomorphs and morphs of affixes, and 4) POS of the base word for each nominal and adjectival lemma in the initial set. This, in turn, enables us to automatically acquire information about: 1) the type of the word-formation process applied (suffixation, prefixation, simultaneous suffixation and prefixation, compounding, simultaneous compounding and suffixation/prefixation, back-formation, conversion, ablaut), 2) the nature of the word-formation process applied (POS-changing or POS-maintaining), 3) the base word / root used in word-formation process.[13]

We plan to include this information for each entry in the lexicon. In the new search interface, the information about grammatical categories (1), morphological structure (2-3), and word-formation properties (4-8) (see the example below) will be available by clicking on the lemma. A link to the base word will be available through the word-formation pattern (4 - <u>poslužiti</u>). The list of all derivatives of the same stem will be available through the link on that stem in the entry (5 - <u>posluži</u>). This will enable users to follow complete derivational paths in both directions: from a root to the final derivative (through the link in 4) and from a particular derived word back to the root (through the link in 5). In the future, we plan to provide links to online dictionaries and inflectional lexica for Croatian and to apply a tool for visualization of derivational relations within families.

The complete structures of entries of different POS are as follows:

1. **lemma:** <u>poslužitelj</u> 'server'

    - **POS:** N
    - **gender:** masculine

2. **morphological structure – surface layer:** po-služ-i-telj-Ø
   (po = prefix, služ = root, i, telj = derivational suffixes, Ø = inflectional suffix)

3. **morphological structure – deep layer:** po-slug-i-telj-Ø
   (po = prefix, slug = root, i, telj = derivational suffixes, Ø = inflectional suffix)

4. **word-formation pattern:** <u>poslužiti</u>[14] + telj

5. **stem (allomorph of the stem):** <u>posluži</u>[15] (posluži)

6. **affix (allomorph of the affix):** telj (telj)

7. **affix sense:** instrument

8. **word-formation process** (POS > POS): suffixation (V > N)

9. **link to the Croatian Language Portal**[16].

---

1. **lemma:** <u>potpisati</u> 'to sign'

    - **POS:** V
    - **aspect:** perfective
    - **reflexivity:** non-reflexive

---

[13] If there is the base word, then the lemma is morphologically complex or motivated; if the lemma is formed directly from the root, then it is morphologically simple or unmotivated. However, both motivated and unmotivated words are included in the lexicon, in order to obtain the complete word-formational path of the lexical entries.

[14] The base word is underlined and functions as a link to the entry of that word in the lexicon.

[15] The stem is underlined and functions as a link to all lemmas derived directly from this stem, e.g. *poslužilac*.

[16] Online dictionary of Croatian: www.hjp.znanje.hr.

2. **morphological structure – surface layer:** pot-pis-a-ti
   (pot = prefix, pis = root, a = derivational suffix, ti = inflectional suffix)

3. **morphological structure – deep layer:** pod-pis-a-ti
   (pod = prefix, pis = root, a = derivational suffix, ti = inflectional suffix)

4. **word-formation pattern:** pod + pisati

5. **stem (allomorph of the stem):** pisati (pisati)

6. **affix (allomorph of the affix):** pod (pot)

7. **affix sense:** location: under

8. **word-formation process** (POS > POS): prefixation (V > V)

9. **link to the Croatian Language Portal.**

---

1. **lemma:** beskrajan 'endless'

   - **POS:** A
   - **gender:** masculine
   - **definiteness:** indefinite

2. **morphological structure – surface layer:** bes-kraj-an-Ø
   (bes = prefix, kraj = root, an = derivational suffix, Ø = inflectional suffix)

3. **morphological structure – deep layer:** bez-kraj-an-Ø
   (bez = prefix, kraj = root, an = derivational suffix, Ø = inflectional suffix)

4. **word-formation pattern:** bez + kraj + an

5. **stem (allomorph of the stem):** kraj (kraj)

6. **affix1 (allomorph of the affix1):** bez (bes)   **affix2 (allomorph of the affix2):** an (an)

7. **affix1 sense:** deprivation   **affix2 sense:** having the property of [meaning of the base]

8. **word-formation process** (POS > POS): simultaneous prefixation and suffixation (N > A)

9. **link to the Croatian Language Portal.**

5   Concluding remarks and future work

In this paper we presented the redesign of the existing version of the Croatian derivational lexicon and its online search interface, required to include non-verbal lemmas into the lexicon, as well as to represent various derivational properties of Croatian lexemes. The Croatian derivational lexicon v. 2.0 is designed to comprise the information about morphological structures, word-formation patterns and derivational relations among Croatian lexemes. We believe that additional information provided for each lemma, e.g. about grammatical categories or external links to online dictionaries, makes this lexicon even more attractive to users.

As mentioned, we intend to use manually analyzed material to build a rule-based automatic procedure for morphological and word-formation analysis. This will facilitate the analysis of new lemmas and their inclusion in the lexicon.

References

Mark Aronoff and Kristen Fudeman. 2011. *What is Morphology. Second Edition*. Wiley-Blackwell, Chichester.

Stjepan Babić. 2002. *Tvorba riječi u hrvatskome književnome jeziku*. Hrvatska akademija znanosti i umjetnosti : Globus, Zagreb.

Elnaz Shafaei Bajestan, Diego Frassinelli, Gabriella Lapesa, and Sebastian Padó. 2017. DErivCelex: Development and Evaluation of a German Derivational Morphology Lexicon based on CELEX. In *Proceedings of the Workshop on Resources and Tools for Derivational Morphology (DeriMo)*. EDUCatt, Milano, pages 117–127.

Eugenija Barić, Mijo Lončarić, Dragica Malić, Slavko Pavešić, Mirko Peti, Vesna Zečević, and Marija Znika. 1995. *Hrvatska gramatika*. Školska knjiga, Zagreb.

Matea Filko and Krešimir Šojat. 2017. Expansion of the Derivational Database for Croatian. In Eleonora Litta and Marco Passarotti, editors, *Proceedings of the Workshop on Resources and Tools for Derivational Morphology (DeriMo)*. EDUCatt, Milan, pages 27–37.

Nizar Habash and Bonnie Dorr. 2003. A categorial variation database for English. In *Proceedings of NAACL-HLT*. AL, Edmonton, pages 17–23.

Nabil Hathout and Fiammetta Namer. 2014. Démonette, a French derivational morpho-semantic network. *Linguistic Issues in Language Technology* 11(5):125–168.

Adrienne Lehrer. 2003. Polysemy in derivational affixes. In Todd Z. Herman V. Nerlich, B. and D. D. Clarke, editors, *Polysemy. Flexible Patterns of Meaning in Mind and Language*, De Gruyter Mouton, New York, pages 218–232.

Rochelle Lieber. 2004. *Morphology and lexical semantics*. Cambridge University Press, New York.

Rochelle Lieber. 2009. *Introducing Morphology*. Cambridge University Press, New York.

Eleonora Litta, Marco Passarotti, and Chris Culy. 2016. Formatio formosa est. Building a Word Formation Lexicon for Latin. In *Proceedings of the Third Italian Conference on Computational Linguistics (CLiC-it 2016)*. aAccademia University Press, Napoli, pages 185–189.

Nikola Ljubešić and Filip Klubička. 2014. {bs,hr,sr}WaC - Web corpora of Bosnian, Croatian and Serbian. In *Proceedings of the 9th Web as Corpus Workshop (WaC-9)*. Association for Computational Linguistics, Gothenburg, pages 29–35.

Ivan Marković. 2012. *Uvod u jezičnu morfologiju*. Number 6 in Biblioteka Thesaurus. Disput, Zagreb. OCLC: 815718585.

Ivan Marković. 2013. O najvećim (i) mogućim hrvatskim riječima. In Stjepan Blažetin, editor, *XI. međunarodni kroatistički znanstveni skup*, Znanstveni zaovd Hrvata u Mađarskoj, Zagreb, pages 43–58.

Milan Moguš, Maja Bratanić, and Marko Tadić. 1999. *Hrvatski čestotni rječnik*. Školska knjiga : Zavod za lingvistiku Filozofskoga fakulteta, Zagreb.

Karel Pala and Pavel Šmerk. 2015. Derivancze — Derivational Analyzer of Czech. In Pavel Král and Václav Matoušek, editors, *Text, Speech, and Dialogue: 18th International Conference, TSD 2015*. Springer, Berlin: Heidelberg, pages 515–523. https://doi.org/10.1007/978-3-319-24033-6$_5$8.

Marco Passarotti and Francesco Mambrini. 2012. First Steps towards the Semi-automatic Development of a Wordformation-based Lexicon of Latin. In Nicoletta Calzolari et al., editor, *Proceedings of the Eighth International Conference on Language Resources and Evaluation*. ELRA, Istanbul, pages 852–859.

Josip Silić and Ivo Pranjković. 2005. *Gramatika hrvatskoga jezika: za gimnazije i visoka učilišta*. Školska knj, Zagreb. OCLC: ocm70847560.

Marko Tadić. 2009. New version of the Croatian National Corpus. In Dana Hlaváčková, Aleš Horák, Klara Osolsobě, and Pavel Rychlý, editors, *After Half a Century of Slavonic Natural Language Processing*, Masaryk University, Brno, pages 199–205.

Luigi Talamo, Chiara Celata, and Pier Marco Bertinetto. 2016. DerIvaTario: An annotated lexicon of Italian derivatives. *Word Structure* 9(1):72–102. https://doi.org/https://doi.org/10.3366/word.2016.0087.

Britta Zeller, Jan Šnajder, and Sebastian Padó. 2013. DErivBase: Inducing and Evaluating a Derivational Morphology Resource for German. In *Proceedings of the 51st Annual Meeting of the Association for Computational Linguistics (Volume 1: Long Papers)*. Association for Computational Linguistics, Sofia, pages 1201–1211.

Magda Ševčíková and Zdeněk Žabokrtský. 2014. Word-Formation Network for Czech. In Nicoletta Calzolari et al., editor, *Proceedings of the Ninth International Conference on Language Resources and Evaluation*. ELRA, Reykjavik, pages 1088–1093.

Jan Šnajder. 2014. DERIVBASE.HR: A High-Coverage Derivational Morphology Resource for Croatian. In Nicoletta Calzolari et al., editor, *Proceedings of the 9th Language Resources and Evaluation Conference (LREC 2014)*. ELRA, Reykjavik, pages 3371–3377.

Krešimir Šojat, Matea Srebačić, and Tin Pavelić. 2014. CroDeriV 2.0.: Initial Experiments. In Adam Przepiórkowski and Maciej Ogrodniczuk, editors, *Advances in Natural Language Processing*, Springer International Publishing, Cham, volume 8686, pages 27–33. https://doi.org/10.1007/978-3-319-10888-9_3.

Krešimir Šojat, Matea Srebačić, and Marko Tadić. 2012. Derivational and Semantic Relations of Croatian Verbs. *Journal of Language Modelling* 0(1):111. https://doi.org/10.15398/jlm.v0i1.34.

Krešimir Šojat, Matea Srebačić, and Vanja Štefanec. 2013. CroDeriV i morfološka raščlamba hrvatskoga glagola. *Suvremena lingvistika* 75:75–96.

Zdeněk Žabokrtský, Magda Ševičková, Milan Straka, Jonáš Vidra, and Adéla Limburská. 2016. Merging Data Resources for Inflectional and Derivational Morphology in Czech. In Nicoletta Calzolari et al., editor, *Proceedings of the Tenth International Conference on Language Resources and Evaluation*. ELRA, Portorož, pages 1307–1314.

DeriNet 2.0: Towards an All-in-One Word-Formation Resource

Jonáš Vidra   Zdeněk Žabokrtský   Magda Ševčíková   Lukáš Kyjánek
Charles University, Faculty of Mathematics and Physics,
Institute of Formal and Applied Linguistics
Malostranské náměstí 25, 118 00 Prague 1, Czech Republic
`{vidra,zabokrtsky,sevcikova,kyjanek}@ufal.mff.cuni.cz`

Abstract

DeriNet is a large linguistic resource containing over 1 million lexemes of Czech connected by almost 810 thousand links that correspond to derivational relations. In the previous version, DeriNet 1.7, it only contained very sparse annotations of features other than derivations – it listed the lemma and part-of-speech category of each lexeme and since version 1.5, a true/false flag with lexemes created by compounding.

The paper presents an extended version of this network, labelled DeriNet 2.0, which adds a number of features, namely annotation of morphological categories (aspect, gender and animacy) with all lexemes in the database, identification of root morphemes in 250 thousand lexemes, annotation of five semantic labels (diminutive, possessive, female, iterative, and aspect) with 150 thousand derivational relations, a pilot annotation of parents of compounds, and another pilot annotation of so-called fictitious lexemes, which connect related derivational families without a common synchronous parent. The new pieces of annotation could be added thanks to a new file format for storing the network, which aims to be general and extensible, and therefore possibly usable to other similar projects.

1 Motivation

The paper deals with extending DeriNet, a lexical database developed for Czech, which contains around 1 million lexemes connected with app. 810 thousand edges representing morphological derivations (Ševčíková and Žabokrtský, 2014), forming app. 220 thousand tree-shaped derivational families. The resulting version is labelled DeriNet 2.0 (Vidra et al., 2019) and it is available for download under a free non-commercial license. The extension is mostly qualitative: we extended the expressive power of the underlying data structure (and of the associated file format) substantially and thus enabled capturing language phenomena which were impossible to handle in the previous versions of DeriNet. More specifically, there are five newly supported annotation components in the DeriNet annotation scheme:

- **morphological categories**: lexemes are assigned morphological categories that remain constant under inflection, such as gender with nouns or aspect with verbs,

- **morpheme segmentation**: lexemes belonging to the largest derivational families have their root morphemes identified,

- **semantic labels**: derivational relations are assigned labels capturing the change that the meaning of the base word undergoes by attaching the affix (in affixation),

- **compounds**: lexemes with two (or even more) roots are linked with their both (or more) base words. The linking of compounds with their base words has not been possible so far due to the highly constrained data structure used in DeriNet 1.7 and older versions,

Proceedings of the 2nd Int. Workshop on Resources and Tools for Derivational Morphology (DeriMo 2019), pages 81–89,
Prague, Czechia, 19-20 September 2019.

- **fictitious lexemes**: lexemes that are attested neither in the corpora nor in the dictionaries but, based on structural analogies, fill a paradigm gap in the derivational family are newly added into the database.

Feature	1.7	2.0
Derivational relations	✓	✓
Part-of-speech category	✓	✓
Morphological categories	✗	✓
Compounding relations	✗[a]	✓
Semantic labels	✗	✓
Morpheme segmentation	✗	✓[b]
Fictitious lexemes	✗	✓

[a] A yes/no flag marking compounds was encoded in the POS category.

[b] In the present version, only root morphs of a subset of lexemes are annotated. The format allows for marking affixes and allomorph resolution as well, but these annotations are not currently available.

Table 1: Comparison of features available in DeriNet 1.7 and 2.0.

The annotations present in DeriNet 2.0 are compared to the previous versions in Table 1.

The actual recall of the newly added annotations is rather limited, but even the incomplete annotations serve as a proof of concept and show the viability of the new annotation scheme. However, the main ambition of our efforts does not lie in adding several new annotation components, but it is more strategical: in the long term we attempt to accumulate virtually all information related to word-formation in a single data resource (similarly to various kind of syntactic and semantic phenomena being annotated), and thus hopefully profit from new synergies due to combining different possible perspectives on word-formation.

Some of the features are already available in existing data resources, so from this viewpoint DeriNet 2.0 is rather eclectic. For instance, detailed information on morphological categories of lexemes is captured in MorfFlex CZ (Hajič and Hlaváčová, 2013), morpheme segmentation is available in the MorphoChallenge dataset (Kurimo et al., 2009), semantic labels of derivations can be found in Démonette (Hathout and Namer, 2014), compounds are identified in CELEX (Baayen et al., 1995), and fictitious lexemes are introduced in Word Formation Latin (Litta Modignani Picozzi et al., 2016). However, none of these resources, to the best of our knowledge, integrate all the features in one data set.

In addition, we believe that the extended annotation scheme is flexible enough to be sustainable for a longer period of time without major changes. At the same time, we plan to apply the scheme to dozens of other languages, so the scheme is designed to be as language agnostic as possible.

2 New features

2.1 Morphological categories

Lexemes were provided with selected morphological categories in DeriNet 2.0, namely with the category of gender and animacy (with nouns) and the category of grammatical aspect (with verbs), in addition to the part-of-speech category already available in the previous versions of the data. These categories do not change in inflection, and are characteristics associated with lexemes as wholes.

The morphological categories to assign were extracted from the MorfFlex CZ dictionary (Hajič and Hlaváčová, 2013), which enumerates all possible word forms and positional part-of-speech tags for each lexeme. The set of part-of-speech tags of a particular lexeme was merged into a single string, tentatively called a *tag mask*, by comparing individual positions of the different tags. If all tags of the lexeme share the same value at a position, it is copied to the tag mask, otherwise it is replaced by the question mark ("?"). For example, exploiting the part-of-speech tags assigned to the individual forms of the noun *chata* 'cottage' (15 tags in total, including e.g. "NNFS1-----A----", "NNFP3-----A----" or "NNFP7-----A---6"), the tag mask "NNF??-----A---?" was compiled, which encodes that the lexeme is a noun (NN), feminine

	Unique combinations	Lexemes
Lemma	2,599	5,342
Lemma + POS category	2,137	4,353
Lemma + POS category + morph. features	518	1,039

Table 2: Counts of homonymous combinations of various lexeme features with the counts of affected lexemes. By definition, the number of lexemes must be at least twice the number of homonymous combinations, since a feature combination that is not shared by at least two lexemes is not a homonym. The number of lexemes is slightly larger, because some lemmas are shared by up to four lexemes: e.g. *stát*, which can mean either 'a country', 'to stand', 'to stop' or 'to melt down'.

gender (F), affirmative polarity (A). The categories associated with the other positions either vary (cf. the question marks in the positions associated with the categories of number, case, and register), or are not applicable to Czech nouns (such as tense, cf. the positions with '-').

In addition to the tag mask format, the morphological categories listed above were extracted from the masks and stored in DeriNet 2.0 using the Universal Features annotation scheme (Nivre et al., 2016).

This approach to extracting the morphological categories has a very high precision: we were unable to find any errors in the grammatical category of gender in an uniformly randomly selected sample of 100 nouns, and we found two errors in the category of aspect in a sample of 100 verbs.

The recall of the annotation is also high, with 99.6% nouns being assigned a gender category and 93.2% of verbs being assigned an aspect category. The nouns with missing gender annotation are mostly foreign words with unclear or varying gender (such as *image* 'image', which can be masculine inanimate, feminine or neuter, depending on the speaker's preference) and words which can be used to denote both male and female persons (such as *šereda* 'ugly (person), gorgon'). The dictionary we use as the lexeme source, MorfFlex CZ, usually handles these cases by having a separate lexeme for each gender (such that all forms of any one lexeme have identical gender), but some lexemes have forms with different genders, resulting in missing gender annotation after extraction. Verbs with missing aspect annotation are mostly missing the aspect category in the source dictionary, but some (about one in six) are marked as biaspectual – we chose to exclude the annotation of these for the time being due to low precision of this part of the annotation.

The morphological categories can in some cases also be used to distinguish homonymous lexemes. Just as there are pairs of lexemes with identical lemmas, but different part-of-speech categories, there are also pairs of lexemes with identical lemmas and part-of-speech categories, but with a different aspect or gender. Using tag masks combined with lemmas, we are able to uniquely identify 3,314 out of 4,353 lexemes with homonymous lemma-POS combinations in DeriNet 2.0; see Table 2 for detailed counts. Therefore, the tag masks serve as auto-generated readable identifiers (distinguishing e.g. masculine inanimate *mol#NNI??-----A---?* 'mole (unit)' and masculine animate *mol#NNM??-----A---?* 'mill moth'), as opposed to e.g. using opaque numerical indices ('mol#1' and 'mol#2') or manually created descriptions ('mol#grammolecule' and 'mol#butterfly') to distinguish homonyms, which are the methods used by the underlying MorfFlex CZ dictionary.

The homonymous lexemes may or may not be parts of the same derivational family. For instance, the noun *růst* 'growth' and the verb *růst* 'to grow', distinguished by the part-of-speech category, are related derivationally, the former one being converted from the latter one. Compared to that, the noun *tulení* 'hugging' and the adjective *tulení* 'seal' are identical in spelling due to truly random coincidence; they belong to different derivational families (with the root lexemes *tulit (se)* 'to hug' and *tuleň* 'seal', respectively).

Morphological categories captured by the tag masks have been exploited also within the semantic labelling task (Section 2.3).

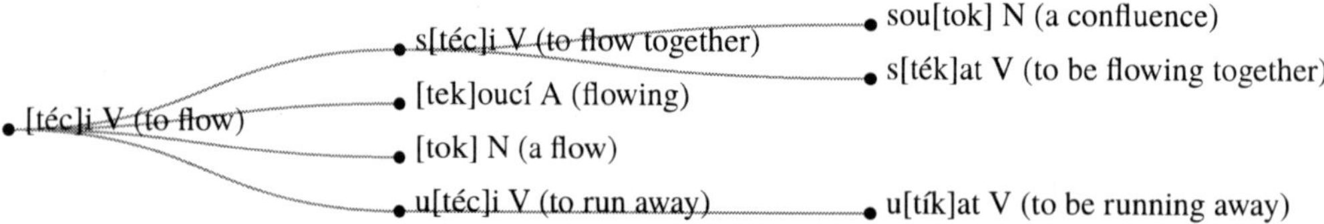

Figure 1: An excerpt from the derivation family of *téci* 'to flow' in DeriNet 2.0, with root morphemes marked by square brackets. Other morphemes are not delimited yet.

2.2 Morpheme segmentation and allomorphy

In DeriNet 2.0, root morphemes of selected lexemes were identified as another new type of annotation. This annotation is currently limited to approx. 250 thousand lexemes and it is supposed to be a sort of pilot approach for a large-coverage morpheme segmentation in the next versions of the data. See Figure 1 for a small sample of the annotation.

Morpheme segmentation, i.e. the task of dividing a word into a sequence of segments corresponding to morphemes as the smallest meaning-bearing language units, is extremely challenging when dealing with Czech. The main reason is the frequent allomorphy of roots and affixes. For instance, in the lexemes that are derivationally related with the verb *jíst* 'to eat' in our data, eight root allomorphs are attested (*jís, jíd, jed, níd, nís, něd, jez,* and *něz*). Notice that there is not a single grapheme shared by all of the allomorphs.

In our first experiment, which aimed at identification of all morphemes in the lexeme structure, we implemented a lemma decision-tree-based segmenter that employed letter n-gram features and was trained using a set of 750 hand-segmented lexemes sampled uniformly randomly from DeriNet. However, the evaluation on an independent dataset showed that the precision of predicted segmentations (95% of identified morphs were correct, resulting in only 85% words being segmented correctly) is below the quality standards usually applied on released versions of DeriNet.[1]

In our second experiment we thus limited the problem to identification of root morphemes and made more intensive use of existing derivational trees. For the 760 biggest trees (in terms of number of nodes), we applied the previously trained segmenter on all lexemes in these trees and tried to distinguish the substring corresponding to the root morpheme in each lexeme using a simple heuristics: for each word, mark its rarest morpheme (measured by the number of occurrences in the whole dataset) as the root; break ties by marking the longer or first such morpheme. We obtained a set of allomorphs of the root morpheme for each tree. The quality of such allomorph sets was relatively low, so the sets were cleaned manually. Then we identified the position of a root allomorph in each lexeme. In case there were multiple matching allomorphs, we preferred the longest one. This process was iterated several times, as applying the allomorph sets to the whole derivational trees uncovered several errors in the annotation of derivational relations. Finally, we added such detected root morpheme boundaries into DeriNet 2.0, which resulted in 243,793 lexemes with identified boundaries of their root morphemes.

There was an interesting side effect of the allomorphy annotations. Some sets of allomorphs for different derivational trees were surprisingly similar. In some cases the string similarity was only due to a random coincidence of etymologically unrelated clusters (such as the derivational family of *řídký* 'sparse' with root allomorphs *řid, říd, řed* and *řeď,* from which three allomorphs overlap with the family of *řídit* 'to direct, to drive' with allomorphs *řid, říz, řed, řiz* and *říd*), or due to a diachronic etymological relation (since DeriNet focuses on synchronic view of the language, diachronic relations which are opacified in modern language are not included; e.g. *medvěd* 'a bear', which is etymologically a compound with bases *med* 'honey' and *jíst* 'to eat', is not connected to any parents in DeriNet) but sometimes we really revealed a missing relation in DeriNet 1.7; such relations were added into DeriNet 2.0.

---

[1]One of our design decisions is that when adding new pieces of information into DeriNet, we prefer precision to recall.

Label	Count
POSSESSIVE	88,718
FEMALE	29,023
ASPECT	15,439
ITERATIVE	11,886
DIMINUTIVE	5,939

Table 3: Counts of the semantic labels in DeriNet 2.0 data.

2.3 Semantic labels

Semantic labels, which capture the change in the meaning of the base word imposed by affixation, were assigned with relations in DeriNet as another new type of annotation.

Derivation in Czech is characterized by homonymy (polyfunctionality)[2] of affixes and, at the same time, by their synonymy. Many affixes convey more than one meaning, cf. the suffix *-ka* deriving the diminutive noun *vlnka* 'small wave' from *vlna* 'wave', the female noun *hráčka* 'female player' derived from *hráč* 'player', the agent noun *mluvka* 'talker' from *mluvit* 'to talk', or the location noun *skládka* 'dump' from *skládat* 'to dump'. From the opposite perspective, a particular meaning is usually expressed by several formally different affixes, cf. the suffixes *-ka* in *stavitelka* 'female builder' derived from *stavitel* 'builder', *-yně* in *kolegyně* 'female colleague' from *kolega* 'colleague', *-ice* in *lékarnice* 'female pharmacist' from *lékárník* 'pharmacist', and *-ová* in *švagrová* 'sister-in-law' from *švagr* 'brother-in-law' for female nouns.

The size of the DeriNet data as well as the fact that the database is still under construction were the main reasons why semantic labels were not assigned manually but a Machine Learning experiment was designed for this task. Five semantic labels were included into this pilot experiment, namely DIMINUTIVE, POSSESSIVE, FEMALE, ITERATIVE, and ASPECT. While the former four labels correspond to semantic concepts proposed for comparative research into affixation (Bagasheva, 2017), the latter label (ASPECT) was introduced to apply to suffixation of verbs that does not affect the lexical meaning but changes the category of aspect (from imperfective to perfective, or the other way round).[3]

Training and test data for the Machine Learning experiment, containing both positive and negative examples of the five labels to assign, were compiled by exploiting several language resources and reference grammars of Czech (cf. Ševčíková and Kyjánek in press for details).

Using morphological categories and character n-grams of both the base words and the derivatives as features and multinomial logistic regression as method, precision and recall achieved in the Machine Learning task (each above 96 %) indicate that the derivational families organized into rooted trees and the features included provide a sufficient basis for resolving the homonymy and synonymy of affixes in most cases. An analysis of incorrectly labelled relations pointed out, for example, to feminines incorrectly assigned the FEMALE label such as *profesura* 'professorship' (derived from *profesor* 'professor') and *krejčovna* 'tailor's workshop' (from *krejčí* 'tailor'); these particular problem could be solved by introducing the animacy feature to feminine nouns because the label is intended to be assigned only with female counterparts of masculines. The resulting annotation of approx. 150 thousand labels was included into the DeriNet 2.0 data. See Table 3 for a breakdown of the counts of the different categories.

2.4 Compounds

In the previous versions of DeriNet, compounding could not be adequately modelled due to the highly constrained data structure used as it allowed to specify a single base word for each derivative. In DeriNet 2.0, we introduce the notion of multi-node relations, which allow specifying any number of parent and child lexemes. Compounding is then annotated as a relation with multiple parent lexemes. For technical reasons, a single parent and a single child must always be marked as the main ones. For example, the adjective *jihoruský* 'south-Russian' points to the adjective *ruský* 'Russian' by the main-parent link

---

[2]The terms "homonymy" / "polyfunctionality" are preferred to "polysemy" in the recent accounts (Karlík et al., 2012; Šimandl, 2016).

[3]As formation of aspectual pairs exploits derivational affixes in Czech, the decision has been made to model this process as deverbal derivation in the DeriNet database (Ševčíková et al., 2017).

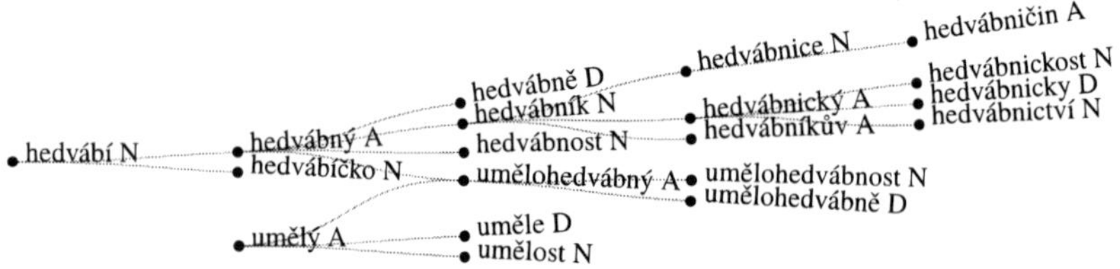

Figure 2: The derivational family of the lexeme *hedvábí* 'silk' and a tiny excerpt from the family of the lexeme *umělý* 'artificial'.

and to the noun *jih* 'south' by a non-main-parent link. The interfix *-o-* is often added between the bases in compounds in Czech.

DeriNet 2.0 contains only a small sample of such compound annotations, serving, again, rather as a proof of concept. Out of around 33 thousand lexemes that were labelled as compounds in DeriNet 1.7 (just by a value of a binary flag, without their compositional parents being identified), we extracted 723 lexemes whose parents can be guessed automatically with relatively high reliability using just a set of string-based heuristics. Subsequently we checked the list manually, which resulted in 600 compounds for which both compositional parents are captured in DeriNet 2.0.

The procedure for guessing the parents works as follows: First, decompose the lemma of a known compound by finding an 'o' in it and extracting the substrings preceding and following it. The first substring is looked up in the dictionary as-is or amended by appending 'ý', 'í', 'y', 'i', 'o' or 'a' (these are common inflectional suffixes and word-final characters in Czech). The second substring is looked up in the dictionary verbatim. If these lookups result in finding only a single pair of candidate parent lemmas, output them, otherwise (if there are no matches or several) end the procedure without producing any output. This selection process is highly biased, as it selects only lexemes whose parents can be conclusively detected by simple string manipulation and ignores ambiguous cases.

2.5   Fictitious lexemes

When climbing from a derived word up to its base parent and continuing upwards, we should ideally end up in a tree root whose lemma is unmotivated (in the synchronous sense, i.e. there is no parent in the contemporary language). However, in some cases there is a strong intuition that a virtual node (corpus- or dictionary unattested) would be helpful, as it would complete a certain analogy pattern. For instance, one is tempted to add a non-existent lemma *bízet*, as it would naturally serve as a derivational base for *nabízet* 'to offer', *vybízet* 'to prompt', *pobízet* 'to urge' and others. In other configurations, a virtual lemma such as *tmívat* could serve as an intermediate node connecting a (corpus-attested) lemma *stmívat se* 'to get dark' with its (corpus-attested) grand-parent *tma* 'darkness', as the derivation is (again, by analogy to other derivational clusters) perceived as two-phase. We call such artificially added lexemes *fictitious lexemes*. As a proof of concept, we added 13 such lexemes into DeriNet 2.0, which allowed adding 41 derivations for prefixed verbs that should clearly not remain in tree root positions.

Our approach to fictitious lexemes is related to the linguistic discussion on cranberry morphemes (Aronoff, 1976) and, more recently, on paradigm gaps (e.g. Stump 2019). However, the basic building unit of DeriNet is still a lexeme, not a morpheme, and thus there is no technical means e.g. for expressing that a set of prefixed verbs makes use of the same morpheme.

3   New data format

Previous versions of DeriNet were published in a simple tab-separated-values text database file, which contained a lemma, part of speech and an optional link to the derivational parent on each line; see Table 4 for an excerpt from DeriNet 1.7. None of the new features can be represented in the old format, and so a new one was required. The old format cannot be easily extended in a backwards-compatible way, as there is no reserved field that identifies the version and the only possible simple extension – adding new columns to the end of each line – is not compatible with existing tooling that uses several extra columns

ID	Lemma	Dictionary ID	POS	Parent ID
205205	hedvábíčko	hedvábíčko	N	205206
205206	hedvábí	hedvábí	N	
205207	hedvábně	hedvábně_(*1ý)	D	205219
205208	hedvábnice	hedvábnice_(*3ík)	N	205215
205209	hedvábničin	hedvábničin_(*3ce)	A	205208
205211	hedvábnickost	hedvábnickost_(*3ý)	N	205213
205212	hedvábnicky	hedvábnicky_(*1ý)	D	205213
205213	hedvábnický	hedvábnický	A	205215
205214	hedvábnictví	hedvábnictví	N	205213
205215	hedvábník	hedvábník	N	205219
205216	hedvábníkův	hedvábníkův_(*2)	A	205215
205218	hedvábnost	hedvábnost_(*3ý)	N	205219
205219	hedvábný	hedvábný	A	205206
...	...	...	...	...
768083	umělohedvábně	umělohedvábně_^(*1ý)	D	768085
768084	umělohedvábnost	umělohedvábnost_^(*3ý)	N	768085
768085	umělohedvábný	umělohedvábný	AC	
...	...	...	...	...
768106	umělý	umělý	A	768197
768020	uměle	uměle_(*1ý)	D	768106

Table 4: The tree below the word "hedvábí" (silk) and excerpts of two related trees in DeriNet 1.7. Since compounding cannot be annotated in this format, the word *umělohedvábný* 'made of artificial silk' is marked as a compound using the 'C' mark in the part-of-speech category (fourth) column, but it is not connected to its parents *umělý* 'artificial' and *hedvábný* 'made of silk'. The Dictionary ID column lists the lemma together with technical suffixes as used by the MorfFlex dictionary – these are stored in DeriNet to allow interlinking the two resources.

for debugging information. Therefore, as compatibility with existing tools has to be broken anyway, we decided to create the new format from the ground up. When designing it, we drew inspiration from the CoNLL-U format (Nivre et al., 2016), which recently became a widely used representation of syntactic annotation.

The new format is still textual and lexeme-based, but it allows for a wider range of annotations. In addition to the lemma and part-of-speech tag, each lexeme can be annotated by key-value pairs specifying its properties (e.g. the morphological categories), a list of its morphemes together with their properties, and by any number of directed word-formation relations. Each relation can connect multiple parents with multiple children, and so the format can express one-to-one relation such as derivation or conversion, as well as many-to-one relations such as compounding. The relations are stored together with their children, connecting them to their parents, but otherwise behave like separate entities, and they can also be annotated with arbitrary key-value pairs (e.g. the semantic labels). Furthermore, there is space for custom (possibly language-specific) extensions of the format in the form of JSON-encoded data (Bray, 2017) stored in the last column. See Table 5 for an excerpt from DeriNet 2.0 showing the new format and Figure 2 for a visualization of this data.

The key-value pairs are serialized into textual form by joining each pair by an equals sign and concatenating all such pairs describing a single entity with ampersands: `key1=value1&key2=value2`. If the field in question describes multiple entities, such as the segmentation, the different entities are concatenated with vertical bars: `key1=value1&key2=value2|keyA=valueA`.

To simplify processing of the data, which has the form of a general graph, we explicitly select tree-shaped substructures from the graph and store the corresponding "main parent" IDs in a dedicated column. The lexemes in the file are grouped according to these trees, which correspond to derivational families, with compounds added to the family of one of its parents. This enables e.g. performing a depth-first search over the structure of the derivational families without having to explicitly avoid cycles by marking

ID	Language-specific ID	Lemma	POS	Morphological features	Morpheme segmentation	Main parent ID	Parent relation
144293.0	hedvábí#NNN??-----A---?	hedvábí	N	Gender=Neut			
144293.1	hedvábný#AA???----??---?	hedvábný	A			144293.0	Type=Derivation
144293.2	hedvábně#Dg-------??---?	hedvábně	D			144293.1	Type=Derivation
144293.3	hedvábník#NNM??-----A---?	hedvábník	N	Animacy=Anim &Gender=Masc		144293.1	Type=Derivation
144293.4	hedvábnice#NNF??-----A---?	hedvábnice	N	Gender=Fem		144293.3	SemanticLabel=Female &Type=Derivation
144293.5	hedvábničin#AU????--------?	hedvábničin	A	Poss=Yes		144293.4	SemanticLabel=Possessive &Type=Derivation
144293.6	hedvábnický#AA???----??---?	hedvábnický	A			144293.3	Type=Derivation
144293.7	hedvábnickost#NNF??-----?---?	hedvábnickost	N	Gender=Fem		144293.6	Type=Derivation
144293.8	hedvábnicky#Dg-------??---?	hedvábnicky	D			144293.6	Type=Derivation
144293.9	hedvábnictví#NNN??-----A---?	hedvábnictví	N	Gender=Neut		144293.6	Type=Derivation
144293.10	hedvábníkův#AU???M--------?	hedvábníkův	A	Poss=Yes		144293.3	SemanticLabel=Possessive &Type=Derivation
144293.11	hedvábnost#NNF??-----?---?	hedvábnost	N	Gender=Fem		144293.1	Type=Derivation
144293.12	umělohedvábný#AA???----??---?	umělohedvábný	A			144293.1	Sources=195833.258,144293.1 &Type=Compounding
144293.13	umělohedvábnost#NNF??-----?---?	umělohedvábnost	N	Gender=Fem		144293.12	Type=Derivation
144293.14	umělohedvábně#Dg-------??---?	umělohedvábně	D			144293.12	Type=Derivation
144293.15	hedvábíčko#NNN??-----A---?	hedvábíčko	N	Gender=Neut		144293.0	SemanticLabel=Diminutive &Type=Derivation
…	…	…	…	…	…	…	…
195833.258	umělý#AA???----??---?	umělý	A		End=2 &Morph=um &Start=0 &Type=Root	195833.4	Type=Derivation
195833.259	uměle#Dg-------??---?	uměle	D		End=2 &Morph=um &Start=0 &Type=Root	195833.258	Type=Derivation

Table 5: The lexeme *hedvábí* 'silk' and derivationally related lexemes (i.e. a derivational family represented as a tree) in DeriNet 2.0. The last column containing language- and resource-specific data has been omitted; in Czech DeriNet 2.0, it contains the technical dictionary ID for linking with MorfFlex and the "compound yes/no" flag from previous versions of DeriNet. The line with dots divides the derivational family of *hedvábí* 'silk' from that of *umělý* 'artificial', which is the second base word for the compound *umělohedvábný* 'made of artificial silk'.
The family containing the lexeme *umělý* is large enough to have been included in the annotation of root morphemes. This annotation is present in the sixth column. The family of *hedvábí* is not annotated yet and its sixth column is therefore empty.

visited lexemes, as it guarantees that a search starting from the base lexeme of the family will visit every lexeme in it exactly once. There are no restrictions on the relations not participating in the tree-shaped substructure, so it is possible to annotate double motivation and other general word-formation structures.

Inside the database, all lexemes are unambiguously specified using an ID. The IDs are hierarchical: they are composed of the number of the tree they are in, followed by the number of the lexeme in the tree. These IDs are used to specify the endpoints of relations. Because the hierarchical numerical IDs are opaque and they change when a lexeme is reconnected, a more permanent identification of a lexeme is possible using a field reserved for this purpose. In the Czech data, this fields contains the lemma and the tag mask introduced above.

Detailed documentation of the file format and the tools created to process it is available in the `doc/` directory of the DeriNet repository at `https://github.com/vidraj/derinet`.

4 Conclusions

The DeriNet database was enriched with several different kinds of information about the lexemes and relations contained therein, which were previously missing. The newly added annotation is useful or even required for many tasks, e.g. the availability of morphological categories was vital to annotating the relations with semantic labels, and the annotation of root morphemes allowed us to cross-check the already present derivational relations with another source of information.

The format we developed for storing and distributing the resulting network is supposed to be general, extensible and language-agnostic enough to be usable by other projects as well. By using a common format, the different networks can benefit from a shared set of tools and services and their users can more easily compare their properties, and through that hopefully also the properties of different languages.

Acknowledgments

This work was supported by the Grant No. GA19-14534S of the Czech Science Foundation, by the Charles University Grant Agency (project No. 1176219) and by the SVV project number 260 453. It has been using language resources developed, stored, and distributed by the LINDAT/CLARIAH CZ project (LM2015071, LM2018101).

References

Mark Aronoff. 1976. *Word Formation in Generative Grammar*, volume 1 of *Linguistic inquiry monographs*. MIT Press, Cambridge, Massachusetts, USA.

R. Harald Baayen, Richard Piepenbrock, and Leon Gulikers. 1995. CELEX2. Linguistic Data Consortium, Catalogue No. LDC96L14. https://catalog.ldc.upenn.edu/LDC96L14.

Alexandra Bagasheva. 2017. Comparative Semantic Concepts in Affixation. In *Competing Patterns in English Affixation*. Peter Lang, Bern, Switzerland, pages 33–65.

Tim Bray. 2017. The JavaScript Object Notation (JSON) Data Interchange Format. RFC 8259.

Jan Hajič and Jaroslava Hlaváčová. 2013. MorfFlex CZ. http://hdl.handle.net/11858/00-097C-0000-0015-A780-9.

Nabil Hathout and Fiammetta Namer. 2014. Démonette, A French Derivational Morpho-Semantic Network. *Linguistic Issues in Language Technology* 11:125–162.

Petr Karlík et al. 2012. *Příruční mluvnice češtiny*. NLN, Prague, Czech Republic.

Mikko Kurimo, Sami Virpioja, Ville T. Turunen, Graeme W. Blackwood, and William Byrne. 2009. Overview and results of Morpho Challenge 2009. In *Workshop of the Cross-Language Evaluation Forum for European Languages*. Springer, pages 578–597.

Eleonora Maria Gabriella Litta Modignani Picozzi, Marco Carlo Passarotti, and Chris Culy. 2016. Formatio Formosa est. Building a Word Formation Lexicon for Latin. In *Proceedings of the 3rd Italian Conference on Computational Linguistics*. pages 185–189.

Joakim Nivre et al. 2016. Universal Dependencies v1: A Multilingual Treebank Collection. In *Proceedings of the 10th International Conference on Language Resources and Evaluation*. ELRA, pages 1659–1666.

Gregory Stump. 2019. Some sources of apparent gaps in derivational paradigms. *Morphology* 29:271–292.

Jonáš Vidra, Zdeněk Žabokrtský, Lukáš Kyjánek, Magda Ševčíková, and Šárka Dohnalová. 2019. DeriNet 2.0. LINDAT/CLARIN digital library at the Institute of Formal and Applied Linguistics (ÚFAL), Faculty of Mathematics and Physics, Charles University. http://hdl.handle.net/11234/1-2995.

Magda Ševčíková, Adéla Kalužová, and Zdeněk Žabokrtský. 2017. Identification of Aspectual Pairs of Verbs Derived by Suffixation in the Lexical Database DeriNet. In *Proceedings of the Workshop on Resources and Tools for Derivational Morphology*. EDUCatt, Milan, Italy, pages 105–116.

Magda Ševčíková and Lukáš Kyjánek. in press. Introducing Semantic Labels into the DeriNet Network. *Jazykovedný časopis* .

Magda Ševčíková and Zdeněk Žabokrtský. 2014. Word-Formation Network for Czech. In *Proceedings of the 9th International Conference on Language Resources and Evaluation*. ELRA, Reykjavik, Iceland, pages 1087–1093.

Josef Šimandl, editor. 2016. *Slovník afixů užívaných v češtině*. Karolinum, Prague, Czech Republic.

Building a Morphological Network for Persian on Top of a Morpheme-Segmented Lexicon

Hamid Haghdoost,[†] **Ebrahim Ansari,**[†‡] **Zdeněk Žabokrtský,**[‡] **and Mahshid Nikravesh**[†]
[†] Department of Computer Science and Information Technology,
Institute for Advanced Studies in Basic Sciences
[‡] Institute of Formal and Applied Linguistics,
Faculty of Mathematics and Physics, Charles University
{hamid.h,ansari,nikravesh}@iasbs.ac.ir
zabokrtsky@ufal.mff.cuni.cz

Abstract

In this work, we introduce a new large hand-annotated morpheme-segmentation lexicon of Persian words and present an algorithm that builds a morphological network using this segmented lexicon. The resulting network captures both derivational and inflectional relations. The algorithm for inducing the network approximates the distinction between root morphemes and affixes using the number of morpheme occurrences in the lexicon. We evaluate the quality (in the sense of linguistic correctness) of the resulting network empirically and compare it to the quality of a network generated in a setup based on manually distinguished non-root morphemes.

In the second phase of this work, we evaluated various strategies to add new words (unprocessed in the segmented lexicon) into an existing morphological network automatically. For this purpose, we created primary morphological networks based on two initial data: a manually segmented lexicon and an automatically segmented lexicon created by unsupervised MORFESSOR. Then new words are segmented using MORFESSOR and are added to the network. In our experiments, both supervised and unsupervised versions of MORFESSOR are evaluated and the results show that the procedure of network expansion could be performed automatically with reasonable accuracy.

1 Introduction

Even though the Natural Language community put more focus on inflectional morphology in the past, one can observe a growing interest in research on derivational morphology (and other aspects of word formation) recently, leading to existence of various morphological data resources. One relatively novel type of such resources are word-formation networks, some of which represent information about derivational morphology in the shape of a rooted tree. In such networks, the derivational relations are represented as directed edges between lexemes (Lango et al., 2018).

In our work, we present a procedure that builds a morphological network for the Persian language using a word segmentation lexicon. The resulting network (a directed graph) represents each cluster of morphologically related word forms as a tree-shaped component of the overall graph. The specific feature of such network is that it captures both derivational and inflectional relations. Figure 1 shows an example of such a tree for the Persian language which represents a base morpheme meaning "to know" and all derived and inflected descendants. In this example, the path from the root to one of the deepest leafs corresponds to the following meanings: (1) "to know", (2) "knowledge"/"science", (3) "scientist", (4) "scientists", (5) "some scientists".

What we use as a primary source of morphological information is a newly created manually annotated morpheme-segmented lexicon of Persian word forms, which is the only segmented lexicon for this language. At the same time, to the best of our knowledge, this lexicon could be considered as the biggest publicly available manually segmented lexicon at all (for any language).

Moreover, we expand the existing morphological network by adding new words into the current network by using our proposed core algorithm. In order to segment new words, we used both supervised and

Proceedings of the 2nd Int. Workshop on Resources and Tools for Derivational Morphology (DeriMo 2019), pages 91–100,
Prague, Czechia, 19-20 September 2019.

unsupervised version of MORFESSOR (Creutz et al., 2007; Grönroos et al., 2014), which is a popular automatic segmentation toolkit. After segmentation, the process of inducing morphological trees is the same as for hand-segmented words.

The paper is organized as follows: Section 2 addresses related work on derivational morphology networks and morphological segmentation. Section 3 introduces our hand-segmented Persian lexicon as well as related pre-processing phases. Section 4 describes the approach used in this work. Section 5 presents experiment results and finally Section 6 concludes the paper.

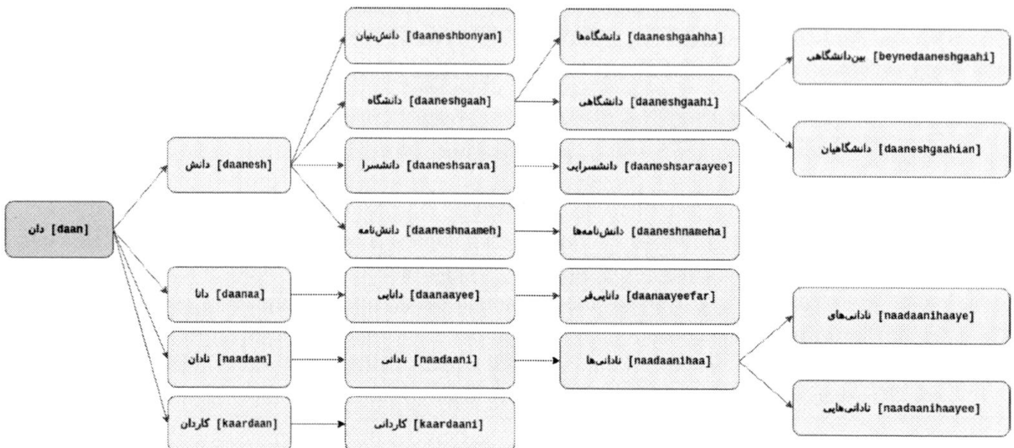

Figure 1: A sample of a Persian morpohological tree for root [dan] which means "to know". The two children of the root node have the meaning of "knowledge" [danesh] and "smart" [dana], respectively. The path from the root to one of the deepest leaf corresponds to the following meanings: (1) "to know", (2) "knowledge"/"science", (3) "scientist", (4) "scientists", (5) "some scientists".

2   Related work

For some languages, intensive research exists with focus on construction of resources specialized in derivation, e.g. DerivBase (Zeller et al., 2013) for German, Démonette (Hathout and Namer, 2014) for French, DerivBase.Hr (Šnajder, 2014) for Croatian, DeriNet (Ševčíková and Žabokrtský, 2014; Žabokrtský et al., 2016) for Czech, (Vilares et al., 2001; Baranes and Sagot, 2014; Lango et al., 2018) for Spanish, Word Formation Latin (Litta et al., 2016), and (Piasecki et al., 2012; Kaleta, 2017; Lango et al., 2018) for Polish. However, for many other languages the data resources which provide information about derived words are scarce or lacking. Simultaneously, inflectional resources are further developed in recent years too (Hajič and Hlaváčová, 2013).

The language studied in our work is Persian, which belongs to morphologically rich languages and is powerful and versatile in word formation. Having many affixes to form new words (a few hundred), the Persian language is considered to be an agglutinative language since it also frequently uses derivational agglutination to form new words from nouns, adjectives, and verb stems. Hesabi (1988) claimed that Persian can derive more than 226 million word forms.

To our knowledge, research on Persian morphology is very limited. Rasooli et al. (2013) claimed that performing morphological segmentation in the pre-processing phase of statistical machine translation could improve the quality of translations for morphology rich and complex languages. Although they segmented only an extremely limited and non-representative sample of Persian words (tens of Persian verbs), the quality of their machine translation system increases by 1.9 points of BLEU score. Arabsorkhi and Shamsfard (2006) proposed an algorithm based on Minimum Description Length with certain improvements for discovering the morphemes of the Persian language through automatic analysis of corpora. However, since no Persian segmentation lexicon was made publicly available, we decided to create a manually segmented lexicon for Persian that contains 45K words now.

As we discussed before, we also trained and evaluated our methods using automatic morph-segmented data. Automatic morphological segmentation was firstly introduced by Harris (1955). More recent research on morphological segmentation has been usually focused on unsupervised learning (Goldsmith, 2001; Creutz and Lagus, 2002; Poon et al., 2009; Narasimhan et al., 2015; Cao and Rei, 2016), whose goal is to find the segmentation boundaries using an unlabeled set of word forms (or possibly a corpus too). Probably the most popular unsupervised systems are LINGUISTICA (Goldsmith, 2001) and MORFESSOR, with a number of variants (Creutz and Lagus, 2002; Creutz et al., 2007; Grönroos et al., 2014). Another version of the latter which includes a semi-supervised extension was introduced by (Kohonen et al., 2010). Poon et al. (2009) presented a log-linear model which uses overlapping features for unsupervised morphological segmentation.

3 Data: New Persian Segmented Lexicon

We extracted our primary word list from a collection composed of three corpora. The first corpus contains sentences extracted from the Persian Wikipedia (Karimi et al., 2018). The second one is a popular Persian corpus **BijanKhan** (Bijankhan et al., 2011), and the last one is the Persian Named Entity corpus[1] (Poostchi et al., 2018). For all those corpora, we used the **Hazm** toolkit (Persian pre-processing and tokenization tools)[2] and the stemming tool presented by Taghi-Zadeh et al. (2015). We extracted and normalized all sentences and lemmatized and stemmed all words using our rule-based stemmer and a lemmatizer that uses our collection of Persian lemmas. Finally all semi-spaces are automatically detected and fixed. An important feature of the Persian and Arabic languages is the existence of semi-space. For example word "کتاب‌ها" (books) is a combination of word "کتاب" and "ها", in which the former is Persian translation of word "book" and the latter is morpheme for a plural form. We can say these semi-space signs segment words into smaller morphemes. However, in formal writing and in all Persian normal corpora, this space is neglected frequently and it could make a lot of problems in Persian and Arabic morphological segmentation task. For example both forms for the previous example, "کتاب‌ها" and "کتابها" , are considered correct in Persian text and have the same meaning.

Words with more than 10 occurrences in our corpus collection were selected for manual annotation, which resulted in a set of around 90K word forms. We distributed them among 16 annotators in a way that each word was checked and annotated by two persons independently. Annotators made decisions about the lemma of a word under question, segmentation parts, plurality, and ambiguity (whether a word had more than one meaning). The manual annotation of segmentation was accelerated by predicting morpheme boundaries by our automatic segmenter and offering the most confident boundaries to the annotators. The annotators were allowed to indicate that a word was not a proper Persian word, while we decided to remove all borrowing words which are not common in the Persian language. For all disagreement in deleted words list, a third reviewer made the final decision for word removing. The whole process led to removing almost 30K words from the lexicon.

The remaining words were sent for resolving inter-annotator differences. All disagreements were reviewed and corrected by the authors of this paper. Finally all annotated words were quickly reviewed by two Persian linguists. The whole process took almost six weeks. Figure 2 shows a snapshot of our morpheme-segmented dataset.

In order to use a hand-annotated lexicon in our work, we extracted the segmentation part from the dataset and converted it into our binary model which is suitable for our algorithm described in Section 4. The total number of words we used in our Persian dataset was 45K. Finally, in order to make the data more appropriate for future segmentation experiments, we divided it into three different sets. The training set includes almost 37K, both test and development sets includes around 4K words each. Moreover, we divided the dataset based on their derivational trees which makes it possible to have all words with the same root in the same set. The dataset which is a rich test set for future experiments on Persian morphological tasks is publicly available in the LINDAT/CLARIN repository (Ansari et al., 2019).

---

[1] https://github.com/HaniehP/PersianNER
[2] https://github.com/sobhe/hazm

X	ملودی	ملودی	1		554	م	ل	و	د	ی					
X	ملودیها	ملودی	1		43	م	ل	و	د	ی	X	ه	ا		
X	ملودیهای	ملودی	1		147	م	ل	و	د	ی	X	ه	ا	X	ی
X	ملونی	ملون	1		20	م	ل	و	ن	X	ی				
X	ملوک	ملوک	1		439	م	ل	و	ک						
X	ملوکسیکام	ملوکسیکام	1		11	م	ل	و	ک	س	ی	ک	ا	م	
X	ملک	ملک	1		3404	م	ل	ک							
X	ملکان	ملک	1		251	م	ل	ک	X	ا	ن				
X	ملکم	ملک	1	N	193	م	ل	ک	X	م					
X	ملکه	ملکه	1		3742	م	ل	ک	X	ه					
X	ملکوتی	ملکوت	1		112	م	ل	ک	و	ت	X	ی			
X	ملکولی	ملکولی	1		115	م	ل	ک	و	ل	X	ی			
X	ملکولها	ملکول	1		28	م	ل	ک	و	ل	X	ه	ا		
X	ملکولهای	ملکول	1		84	م	ل	ک	و	ل	X	ه	ا	X	ی
X	ملکیان	ملک	1	N	115	م	ل	ک	X	ی	X	ا	ن		
X	ملکآباد	ملکآباد	1	N	61	م	ل	ک	X	آ	ب	ا	د		

Figure 2: A snapshot of the annotated dataset.

4 Morphological Network Construction

In this section, the method used in our work is described. Subsection 4.1 introduces our algorithm developed for the task and Subsection 4.2 describes the idea of using automatic segmented lexicon.

4.1 Automatic Network Construction

The core idea of this work is to construct a morphological network using a morpheme-segmented lexicon. First we need to partition the set of word forms into subsets based on same root morphemes. We approximate the distinction between root morphemes and affixes using the frequency of individual morphemes in the segmented lexicon. After calculating the frequencies, the m most frequent segments (we used 100 and 200 for m in our experiments) are removed from the set of potential root morphemes; all the remaining morphemes are stored in a set named *roots*. While the first m frequent segments are repeated more than other segments in our dataset, usually they are not root morphemes and could be considered as affixes. Table 1 shows an example of the most frequent segments based on our Persian segmented lexicon; none of them are none-root morphemes.

The next phase is to add nodes to our morphological graph (i.e., the network contains morphological trees) based on the assembled set of root morphemes. For each r_i from the *roots* set, we create a set of words that contain r_i. We name this set $words_i$. Now, we add r_i as a new node to our derivational graph. In the next step, we find and connect all the words in $words_i$ in the network. We divide all the words in $words_i$ into n smaller sets $words_{i,2}, words_{i,3}, ..., words_{i,n}$ based on the number of their segments. The set $words_{i,j}$ includes all words containing r_i and their number of segments is equal to j. First, we check all w in $words_{i,2}$ and if it contains a node in the tree that includes r_i, we add it to the network graph, otherwise we add w to the *remaining* set. Then, for the next group, $words_{i,3}$, we follow a similar procedure, however, we add all w in $words_{i,3}$ when it contains a node existing in $words_{i,2}$ (i.e., set of words with two segments). Then we add them to *remaining* if there is not any subset in our current graph. We iterate this procedure until we pass all sets. Now, for each w in *remaining* set, we check all added nodes and add w as a child of any node with maximum number of segments. It means it would be connected to the root if there is no other option available. Figure 3 shows a simple pseudo code of the segmentation graph generating procedure. the *generate* function is recursive and gets *root*, current *tree*, remaining *words* and current *step* as the input parameters and returns a new *tree* and remaining *words*. The *overlap* function gets two words as the input and checks direct and reverse overlap count of the morphemes and returns maximum of them.

4.2 Semi-automatic Network Construction

After our primary experiments, we observed some root morphemes such as [shah] "king" (clearly not an affix) among the first 200 frequent segments. In order to quantify the influence of such wrongly classified affixes, we performed a modified versions of the above described experiment. This time, after frequency

```
def generate(root, tree, words, n):
    tree[root] = root
    for word in words[n] and for leaf in leafs(tree[root]) :
        if overlap(leaf, word) > n:
            set_child_to_leaf(tree, leaf, word) and break
        else:
            remains.append(word)
        for leaf in leafs(tree):
            tree , remains = generate(leaf, tree, remains, n + 1)
    return tree, remains

def overlap(x, y):
    return max(direct_overlap_from_start_to_end(x, y), reverse_overlap_from_end_to_start(x, y))

sets = [s for segmentation_sets()]

for s in sets:
    tree, remains = generate(root, {}, s, 1)
```

Figure 3: A pseudo-code of generating derivational graphs.

counting, we selected the m most frequent morphemes and two annotators decided in parallel whether they are root morphemes or not (such annotation is not a time-consuming task for a human at all). The rest of the experiment remained the same. Again, we set m equal to 100 or 200.

Table 1: 40 most frequent morphemes in the hand-segmented segmented lexicon.

rank	segment	freq.	rank	segment	freq.	rank	segment	freq.	rank	segment	freq.
1	ى [y]	9118	11	اى [ee]	583	21	هم [ham]	278	31	است [ast]	216
2	ها [haa]	4819	12	ال [al]	561	22	يد [id]	274	32	ش [ash]	206
3	ه [h]	2898	13	تر [tar]	746	23	ا [aa]	274	33	دان [daan]	198
4	ان [aan]	1708	14	ات [aat]	425	24	م [m]	267	34	شان [shaan]	193
5	می [mi]	1112	15	ب [b]	422	25	در [dar]	260	35	گاه [gaah]	192
6	یی [yee]	941	16	ين [een]	396	26	کار [kaar]	258	36	کن [kan]	189
7	ش [sh]	891	17	ده [deh]	383	27	ساز [saaz]	254	37	پر [por]	187
8	ن [n]	864	18	شد [shod]	359	28	دو [do]	241	38	نا [naa]	178
9	ند [nd]	782	19	دار [daar]	337	29	بر [bar]	239	39	ت [t]	173
10	د [d]	658	20	و [oo]	308	30	گر [gar]	232	40	شاه [shaah]	164

4.3 Automatic Network Expansion Using Morpheme-Segmented Data Created by MORFESSOR

In this part of our work, we decided to propose an automatic procedure to expand the existing derivational network by adding selected new and unseen words into the graph. In other words, when the primary network is ready, we try to add new words into it using the core algorithm explained in Section 4.1. However, the segmentation process for these new words is done by MORFESSOR. Figure 4 shows a flowchart of segmentation process workflow.

As is shown in Figure 4, the effect of using MORFESSOR could be evaluated in two different ways. First, in the initial data segmentation which is used to create the primary morphological network. Second way of adopting MORFESSOR is when we have some new words (i.e. test words) and we want to add them into our existing network and we can use MORFESSOR to segment them in an automatic way. In other words, in the testing phase, we have words that do not exist in our hand-annotated dataset and for creating derivational network of morphemes we need a segmentation for them. In order to resolve this problem, we decided to use an automatic segmentation algorithm to segment these unseen words and we selected MORFESSOR for this purpose. It works in two ways; supervised and unsupervised: we created two models of MORFESSOR and in the testing phase when a new word is under question, we segment it and add it to our existing tree based on that segmentation.

In this experiment, the unsupervised model is created based on all 97K raw data that we collected in our work and supervised MORFESSOR is trained using the 45K hand-annotated dataset. Experimental results in Section 5 show that the supervised model has better performance in comparison with the unsupervised one in the final tree accuracy.

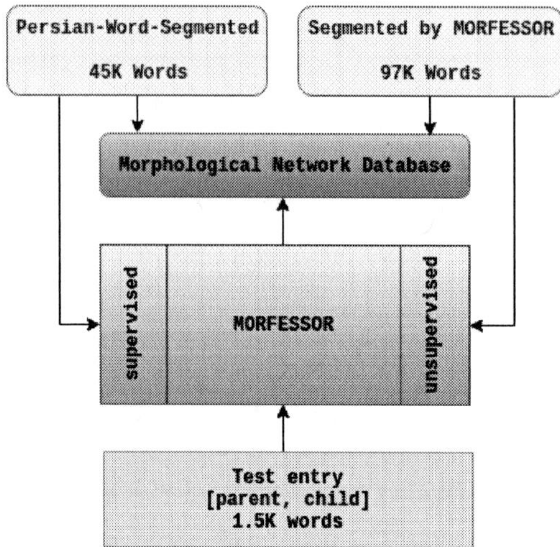

Figure 4: Morphological Network Database construction flowchart which shows the primary network construction and the expansion procedure.

5   Experiments

In order to estimate the quality of the resulting network, we randomly selected 400 nodes and checked if their parent node is identified correctly. We ran our automatic and semi-automatic versions of the algorithm using two thresholds for skipped root morphemes, 100 and 200. Table 2 summarizes the results for the individual experiment configurations. In all cases, the number of nodes in the generated graphs is 45K, which is equal to the total number of words in our manually segmented lexicon. Finally, Figure 5 shows three sample sub-graphs extracted by our algorithms.

Table 2: Accuracy for both automatic and semi-automatic methods using different numbers of non-roots in primary phase on 400 randomly selected nodes (i.e., words).

non-root selection	# of non-roots	accuracy
automatic	100	89.5%
automatic	200	86.3%
semi-automatic	100	91.0%
semi-automatic	200	92.8%

In the next experiment, we tried to evaluate our strategy to expand the morphological network when new unseen words were supposed to be added to the graph. Table 3 shows results of eight configurations of our experiments with using MORFESSOR as the automatic morpheme segmentation tool. In the first half of the table, we used all available words to create out initial network and to make the segmentation, the unsupervised version of MORFESSOR is used. In the bottom half of Table 3, all rows show the results when the hand-annotated segmented data is used. Similarly to the previous experiment, we removed and

Figure 5: Samples of trees generated by our procedures describe in Sections 4.1 and 4.1.

cleaned most frequent non-root morphemes in two ways: in automatic removing during which we ignore all first 200 frequent morphemes, and in manual removing during which the selection and removing is done by an annotator. In other words, the first two columns of this table represents the configuration of the initial tree creation. The third column of Table 3 represents the method we used for segmenting the new words and in this column. Caption "Supervised" declares we used supervised MORFESSOR which is trained using 45K hand-annotated data and "Unsupervised" indicates that the segmentation is done by using fully unsupervised version of MORFESSOR. For all tests in this experiment, we provided a hand-annotated morphological network with 1500 words.

Table 3: Accuracy for tree structures on 1.2K dataset.

init. network creation	non-root selection	test words segmentation	Accuracy
97K/Segmented by MORFESSOR	automatic	sup. MORFESSOR	0.893
97K/Segmented by MORFESSOR	automatic	uns. MORFESSOR	0.777
97K/Segmented by MORFESSOR	manual	sup. MORFESSOR	0.893
97K/Segmented by MORFESSOR	manual	uns. MORFESSOR	0.777
45K Persian-Word-Segmented	automatic	sup. MORFESSOR	0.919
45K Persian-Word-Segmented	automatic	uns. MORFESSOR	0.846
45K Persian-Word-Segmented	manual	sup. MORFESSOR	0.934
45K Persian-Word-Segmented	manual	uns. MORFESSOR	0.866

5.1 Error Analysis

In this section we present an error analysis based on our observations. In the first experiment, when we created a morphological network using the hand-segmented lexicon and the whole procedure was automatic (Section 4.1), we explored two different error types. The first one happened when we wrongly labeled a root morpheme as the non-root which was ranked among top frequent morphemes. For example, as can be seen in in Table 1, the word "شاه [shaah]" which means "king" and ranked 40 is a root morpheme, but we automatically labeled it as a non-root. The second common type of errors happened when our method classified a non-root morpheme as a root morpheme. For example, morpheme "ون [oon] (plural suffix)" was classified wrongly as a root morpheme by our algorithm.

In the second experiment (Section 4.2), we solved the first problem by checking the frequent morphemes manually, and as we expected, the accuracy of the result was better comparing with automatic non-root selection. However, the second problem (false roots) still existed. The main reason of this problem is that there are not enough words in our segmented lexicon, and thus our algorithm is not able to identify correct parts of rare words as their root morphemes.

In our last experiment (i.e. expanding the existing graph by adding the new unseen words) which is described in Section 4.3 the main reason of seen errors was the wrong segmentation for some new test words. It means in some cases MORFESSOR did the segmentation wrong which consequently led to wrong morpheme detection and wrong parent/child identification. Table 4 shows five examples of wrong segmentation of supervised and unsupervised MORFESSOR for our test words. Moreover, in some cases, there was not any child and parent word for test words and consequently our algorithm could not expand the graph correctly based on them. However, this error happened very few times while our primary graph was big enough.

Table 4: Sample segmentation of supervised and unsupervised MORFESSOR for test words.

word	correct segmentation	unsup. MORFESSOR	sup. MORFESSOR
آبزی [aabzi]	آب-زی	آبزی	آب-ز-ی
آبشش‌ها [aabshoshha]	آب-شش-ها	آبشش-ها	آب-ش-ش-ها
تعهدنامه [taahodnameh]	تعهد-نامه	ت-عهدنامه	ت-عهد-نامه
بی‌اجازه [biejaazeh]	بی-اجازه	ب-ی-اجازه	ب-ی-اجازه
حاکمیت [haakemiat]	حاکم-یت	حاکمیت	ح-اک-میت

6 Conclusions and future work

In this work, we developed and empirically evaluated an algorithm for creating a morphological (derivational and inflectional) network using a morpheme-segmented lexicon. Our algorithm tries to find all root candidates automatically and creates connections for all words of the lexicon. In addition, we evaluated a modification of our procedure based on hand-validated set of non-root morphemes. To prepare input for our presented algorithm, we presented a large manually annotated Persian lexicon which is the only segmented corpus for Persian words and which currently includes 45K words. In the second part of this work, we tried to expand the morphological network by adding 1500 new words into the existing network. While this procedure is automatic, we tried to segment new test words using both supervised and unsupervised versions of MORFESSOR, the automatic segmentation toolkit. These segmented morphemes are used as the input of our proposed algorithm to find the parents of new words.

Acknowledgments

The research was supported by OP RDE project No. CZ.02.2.69/0.0/0.0/16_027/0008495, International Mobility of Researchers at Charles University, and by grant No. 19-14534S of the Grant Agency of the Czech Republic. It has been using language resources developed, stored, and distributed by the LINDAT/CLARIAH CZ project (LM2015071, LM2018101).

References

Ebrahim Ansari, Zdeněk Žabokrtský, Hamid Haghdoost, and Mahshid Nikravesh. 2019. Persian Morphologically Segmented Lexicon 0.5. LINDAT/CLARIN digital library at the Institute of Formal and Applied Linguistics (ÚFAL), Faculty of Mathematics and Physics, Charles University. https://hdl.handle.net/11234/1-3011.

Mohsen Arabsorkhi and Mehrnoush Shamsfard. 2006. Unsupervised Discovery of Persian Morphemes. In *Proceedings of the Eleventh Conference of the European Chapter of the Association for Computational Linguistics: Posters & Demonstrations*. Association for Computational Linguistics, Stroudsburg, PA, USA, EACL '06, pages 175–178. http://dl.acm.org/citation.cfm?id=1608974.1609002.

Marion Baranes and Benoît Sagot. 2014. A language-independent approach to extracting derivational relations from an inflectional lexicon. In *Proceedings of the Ninth International Conference on Language Resources and Evaluation (LREC'14)*. European Language Resources Association (ELRA), Reykjavik, Iceland, pages 2793–2799.

Mahmood Bijankhan, Javad Sheykhzadegan, Mohammad Bahrani, and Masood Ghayoomi. 2011. Lessons from building a Persian written corpus: Peykare. *Language Resources and Evaluation* 45(2):143–164.

Kris Cao and Marek Rei. 2016. A joint model for word embedding and word morphology. In *Proceedings of the 1st Workshop on Representation Learning for NLP*. Association for Computational Linguistics, Berlin, Germany, pages 18–26. https://doi.org/10.18653/v1/W16-1603.

Mathias Creutz, Teemu Hirsimäki, Mikko Kurimo, Antti Puurula, Janne Pylkkönen, Vesa Siivola, Matti Varjokallio, Ebru Arisoy, Murat Saraçlar, and Andreas Stolcke. 2007. Morph-based Speech Recognition and Modeling of Out-of-vocabulary Words Across Languages. *ACM Trans. Speech Lang. Process.* 5(1):3:1–3:29. https://doi.org/10.1145/1322391.1322394.

Mathias Creutz and Krista Lagus. 2002. Unsupervised Discovery of Morphemes. In *Proceedings of the ACL-02 Workshop on Morphological and Phonological Learning.* Association for Computational Linguistics, pages 21–30. https://doi.org/10.3115/1118647.1118650.

John Goldsmith. 2001. Unsupervised Learning of the Morphology of a Natural Language. *Computational Linguistics* 27(2):153–198. https://doi.org/10.1162/089120101750300490.

Stig-Arne Grönroos, Sami Virpioja, Peter Smit, and Mikko Kurimo. 2014. Morfessor FlatCat: An HMM-Based Method for Unsupervised and Semi-Supervised Learning of Morphology. In *Proceedings of COLING 2014, the 25th International Conference on Computational Linguistics: Technical Papers.* Dublin City University and Association for Computational Linguistics, Dublin, Ireland, pages 1177–1185. https://www.aclweb.org/anthology/C14-1111.

Jan Hajič and Jaroslava Hlaváčová. 2013. MorfFlex CZ. LINDAT/CLARIN digital library at the Institute of Formal and Applied Linguistics (ÚFAL), Faculty of Mathematics and Physics, Charles University. http://hdl.handle.net/11858/00-097C-0000-0015-A780-9.

Zellig Harris. 1955. From phoneme to morpheme. *Language* 31:209–221.

Nabil Hathout and Fiammetta Namer. 2014. Démonette, a French derivational morpho-semantic network. *Linguistic Issues in Language Technology* 11(5):125–168.

Mahmoud Hesabi. 1988. *Persian Affixes and Verbs*, volume 1. Javidan.

Zbigniew Kaleta. 2017. Automatic Pairing of Perfective and Imperfective Verbs in Polish. In *Proceedings of the 8th Language and Technology Conference.*

Akbar Karimi, Ebrahim Ansari, and Bahram Sadeghi Bigham. 2018. Extracting an English-Persian Parallel Corpus from Comparable Corpora. In *Proceedings of the Eleventh International Conference on Language Resources and Evaluation, LREC 2018, Miyazaki, Japan, May 7-12, 2018.*.

Oskar Kohonen, Sami Virpioja, Laura Leppänen, and Krista Lagus. 2010. Semi-supervised extensions to Morfessor baseline. In *Proceedings of the Morpho Challenge 2010 Workshop.* pages 30–34.

Mateusz Lango, Magda Ševčíková, and Zdeněk Žabokrtský. 2018. Semi-Automatic Construction of Word-Formation Networks (for Polish and Spanish). In *Proceedings of the 11th Language Resources and Evaluation Conference.* European Language Resource Association, Miyazaki, Japan. https://www.aclweb.org/anthology/L18-1291.

Eleonora Litta, Marco Passarotti, and Chris Culy. 2016. Formatio formosa est. Building a Word Formation Lexicon for Latin. In *Proceedings of Third Italian Conference on Computational Linguistics (CLiC-it 2016) & Fifth Evaluation Campaign of Natural Language Processing and Speech Tools for Italian. Final Workshop (EVALITA 2016), Napoli, Italy, December 5-7, 2016.*. http://ceur-ws.org/Vol-1749/paper32.pdf.

Karthik Narasimhan, Regina Barzilay, and Tommi Jaakkola. 2015. An unsupervised method for uncovering morphological chains. *Transactions of the Association for Computational Linguistics* 3:157–167.

Maciej Piasecki, Radoslaw Ramocki, and Marek Maziarz. 2012. Recognition of Polish Derivational Relations Based on Supervised Learning Scheme. In *Proceedings of the Eighth International Conference on Language Resources and Evaluation (LREC-2012).* European Language Resources Association (ELRA), Istanbul, Turkey, pages 916–922.

Hoifung Poon, Colin Cherry, and Kristina Toutanova. 2009. Unsupervised morphological segmentation with log-linear models. In *Proceedings of Human Language Technologies: The 2009 Annual Conference of the North American Chapter of the Association for Computational Linguistics.* Association for Computational Linguistics, Stroudsburg, PA, USA, NAACL '09, pages 209–217. http://dl.acm.org/citation.cfm?id=1620754.1620785.

Hanieh Poostchi, Ehsan Zare Borzeshi, and Massimo Piccardi. 2018. BiLSTM-CRF for Persian Named-Entity Recognition ArmanPersoNERCorpus: the First Entity-Annotated Persian Dataset. In *Proceedings of the Eleventh International Conference on Language Resources and Evaluation, LREC 2018, Miyazaki, Japan, May 7-12, 2018.*.

Mohammad Sadegh Rasooli, Ahmed El Kholy, and Nizar Habash. 2013. Orthographic and Morphological Processing for Persian-to-English Statistical Machine Translation. In *Proceedings of the Sixth International Joint Conference on Natural Language Processing*. Asian Federation of Natural Language Processing, Nagoya, Japan, pages 1047–1051. https://www.aclweb.org/anthology/I13-1144.

Magda Ševčíková and Zdeněk Žabokrtský. 2014. Word-formation network for Czech. In *Proceedings of the Ninth International Conference on Language Resources and Evaluation (LREC'14)*. European Language Resources Association (ELRA), Reykjavik, Iceland, pages 1087–1093.

Jan Šnajder. 2014. DerivBase.hr: A high-coverage derivational morphology resource for Croatian. In *Proceedings of the Ninth International Conference on Language Resources and Evaluation (LREC'14)*. European Language Resources Association (ELRA), Reykjavik, Iceland, pages 3371–3377.

Hossein Taghi-Zadeh, Mohammad Hadi Sadreddini, Mohammad Hasan Diyanati, and Amir Hossein Rasekh. 2015. A new hybrid stemming method for Persian language. *Digital Scholarship in the Humanities* 32(1):209–221. https://doi.org/10.1093/llc/fqv053.

Jesús Vilares, David Cabrero, and Miguel A. Alonso. 2001. Applying Productive Derivational Morphology to Term Indexing of Spanish Texts. In Alexander Gelbukh, editor, *Computational Linguistics and Intelligent Text Processing*. Springer Berlin Heidelberg, Berlin, Heidelberg, pages 336–348.

Zdeněk Žabokrtský, Magda Ševčíková, Milan Straka, Jonáš Vidra, and Adéla Limburská. 2016. Merging data resources for inflectional and derivational morphology in Czech. In *Proceedings of the Tenth International Conference on Language Resources and Evaluation (LREC 2016)*. European Language Resources Association (ELRA), Portorož, Slovenia, pages 1307–1314. https://www.aclweb.org/anthology/L16-1208.

Britta Zeller, Jan Šnajder, and Sebastian Padó. 2013. DErivBase: Inducing and evaluating a derivational morphology resource for German. In *Proceedings of the 51st Annual Meeting of the Association for Computational Linguistics (Volume 1: Long Papers)*. Association for Computational Linguistics, Sofia, Bulgaria, pages 1201–1211. https://www.aclweb.org/anthology/P13-1118.

Universal Derivations Kickoff:
A Collection of Harmonized Derivational Resources for Eleven Languages

Lukáš Kyjánek   **Zdeněk Žabokrtský**   **Magda Ševčíková**   **Jonáš Vidra**
Charles University, Faculty of Mathematics and Physics,
Institute of Formal and Applied Linguistics
Malostranské náměstí 25, 118 00 Prague 1, Czech Republic
`{kyjanek,zabokrtsky,sevcikova,vidra}@ufal.mff.cuni.cz`

Abstract

The aim of this paper is to open a discussion on harmonization of existing data resources related to derivational morphology. We present a newly assembled collection of eleven harmonized resources named "Universal Derivations" (clearly being inspired by the success story of the Universal Dependencies initiative in treebanking), as well as the harmonization process that brings the individual resources under a unified annotation scheme.

1 Introduction

There are several dozen of language resources that either focus specifically on derivational morphology, or capture some derivational features in addition to other types of annotation. Being rooted in different approaches, the language resources differ greatly in many aspects. This fact complicates usability of the data in multilingual projects, including a potential data-oriented research in derivational morphology across languages. Last but not least, for developers of new data, it can be highly time-consuming to deal with various technical and other issues that somebody else may have already successfully solved.

The current situation with derivational resources is sort of similar to recent developments in treebanking. Efforts have been made to harmonize syntactic treebanks, for instance, in the CoNLL Shared Task 2006 (Buchholz and Marsi, 2006), in the HamleDT treebank collection (Zeman et al., 2014), or in Google Universal Treebanks (McDonald et al., 2013), converging into the Universal Dependencies project (Nivre et al., 2016), and that has become a significant milestone in the applicability of the treebanks.[1]

Being inspired by the harmonization of syntactic treebanks, we harmonized eleven selected derivational resources to a unified scheme in order to verify the feasibility of such undertaking, and to open a discussion on this topic, so far without any specific NLP application in mind. The collection is introduced under the, admittedly imitative, title *Universal Derivations* (UDer).

A brief overview of existing derivational resources and underlying data structures is given in Section 2; some details on the eleven resources to harmonize can be found in Section 3. The harmonization process is described in Section 4, followed by basic quantitative characteristics of the resulting UDer collection (Section 5).

2 Existing data resources for individual languages

Kyjánek (2018) listed 51 resources that capture information on derivational morphology of 22 different languages. The resources differ in many aspects, out of which the most important for us is the data structure, but other essential characteristics include the file format, the size in terms of both lexemes and derivational relations, and the licence under which the data were released.

To be able to compare the resources, we describe the content of the derivational resources for various languages using graph theory terminology. Such interpretation leads to a typology, dividing the resources

---

[1] Similarly to the evolution of multilingual syntactic datasets, we hope that the existence of our harmonized collection may lead to a snowball effect, as it could facilitate annotating word-formation resources for other languages, performing cross-lingual transfer experiments, allowing typological studies etc. On the other hand, the analogy is limited by the different nature of the two types of resources since, for instance, parsers trained on syntactic annotations can be applied on astronomical amounts of unseen texts, while vocabulary of a language whose word-formation is studied is growing only very slowly.

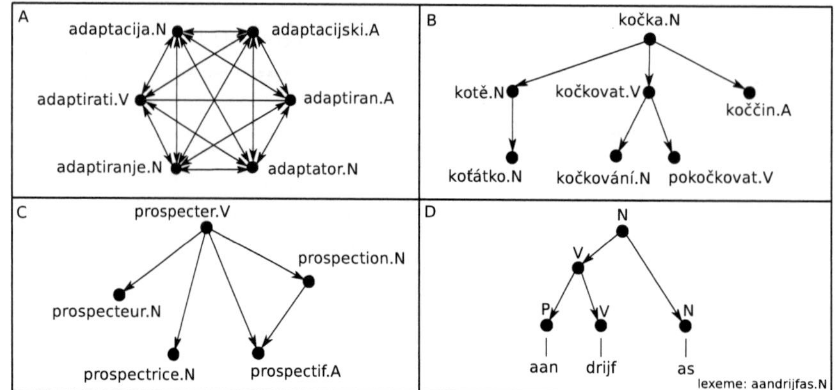

Figure 1: Data structures in available derivational resources: A. complete directed subgraph, B. rooted tree, C. weakly connected subgraph, D. derivation tree.

into four types listed below. In the first three types, lexemes are represented as nodes and derivational relations as directed edges, pointing to a derived lexeme from its base lexeme, while in the fourth type the basic building unit is the morpheme.

A. In some resources, derivationally related lexemes (i.e. lexemes that share a common root morpheme; hereafter, a derivational family) are simply grouped together, leaving particular derivational relations within the groups underspecified (cf. DerivBase.hr for Croatian, Šnajder, 2014). Such derivational families could be represented as complete subgraphs. However, given that the structure models linguistic derivation, we should represent such derivational families rather by *complete directed subgraphs* (see A in Figure 1).[2]

B. If at most one base lexeme is captured for any derived lexeme, then the derivational family can be naturally represented as a *rooted tree* with a designated root node representing a lexeme that is considered as further unmotivated (cf. DeriNet for Czech, Vidra et al., 2019a; B in Figure 1).

C. A *weakly connected subgraph* (in which any lexeme can have more than one base lexeme) is used for representing derivational families in resources in which the rooted-tree constraint does not hold, e.g. in Démonette for French (Hathout and Namer, 2014; C in Figure 1).

D. A *derivation tree* (in the terminology of Context Free Grammars), with morphemes in its leaf nodes and artificial symbols in non-terminal nodes, can be used for describing how a lexeme is composed of individual morphemes (cf. Dutch section of CELEX2, Baayen et al., 1995, D in Figure 1); derivational relations between lexemes are then present only implicitly (based on shared sequences of morphemes).

3   Data resources selected for harmonization

For the pilot stage of the harmonization project, we selected 11 data resources, all of them based either on rooted trees or weakly connected subgraphs (see B and C in Figure 1). The original resources (in alphabetical order) are briefly described below in this section.

Démonette is a network containing lexemes assigned with morphological and semantic features. It was created by merging existing derivational resources for French (cf. Morphonette, Hathout, 2010; VerbAction, Tanguy and Hathout, 2002; and DériF, Namer, 2003). Démonette focuses on suffixation and captures also so-called *indirect relations* (representing *sub-paradigms*) and derivational series among lexemes. Derivational families are represented by weakly connected subgraphs.

---

[2]Keeping the quadratic number of edges in the data might seem rather artificial at the beginning, however, it is a good starting point as it allows for applying graph algorithms analogously to other types.

DeriNet is a lexical database of Czech that captures derivational relations between lexemes. Each derivational family is represented as a rooted tree.

DeriNet.ES is a DeriNet-like lexical database for Spanish which is based on a substantially revised lexeme set used originally in the Spanish Word-Formation Network (Lango et al., 2018). In DeriNet.ES, derivational relations were created using substitution rules covering Spanish affixation (Faryad, 2019). Resulting derivational families are organized into rooted trees.

DeriNet.FA is a lexical database capturing derivations in Persian, which was created on top of manually compiled Persian Morphologically Segmented Lexicon (Ansari et al., 2019). By using automatic methods, derivationally related lexemes were identified and organized into DeriNet-like rooted trees (Haghdoost et al., 2019).

DErivBase is a large-coverage lexicon for German (Zeller et al., 2013) in which derivational relations were created by using more than 190 derivational rules extracted from reference grammars of German. The resulting derivational families were automatically split into semantically consistent clusters, forming weakly connected subgraphs.

The Morphosemantic Database from English WordNet 3.0 (hereafter, English WordNet) is a stand-off database linking morphologically related nouns and verbs from English WordNet (Miller, 1995) in which synonymous lexemes are grouped into so-called *synsets*, which are further organized according to the hyponymy/hyperonymy relations. Derivational relations were identified and assigned 14 semantic labels (Fellbaum et al., 2007). Derivational families are represented by weakly connected subgraphs.

EstWordNet (Kerner et al., 2010) is a WordNet-like lexical database for Estonian, which did not cover derivational morphology originally. Derivational relations were added by Kahusk et al. (2010); derivational families are represented by weakly connected subgraphs.

FinnWordNet is another WordNet-like database; it is based on the English database which was translated into Finnish (Lindén and Carlson, 2010). Derivational relations were added later by Lindén et al. (2012). Derivational families are represented by weakly connected subgraphs.

NomLex-PT is a lexicon of nominalizations in Portuguese (De Paiva et al., 2014), which were extracted from existing resources. Resulting derivational families are represented by weakly connected subgraphs.

The Polish Word-Formation Network is a DeriNet-like lexical network for Polish created by using pattern-mining techniques and a machine-learned ranking model (Lango et al., 2018). The network was enlarged with the derivational relations extracted from the Polish WordNet (Maziarz et al., 2016). Each derivational family is represented as a rooted tree.

Word Formation Latin is a resource specialized in word-formation of Latin (Litta et al., 2016). The lexeme set is based on the Oxford Latin Dictionary (Glare, 1968). In the Word Formation Latin database, the majority of derivational families is represented by rooted trees but weakly connected subgraphs are used to capture compounds.

4 Harmonization process

4.1 Target representation

The data structure of the DeriNet database is used as the target representation for the remaining ten resources to harmonize. In DeriNet, each tree corresponds to a derivational family. In each tree, the derivational family is internally organized according to the morphemic complexity of the lexemes, from the morphematically simplest lexeme in the root of the tree to the most complex ones in the leaves of the structure, concurring thus with the linguistic account of derivation as a process of adding an affix to a base in order to create a new lexeme (Dokulil, 1962; Iacobini, 2000; Lieber and Štekauer, 2014).

This simple but, at the same time, highly constrained data structure makes it possible to organize massive amounts of language data in a unified way, but it is not sufficient for modelling compounding and other more intricate phenomena, such as double motivation. In the DeriNet 2.0 format, which was released recently (Vidra et al., 2019b) and which is used as the target representation in the presented harmonization process, some of the issues have been solved by introducing *multi-node relations* and other features modelling the language phenomena in a more adequate way.

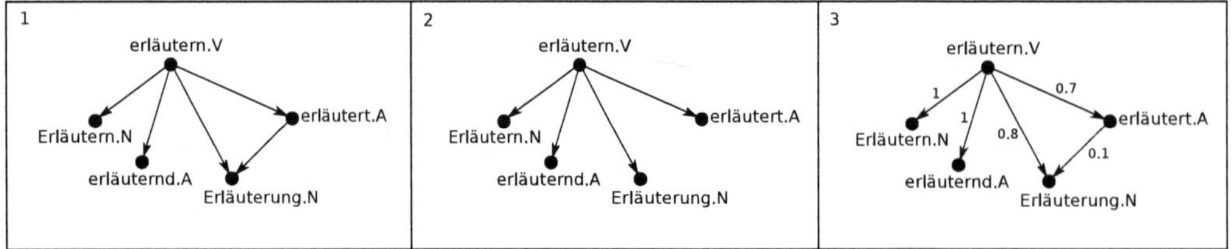

Figure 2: The process of harmonization of a weakly connected graph (an example from DErivBase).

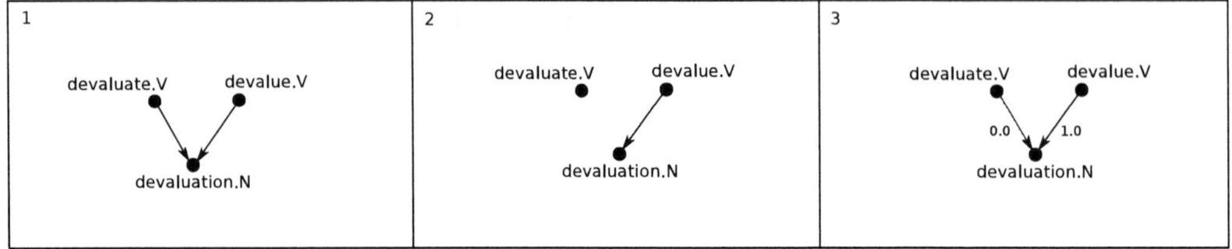

Figure 3: The process of harmonization of a weakly connected graph (an example from English WordNet) that leads to the splitting of the graph (due to spelling variants).

During any harmonization effort, one faces the trade-off between expressiveness and uniformity. A target framework with high expressiveness and flexibility might be able to subsume information exactly as it is present in any input data resource (preserving the annotation scheme with all its linguistic and technical decisions), but it would be just a mere file format conversion without offering any new or more general insights. On the other hand, if the target framework pushes too much on simplicity and uniformity, it could leads to ignoring some features that are important in a particular language. We have to search for something between these two extremes, as we really cannot keep both perfect flexibility and generalization at the same time. We believe that choosing rooted trees is a reasonable compromise: we keep selected word-formation relations in a tree-shaped skeleton (and we hope that multilingual analogies will be enlightened this way), while non-tree edges from the original resources are memorized too in the resulting collection, however, on a less prominent place. Last but not least, choosing the tree approach is hard to resist from the practical perspective: it simplifies many technical aspects (compared to less constrained graphs), such as data traversing, visualization, and evaluating annotator agreement.[3]

4.2 Importing data from existing resources

Derivational resources differ in the formats in which they are distributed. Therefore, as the first step of the harmonization process, the data files were converted into a common file format.

From all resources, we imported as much information as possible about lexemes and word-formation, e.g. morphological features, semantic labels, segmentation, compounding etc., however, we could not preserve all the information present in the original data. For instance, we did not import explicit information about the origin of each feature in Démonette. From Estonian and Finnish WordNet, we extracted all lexemes but processed only derivationally related ones, disregarding synonymy relations and the hyponymic/hyperonymic architecture completely.

4.3 Identifying rooted trees in weakly connected graphs

According to the typology sketched in Section 2, the DeriNet, DeriNet.ES and DeriNet.FA databases, and the Polish Word-Formation Network contain rooted trees, while all the other selected resources consist of weakly connected graphs, in which the spanning tree (tree-shaped skeleton) has to be identified.

---

[3]Again, this resembles the case of UD, where it was also clear from the very beginning that trees are insufficient for capturing all syntactic relations (e.g. with more complex coordination expressions). The recent UD solution is similar to ours: for each sentence there is a core tree-shaped structure, possibly accompanied with a set of secondary (non-tree) edges.

Therefore, a procedure of selecting rooted tree edges out of a weakly connected graph was applied to the French Démonette, German DErivBase, English WordNet, Estonian EstWordNet, Finnish FinnWordNet, Portuguese NomLex-PT, and Word Formation Latin; see Figure 2 for individual steps. In these resources, a lexeme was allowed to refer to two or more base lexemes, for example, due to compounding, double motivation, or spelling variants (see step 1 in Figure 2).

The data of Démonette, English WordNet, EstWordNet, NomLex-PT, and Word Formation Latin contained a small number of derivational families represented by non-tree structures, therefore, we could select the most appropriate incoming link manually for all those families. In the case of DErivBase and FinnWordNet, there were many such non-tree edges, so we decided to apply Machine Learning. We annotated a small sample of both resources (see step 2 in Figure 2) to train classifiers that predict scores estimating a chance of a derivational relation between two lexemes to be present, or absent, respectively.

Our feature set employed in the classifiers consisted of part-of-speech categories, Levenshtein distance (Levenshtein, 1966), length difference and character n-grams of both the base lexeme and the derived lexeme, and boolean features manifesting whether the initial and final unigrams and bigrams of the base lexeme and the derivative were identical. We tested a number of classification techniques and evaluated them using held-out data in terms of F-score. Logistic Regression performed best for FinnWordNet (F-score = 76.13 %), while Decision Trees achieved the highest F-score for DErivBase (F-score = 82.71 %). Using the classification models, we assigned estimated edge-presence scores to all edges except for leaf nodes, for which no decision-making was needed (see step 3 in Figure 2).

We chose resulting trees by maximizing the sum of scores using the Maximum Spanning Tree algorithm introduced by Chu and Liu (1965) and Edmonds (1967) implemented in a Python package NetworkX (Hagberg et al., 2008). The resulting tree-shaped skeleton is drawn with solid lines and the non-tree edges are drawn with dashed lines in the step 3 in Figure 2. In the harmonized data, we saved both types of edges, but the non-tree ones were processed as secondary ones.

However, some derivational families did not contain a rooted tree in the respective weakly connected graphs. This situation can be caused, for example, by spelling variants, that is illustrated on the data from English WordNet in Figure 3. English verbs "devalue" and "devaluate" are proposed as base lexemes for lexeme "devaluation" (see step 1 in Figure 3) but only one is allowed in the rooted tree (see step 2 in Figure 3), which leads to splitting the family into two (see step 3 in Figure 3). One of the families contains the lexemes "devalue" and "devaluation", the second one has a single lexeme "devaluate". Using links between the new roots ("devalue" and "devaluate"), we kept information about splitting the family in the harmonized data.

4.4   Converting the data into the DeriNet 2.0 format

Using the application interface developed for DeriNet 2.0,[4] we stored the trees resulting from the previous steps into the DeriNet 2.0 format, which was designed to be as language agnostic as possible; see Vidra et al. (2019b) in this volume.

The lemma set of each resource and all features assigned to the lexemes (e.g. morphological features) were converted first. It was also necessary to create a unique identifier for each lexeme to prevent technical problems caused by the same string form or homonymy of lexemes. An identifier pattern consisting of the string and the part-of-speech category of the lexeme was sufficient for all harmonized resources except for Démonette, DeriNet, DErivBase and Word Formation Latin.

DeriNet uses so-called *tag masks*[5] instead of part-of-speech category. In Démonette and DErivBase, the identifier contains also a gender (for nouns only) of the lexeme, and Word Formation Latin needs to use the ID from its original version due to the subtle differentiation of lexeme meanings. For example, there are three meanings of the lexeme "gallus" captured in the Word Formation Latin resource ("a farmyard cock", "an inhabitant of Gaul", and "an emasculated priest of Cybele"; Glare 1968), i.e. three entries with the same graphemic form and morphological features but with the different derivational families.

---

[4] https://github.com/vidraj/derinet

[5] The tag mask represents the intersection of the set of part-of-speech tags of all inflected forms of a particular lexeme. By comparing positions of values in each tag, the tag mask consists of values (whether the value was the same across all tags) or question marks (otherwise). For more details, see Vidra et al. (2019b).

Resource	Language	Extracted from original			After harmonization			License
		Lexemes	Relations	Families	Lexemes	Relations	Families	
Démonette 1.2	French	21,290	14,152	7,336	21,290	13,808	7,482	CC BY-NC-SA 3.0
DeriNet 2.0	Czech	1,027,665	808,682	218,383	1,027,665	808,682	218,383	CC BY-NC-SA 3.0
DeriNet.ES	Spanish	151,173	36,935	114,238	151,173	36,935	114,238	CC BY-NC-SA 3.0
DeriNet.FA	Persian	43,357	35,745	7,612	43,357	35,745	7,612	CC BY-NC-SA 4.0
DErivBase 2.0	German	280,775	55,010	235,287	280,775	44,830	235,945	CC BY-SA 3.0
English WordNet 3.0	English	13,813	8,000	5,818	13,813	7,855	5,958	CC BY-NC-SA 3.0
EstWordNet 2.1	Estonian	115,318	535	456	988	507	481	CC BY-SA 3.0
FinnWordNet 2.0	Finnish	44,173	29,783	6,347	20,035	13,687	6,348	CC BY 3.0
Nomlex-PT 2017	Portuguese	7,020	4,235	2,785	7,020	4,201	2,819	CC BY 4.0
Polish WFN 0.5	Polish	262,887	189,217	73,670	262,887	189,217	73,670	CC BY-NC-SA 3.0
Word Formation Latin	Latin	29,708	22,687	5,273	29,708	22,641	5,320	CC BY-NC-SA 4.0

Resource	Singleton nodes	#Nodes	Tree depth	Tree out-degree	Part-of-speech distribution [%]				
					Noun	Adj	Verb	Adv	Other
Démonette 1.2	69	2.8 / 12	1.1 / 4	1.8 / 8	63.0	2.5	34.5	–	–
DeriNet 2.0	96,208	4.7 / 1638	0.8 / 10	1.1 / 40	44.0	34.8	5.5	15.7	–
DeriNet.ES	98,325	1.3 / 35	0.2 / 5	0.3 / 14	–	–	–	–	–
DeriNet.FA	0	5.7 / 180	1.5 / 6	3.3 / 114	–	–	–	–	–
DErivBase 2.0	215,823	1.2 / 51	0.1 / 7	0.1 / 13	85.5	9.9	4.6	–	–
English WordNet 3.0	65	2.3 / 6	1.0 / 1	1.3 / 6	56.9	–	43.1	–	–
EstWordNet 2.1	21	2.1 / 3	1.0 / 2	1.0 / 3	15.9	29.0	7.9	47.2	–
FinnWordNet 2.0	3	3.2 / 36	1.5 / 9	1.5 / 13	55.3	29.2	15.5	–	–
Nomlex-PT 2017	17	2.5 / 7	1.0 / 1	1.5 / 7	59.8	–	40.2	–	–
Polish WFN 0.5	41,332	3.6 / 214	1.0 / 8	1.1 / 38	–	–	–	–	–
Word Formation Latin	63	5.6 / 130	1.5 / 6	3.0 / 42	46.0	27.4	23.8	–	2.8

Table 1: Ten language resources of the UDer collection before and after the harmonization, and some basic quantitative features of the UDer collection. Columns #Nodes, Tree depth, and Tree outdegree are presented in average / maximum value format.

In the second step, we converted tree-shaped derivational relations and added details about each relation, e.g. semantic label, type of relation, affix, depending on the annotation in the original resource. Because Word Formation Latin captures also compounding, these relations were included too.

The rest of the imported data and some by-products of the harmonization process (esp. the non-tree derivational relations, links between roots in the case of splitting the original family, and resource-specific annotation, e.g. indirect relations in Démonette) were converted for each resource in the last step.

5 UDer Collection

The resulting collection, Universal Derivations version 0.5 (UDer 0.5), includes eleven resources covering eleven different languages listed in Table 1. Using the DeriNet 2.0 file format, UDer provides derivational data in the same annotation scheme, in which a rooted tree is the backbone of each derivational family, however, other original derivational relations that are not involved in the trees due to the harmonization process are also included as the secondary relations to the harmonized data. Tree-shaped derivational families with the verb "evaluate" (and their equivalents in particular languages) in all harmonized resources are displayed in Figure 4. Basic quantitative properties of the collection are summarized in the following subsections; information about the availability of the collection is provided, too.

5.1 Selected quantitative properties

Selected quantitative characteristics of the resources involved in the harmonized collection can be compared in Table 1. The lexeme sets were adopted from the original data resources, except for WordNets. From FinnWordNet and EstWordNet, only derivationally related lexemes were admitted.

After the harmonization process, the number of derivational relations decreased in resources capturing derivational families in weakly connected graphs, however, the number of relations after the harmonization as given in the table includes only tree-shaped relations. Non-tree relations are also stored but on a less prominent place (the number of them can be calculated as a difference between extracted relations and

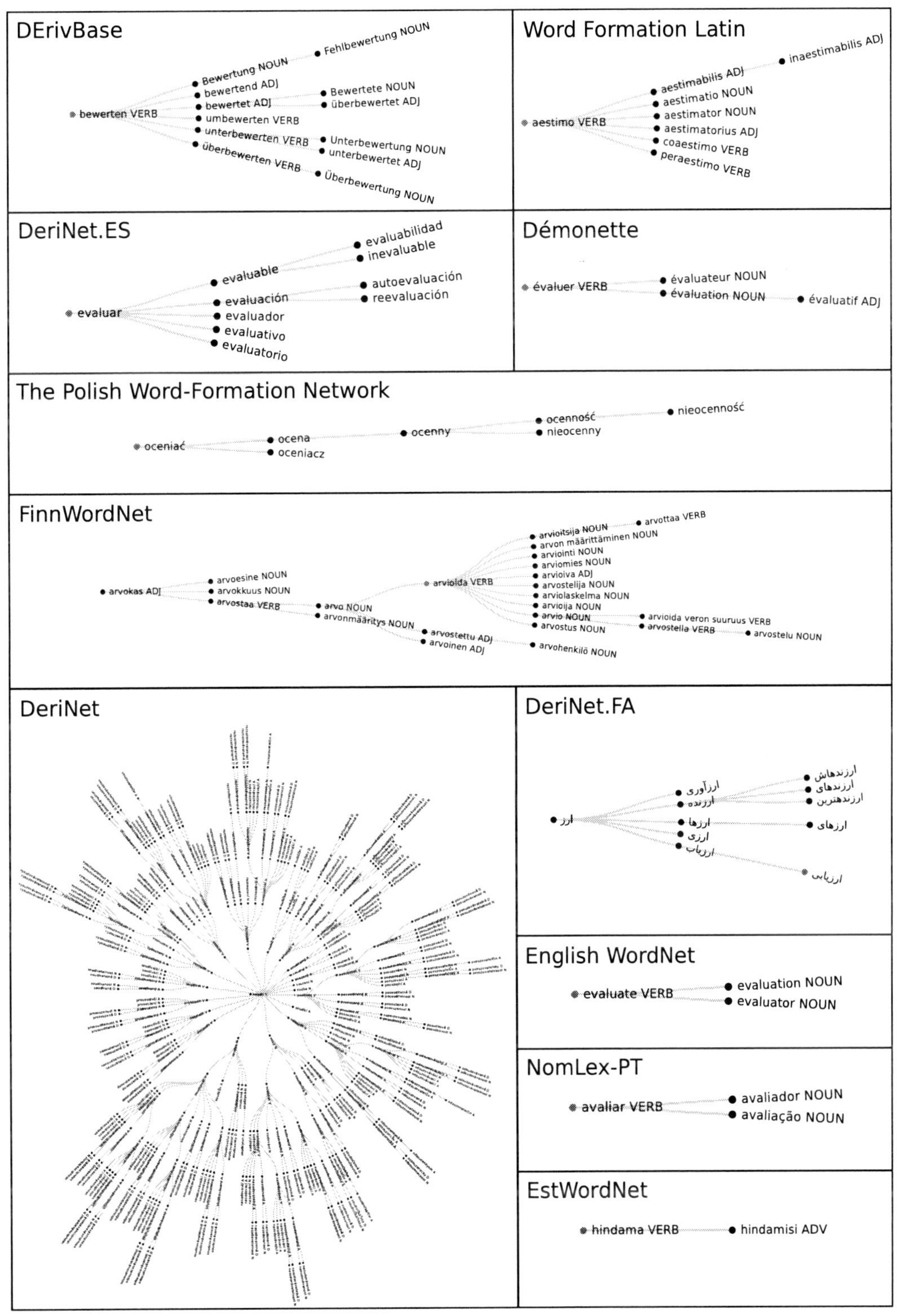

Figure 4: Harmonized rooted trees for verb "evaluate" in UDer v0.5 collection.

relations after the harmonization).

The number of derivational families after the harmonization process remained the same for resources representing derivational families as rooted trees, but it increased in resources that organized derivational families in the weakly connected graphs. The growth is caused by splitting the original family because some weakly connected graphs did not contain the rooted tree (cf. Figure 3 and Section 4.3). Nevertheless, the information about splitting the original family is stored in form of links between roots of the rooted trees in the harmonized data.

The second part of Table 1 indicates the number of singleton nodes (some derivational families contain just a single lexeme). The number of singleton nodes correlates with the way the resource was created. The high number of singleton nodes occurs in resources that were built-up from lexeme set to finding derivational relations within them, i.e. DeriNet, DeriNet.ES, DErivBase, and The Polish Word-Formation Network, whereas the lower number of singleton nodes is documented in resources that included lexemes depending on whether the lexeme was derivationally related to another lexeme. The number of singleton nodes could increase due to splitting the original family during the harmonization of these resources.

As for the average and maximum size of derivational families, their average and maximum depth (i.e. the distance of the furthest node from the tree root) and out-degree (i.e. the highest number of direct children of a single node) is compared across the harmonized resources which illustrate a general condition of the resources after the harmonization process. On average, the biggest derivational families can be found in DeriNet.FA, Word Formation Latin, and DeriNet, while the smallest families are in DErivBase and DeriNet.ES, as their data are made up mostly of singletons. A similar tendency can also be seen for the maximum size of nodes (lexemes) in the trees (families). DeriNet contains the biggest tree with the root "dát" ("give") having more than 1.6 thousand nodes. On the other hand, in the small and sparse data of EstWordNet, all trees contain three or even fewer nodes.

As for the part-of-speech categories, DeriNet and EstWordNet cover nouns, adjectives, verbs, and adverbs. Word Formation Latin lacks adverbs but it contains pronouns, auxiliaries and lexemes unspecified for the part of speech. Démonette, DErivBase and FinnWordNet also lacks adverbs, and both Démonette and DErivBase have a low number of adjectives. English WordNet and NomLex-PT are limited to nouns and verbs. The part-of-speech categories are not available for DeriNet.ES, DeriNet.FA, and the Polish Word-Formation Network.

5.2 Publishing and licensing

The presented UDer 0.5 collection is freely available in a single data package in the LIN-DAT/CLARIAH CZ repository[6] under the licenses listed in Table 1. The UDer data can be also queried using DeriSearch tool[7] (Vidra and Žabokrtský, 2017) and processed using other software developed within the DeriNet project, especially the Python application interface for DeriNet 2.0.

6 Conclusions and final remarks

This paper introduced a collection of derivational resources which have been harmonized to a common annotation scheme. The collection is publicly available. In the near future, we plan to evaluate the harmonization process in terms of consistency and adequacy across languages, and we are going to harmonize data resources for other languages and from other types of data structures, too.

The process of harmonization of linguistic data resources is always a compromise between expressiveness and uniformity. It is impossible to keep all the information stored in the diverse original resources and allow processing them all in an efficient unified way at the same time to allow multilingual or cross-lingual research. However, we believe that the benefits of the presented harmonization efforts outweigh the negatives and, above all, that it will open a (previously almost non-existent) discussion on the harmonization of derivational resources.

---

[6]http://hdl.handle.net/11234/1-3041
[7]http://ufal.mff.cuni.cz/derinet/derinet-search

Acknowledgments

This work was supported by the Grant No. GA19-14534S of the Czech Science Foundation, by the Charles University Grant Agency (project No. 1176219) and by the SVV project number 260 453. It has been using language resources developed, stored, and distributed by the LINDAT/CLARIAH CZ project (LM2015071, LM2018101).

References

Ebrahim Ansari, Zdeněk Žabokrtský, Hamid Haghdoost, and Mahshid Nikravesh. 2019. Persian Morphologically Segmented Lexicon 0.5. LINDAT/CLARIN digital library at the Institute of Formal and Applied Linguistics (ÚFAL), Faculty of Mathematics and Physics, Charles University. http://hdl.handle.net/11234/1-3011.

Harald R. Baayen, Richard Piepenbrock, and Leon Gulikers. 1995. CELEX2. Linguistic Data Consortium, Catalogue No. LDC96L14.

Sabine Buchholz and Erwin Marsi. 2006. CoNLL-X Shared Task on Multilingual Dependency Parsing. In *Proceedings of the 10th Conference on Computational Natural Language Learning*. ACL, pages 149–164.

Yoeng-Jin Chu and T. H. Liu. 1965. On the Shortest Arborescence of a Directed Graph. *Scientia Sinica* 14:1396–1400.

Valeria De Paiva, Livy Real, Alexandre Rademaker, and Gerard de Melo. 2014. NomLex-PT: A Lexicon of Portuguese Nominalizations. In *Proceedings of the 9th International Conference on Language Resources and Evaluation*. ELRA, pages 2851–2858.

Miloš Dokulil. 1962. *Tvoření slov v češtině 1: Teorie odvozování slov*. Academia, Prague.

Jack Edmonds. 1967. Optimum Branchings. *Journal of Research of the national Bureau of Standards* 71B(4):233–240.

Ján Faryad. 2019. Identifikace derivačních vztahů ve španělštině. Technical Report TR-2019-63, Faculty of Mathematics and Physics, Charles University.

Christiane Fellbaum, Anne Osherson, and Peter E Clark. 2007. Putting Semantics into WordNet's "Morphosemantic" Links. In *Language and Technology Conference*. Springer, pages 350–358.

P. G. W. Glare. 1968. *Oxford Latin dictionary*. Clarendon Press, Oxford.

Aric A. Hagberg, Daniel A. Schult, and Pieter J. Swart. 2008. Exploring Network Structure, Dynamics, and Function using NetworkX. In *Proceedings of the 7th Python in Science Conference*. pages 11–15.

Hamid Haghdoost, Ebrahim Ansari, Zdeněk Žabokrtský, and Mahshid Nikravesh. 2019. Building a Morphological Network for Persian on Top of a Morpheme-Segmented Lexicon. In *Proceedings of the 2nd Workshop on Resources and Tools for Derivational Morphology*. Charles University.

Nabil Hathout. 2010. Morphonette: A Morphological Network of French. *arXiv preprint arXiv:1005.3902* .

Nabil Hathout and Fiammetta Namer. 2014. Démonette, a French Derivational Morpho-Semantic Network. *Linguistic Issues in Language Technology* 11:125–162.

Claudio Iacobini. 2000. Base and Direction of Derivation. In *Morphology. An International Handbook on Inflection and Word-formation*, Mouton de Gruyter, volume 1, pages 865–876.

Neeme Kahusk, Kadri Kerner, and Kadri Vider. 2010. Enriching Estonian WordNet with Derivations and Semantic Relations. In *Baltic hlt*. pages 195–200.

Kadri Kerner, Heili Orav, and Sirli Parm. 2010. Growth and Revision of Estonian WordNet. In *Principles, Construction and Application of Multilingual WordNets*. Narosa Publishing House, pages 198–202.

Lukáš Kyjánek. 2018. Morphological Resources of Derivational Word-Formation Relations. Technical Report TR-2018-61, Faculty of Mathematics and Physics, Charles University.

Mateusz Lango, Magda Ševčíková, and Zdeněk Žabokrtský. 2018. Semi-Automatic Construction of Word-Formation Networks (for Polish and Spanish). In *Proceedings of the 11th International Conference on Language Resources and Evaluation*. ELRA, pages 1853–1860.

Vladimir I. Levenshtein. 1966. Binary Codes Capable of Correcting Deletions, Insertions and Reversals. *Soviet Physics Doklady* 10:707.

Rochelle Lieber and Pavol Štekauer. 2014. *The Oxford handbook of derivational morphology*. Oxford University Press, Oxford.

Krister Lindén and Lauri Carlson. 2010. FinnWordNet–Finnish WordNet by Translation. *LexicoNordica – Nordic Journal of Lexicography* 17:119–140.

Krister Lindén, Jyrki Niemi, and Mirka Hyvärinen. 2012. Extending and updating the Finnish Wordnet. In *Shall We Play the Festschrift Game?*, Springer, pages 67–98.

Eleonora Litta, Marco Passarotti, and Chris Culy. 2016. Formatio Formosa est. Building a Word Formation Lexicon for Latin. In *Proceedings of the 3rd Italian Conference on Computational Linguistics*. pages 185–189.

Marek Maziarz, Maciej Piasecki, Ewa Rudnicka, Stan Szpakowicz, and Paweł Kędzia. 2016. plWordNet 3.0 – a Comprehensive Lexical-Semantic Resource. In *Proceedings of the 26th International Conference on Computational Linguistics*. The COLING 2016 Organizing Committee, Osaka, Japan, pages 2259–2268.

Ryan McDonald, Joakim Nivre, Yvonne Quirmbach-Brundage, Yoav Goldberg, Dipanjan Das, Kuzman Ganchev, Keith Hall, Slav Petrov, Hao Zhang, Täckström Oscar, Bedini Claudia, Castelló B. Núria, and Lee Jungmee. 2013. Universal Dependency Annotation for Multilingual Parsing. In *Proceedings of the 51st Annual Meeting of the Association for Computational Linguistics*. ACL, volume 2, pages 92–97.

George A Miller. 1995. WordNet: A Lexical Database for English. *Communications of the ACM* 38(11):39–41.

Fiammetta Namer. 2003. Automatiser l'analyse morpho-sémantique non affixale: le système DériF. *Cahiers de grammaire* 28:31–48.

Joakim Nivre, Marie-Catherine De Marneffe, Filip Ginter, Yoav Goldberg, Jan Hajič, Christopher D Manning, Ryan McDonald, Slav Petrov, Sampo Pyysalo, Natalia Silveira, Tsarfaty Reut, and Zeman Daniel. 2016. Universal Dependencies v1: A Multilingual Treebank Collection. In *Proceedings of the 10th International Conference on Language Resources and Evaluation*. ELRA, pages 1659–1666.

Ludovic Tanguy and Nabil Hathout. 2002. Webaffix: un outil d'acquisition morphologique dérivationnelle à partir du Web. In *Actes de la 9e Conférence Annuelle sur le Traitement Automatique des Langues Naturelles (TALN-2002)*. ATALA, Nancy, France.

Jonáš Vidra and Zdeněk Žabokrtský. 2017. Online Software Components for Accessing Derivational Networks. In *Proceedings of the Workshop on Resources and Tools for Derivational Morphology*. EDUCatt, pages 129–139.

Jonáš Vidra, Zdeněk Žabokrtský, Lukáš Kyjánek, Magda Ševčíková, and Šárka Dohnalová. 2019a. DeriNet 2.0. LINDAT/CLARIN digital library at the Institute of Formal and Applied Linguistics (ÚFAL), Faculty of Mathematics and Physics, Charles University. http://hdl.handle.net/11234/1-2995.

Jonáš Vidra, Zdeněk Žabokrtský, Magda Ševčíková, and Lukáš Kyjánek. 2019b. DeriNet 2.0: Towards an All-in-One Word-Formation Resource. In *Proceedings of the 2nd Workshop on Resources and Tools for Derivational Morphology*. Charles University.

Britta Zeller, Jan Šnajder, and Sebastian Padó. 2013. DErivBase: Inducing and Evaluating a Derivational Morphology Resource for German. In *Proceedings of the 51st Annual Meeting of the Association for Computational Linguistics*. ACL, volume 1, pages 1201–1211.

Daniel Zeman, Ondřej Dušek, David Mareček, Martin Popel, Loganathan Ramasamy, Jan Štěpánek, Zdeněk Žabokrtský, and Jan Hajič. 2014. HamleDT: Harmonized Multi-Language Dependency Treebank. *Language Resources and Evaluation* 48(4):601–637.

Jan Šnajder. 2014. DerivBase.hr: A High-Coverage Derivational Morphology Resource for Croatian. In *Proceedings of the 9th International Conference on Language Resources and Evaluation*. ELRA, pages 3371–3377.

A Parametric Approach to Implemented Analyses: Valence-changing Morphology in the LinGO Grammar Matrix

Christian Curtis
University of Washington
Department of Linguistics
cmc3c@uw.edu

Abstract

I describe an analysis of valence-changing verbal morphology implemented as a library extending the LinGO Grammar Matrix customization system. This analysis is based on decomposition of these operations into rule components, which in turn are expressed as lexical rule supertypes that implement specific, isolatable constraints. I also show how common variations of these constraints can be abstracted and parameterized by their axes of variation. I then demonstrate how these constraints can be recomposed in various combinations to provide broad coverage of the typological variation of valence change found in the world's languages. I evaluate the coverage of this library on five held-out world languages that exhibit these phenomena, achieving 79% coverage and 2% overgeneration.

1 Introduction

The LinGO Grammar Matrix (Bender et al., 2002) is a resource, rooted in the Head-driven Phrase Structure Grammar (HPSG) formalism (Pollard and Sag, 1994), that enables linguists to create implemented precision grammars. The core of the Grammar Matrix is a collection of types and constraints expected to be cross-linguistically useful, such as lexical and phrase rule types, feature geometry, and types implementing compositionality and long-distance dependency resolution. These analyses embed linguistic knowledge developed and tested by linguists and grammar writers over many years, in implementations of grammars at both large and small scales, in a framework that provides infrastructure and context for reuse in development of new grammars. Beyond reuse and rapid development of new grammars, aspects of the *engineering* purpose of the Grammar Matrix, the Matrix also serves two scientific goals, as articulated by Bender et al. (2010): first, to support linguistic hypothesis testing through grammar engineering; and, second, to combine both breadth of typological research and depth of syntactic analysis into a single computational resource.

In this work I present an analysis of valence-changing verbal morphology in order to test two primary hypotheses: first, that a typologically-informed set of implemented valence-changing operations can cover a meaningful proportion of the incidence of valence change in the world's languages; and, second, that these valence-changing operations can be implemented in a "building-block" fashion by building up complete valence change operations from isolated, common elements that can be reused and recombined in varying combinations. In order to test these hypotheses, I developed a library for valence-changing verbal morphology for the Grammar Matrix customization system, and evaluated its performance when modeling valence change from five held-out languages from different familial and areal groups.

2 Relevant elements of HPSG and the Grammar Matrix

The foundation of HPSG is the representation of each linguistic sign as a typed feature structure. This typed feature structure (Carpenter, 1992) is a structured object consisting of defined attributes, or features, the values of which are themselves other typed feature structures. The type of a feature structure determines which features appear in it. Thus, the entire feature structure of a sign forms a directed graph, where each node is a feature structure, and each edge is labeled with a feature name. Each node in the graph can be reached by following a sequence of labeled edges from the root. However, this path need not be unique; two (or more) paths through different feature structures may reach the same node.

Proceedings of the 2nd Int. Workshop on Resources and Tools for Derivational Morphology (DeriMo 2019), pages 111–120,
Prague, Czechia, 19-20 September 2019.

Disjoint feature structures can be combined, or *unified*, where their graphs (or a graph and a subgraph) are isomorphic. Unification is constrained such that the types of each node must be compatible; that is, that (a) the features present at the node must be valid for both node types, and (b) the types of each value the nodes have in common are also compatible. In this way the constraints expressed by each feature structure are satisfied. Note that this definition is recursive: each node must unify as well as each descendant node.

A grammar in this paradigm is comprised of the following main elements:

- **lexical types**, constraints inherited by words in the lexicon;
- **lexical rule types**, constraints on how stems give rise to inflected and derived forms;
- **grammar rule types**, constraints on how words combine into phrases, and how phrases combine;
- **foundational types**, types that constrain feature values (*e.g.* valid values of the CASE feature); and
- **instances**, instantiations of lexical types and lexical and grammar rule types.

This brief description illustrates two distinctive attributes of HPSG,[1] as described in Sag et al. 2003, Chapter 9. First, grammars are based on constraint satisfaction through unification (as contrasted with a transformational approach). Second, the grammar's view of syntax is strongly lexical: constraints originate with instances of lexical types and a distinction is made between word-internal rules and syntactic rules, the latter having no access to the former.

The Grammar Matrix implements a restricted formalism, described in Copestake (2002) and referred to as the DELPH-IN joint reference formalism, that significantly limits the available operations on feature structures. For example, the Joint Reference Formalism disallows set-valued features and relational constraints, and all structures must be acyclic.

2.1 Valence and argument structure

In the revised[2] conception of HPSG, the valence of a particular sign—that is, the specification of what other signs it must combine with to become saturated—is conveyed by the SUBCAT feature, which is defined as the append of the SUBJ, SPR, and COMPS lists (representing, respectively, the subject, specifier, and complements of the sign) (Pollard and Sag, 1994, p. 375). Subsequently, Manning and Sag (1998) proposed a modification whereby SUBCAT became a means to express the argument structure of a lexical sign, and specifically as a distinct entity from the SUBJ, SPR, and COMPS valence lists. The SUBCAT feature was renamed to ARG-ST to indicate this revised role.

This separation and its concomitant materialization of the mechanisms for linking argument structure and valence lists, making them available for manipulation, is essential to the implementation of valence change in this work. As I describe in more detail below, operations such as the passive rely on changing the relationship between syntactic and semantic roles played by a verb's arguments.

2.1.1 Grammar Matrix customization system

The Grammar Matrix customization system (Bender et al., 2010) combines a structured means of eliciting typological characteristics, validating responses for consistency, and using those choices to combine Matrix core grammar elements with stored analyses of various linguistic phenomena into a customized grammar. These stored analyses can include both static representations of cross-linguistically common phenomena as well as dynamically-generated implementations that embody language-specific variations. Elicitation is accomplished via a dynamic, iteratively-generated HTML questionnaire, which records the responses (while validating the consistency of both individual responses and their combination) in a structured choices file. This choices file is then processed by the customization script to produce the customized grammar. The system components and their relationships are shown in Figure 1 (from Bender et al., 2010, p. 31).

The stored analyses of linguistic phenomena in the customization system are organized into conceptual "libraries." These libraries also provide elements of the questionnaire, customization routines, and validation logic associated with the phenomena analyses they control. Representative libraries include word order (Fokkens, 2010), sentential negation (Crowgey, 2012), argument optionality (Saleem, 2010;

---

[1]These attributes also apply to other grammar approaches in the same tradition.

[2]With respect to earlier chapters of Pollard and Sag 1994.

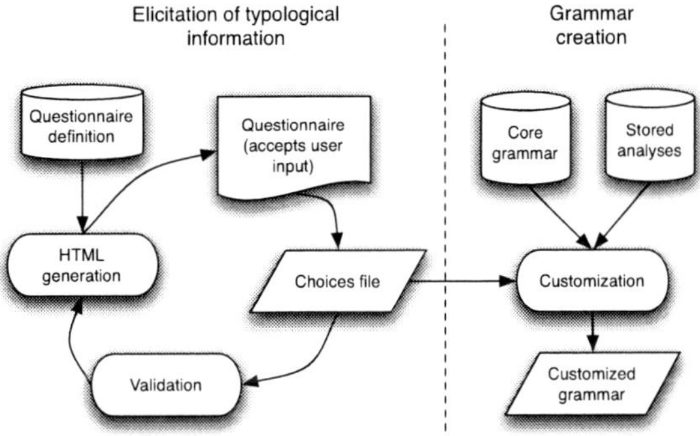

Figure 1: Customization system overview

Saleem and Bender, 2010), and information structure (Song, 2014), among others. Libraries may also interact and depend on facilities provided by other libraries; libraries such as the one presented here that implicate morphology may have relatively tighter coupling to the morphotactics library, for example.

2.2 Morphotactics

The Grammar Matrix customization system includes mechanisms for implementing morphosyntax, including the obligatoriness, ordering, and co-occurrence of position classes, and the definition and instantiation of lexical rules to implement inflectional (and, to a limited degree, derivational) morphology. The original morphotactics library was developed by O'Hara (2008), with argument optionality added by Saleem (2010). The current morphotactics framework is the result of significant modification and improvement by Goodman (2013).

2.3 Minimal Recursion Semantics

The Grammar Matrix uses Minimal Recursion Semantics (MRS; Copestake et al. 2005) as its semantic representation, integrated into its HPSG mechanisms and feature structures. In MRS, the primary unit of interest for semantics is the elementary predication (EP), which is a single relation and its arguments, identified by a label. EPs are never embedded in other EPs, but are instead grouped as flat elements in a bag.[3] Typical lexical items contribute a single EP; phrase structure rules construct a bag of EPs by appending the bags of EPs of all the phrase daughters and may contribute EPs themselves. This flat representation is underspecified as to scope, so an additional set of constraints are applied that define a restricted set of ways in which EPs can be related via scope relations. Scopal arguments are expressed via handle relationships, in which a handle is equal, modulo quantifiers, to a label. This relationship, denoted as qeq or $=_q$, allows semantic composition to be defined simply while preserving the scope constraints that could contain intervening quantifiers. This distinction between scopal and non-scopal relationships is essential to expressing certain valence-changing phenomena such as the causative.

3 Typology of valence change

Valence, by analogy to the valence of atoms in chemistry (Tesnière, 1959), refers to the number of core syntactic arguments a verb in a given clause type takes. All human languages have both intransitive and transitive clauses: intransitive clauses have a single argument, the subject (denoted S); transitive clauses have two arguments, the transitive subject (denoted A) and the transitive object (denoted O) (Dixon, 1979).

Many languages permit verbal derivations that alter the argument structure of verbs, either increasing or decreasing the valence and changing the relationship of realized arguments to syntactic roles. In analyzing the cross-linguistic range of these operations below, I follow the broad conceptual framework provided by Haspelmath and Müller-Bardey (2004) (henceforth H&MB) and group the operations first by whether

---

[3]In a bag, unlike in a set, EPs may be repeated.

they reduce or increase valence, and second by whether they affect the subject or object. I also retain
their focus on verbal valence-changing morphology (thus excluding, e.g., periphrastic constructions).

3.1 Valence-reducing operations

The primary types of subject-removing operation to consider are the anticausative and the passive. Both
remove the subject (A) and move the former object (O) into the subject position; the essential distinction
between them is that the anticausative removes the A argument entirely, while the passive merely moves
it to the periphery (H&MB). The Turkish [tur] anticausative and passive in Mam [mam] (Mayan family),
are illustrated in (1) and (2), respectively:

(1) a. *Anne-m   kapı-yı   aç-tı*
         mother-1SG door-ACC open-PAST(3SG)
         'My mother opened the door.' [tur]

     b. *Kapı aç-tı-dı*
         door open-ANTIC-PAST(3SG)
         'The door opened.' [tur]   (H&MB, p. 5)

(2) a. *ma   ch-ok   t-b'iyo-'n   Cheep kab' xjaa*
         PAST 3PL+O-DIRectional 3SG+A-hit-DIR José   two   person
         'José hit two people.' [mam]

     b. *ma   chi   b'iy-eet kab' xjaa   (t-u'n   Cheep)*
         PAST 3PL+S hit-PASS two   person 3SG-REL/AGENT José
         'Two people were hit (by José).' [mam]

                                              (England, 1983, in Dixon and Aikhenvald, 1997, p. 75)

Analogous to the anticausative, the object-removing operation where the object O is completely removed is referred to as the deobjective (H&MB) or the absolutive antipassive (Dayley, 1989, as cited in
H&MB). A related form, the "potential deobjective," expresses disposition of an agent rather than a real
action; however, this semantic distinction is not relevant to this analysis.

(3) a. *Sake a-ku*
         sake 1SG.TR-drink
         'I drink sake.' [ain]

     b. *I-ku-an*
         DEOBJ-drink-1SG.INTR
         'I drink.' [ain]   (Shibatani, 1990, in H&MB, p. 3)

The deaccusative (H&MB) or antipassive[4] (Dixon and Aikhenvald, 2000) is similar, but instead of
completely removing the underlying O argument, moves it out of the core to the periphery, as illustrated
by the Hungarian [hun] deaccusative in (4).

(4) a. *Az orvos szán-ja a   beteg-et*
         the doctor pity-3SG the patient-ACC
         'The doctor pities the patient.' [hun]

     b. *Az orvos szán-akoz-ik   a   beteg-en*
         the doctor pity-DEACC-3SG the patient-SUPERESS
         'The doctor feels pity for the patient.' [hun]   (Károly, 1982, in H&MB, p. 4)

3.2 Valence-increasing operations

3.2.1 Subject-adding

Cross-linguistically the most common valence-changing category (Bybee, 1985), the causative adds a
new subject (A), the causer of the event described by the verb. The addition of a causer to an intransitive

---

[4]Dixon and Aikhenvald use 'antipassive' to refer to both constructions, noting simply that "the [underlying O] argument
may be omitted" (p. 9)

verb can simply move the underlying subject (S) into an object (O) position, as illustrated by the Vengo [bav] (Grassfields Bantu) causative in (5):

(5) a. *nw nìi   táa nìì*
      he enter in house
      'He entered the house.' [bav]

    b. *m nìi-s   nw táa nìì*
      I enter-CAUS him in house
      'I made him enter the house.' [bav]   (Schaub, 1982, in H&MB, p. 11)

The situation with underlying transitive verbs is more complex, as there are different strategies for dealing with the underlying subject (causee), given the presence of an already-existing direct object (O). H&MB identify three such strategies, illustrated in (6): (6a) causee as an indirect object, as in Georgian [kat], (6b) causee as instrumental phrase, as in Kannada [kan], and (6c) causee as second direct object, as in Imbabura Kwicha [qvi].

(6) a. *Mama-m Mzia-s   daanteb-in-a   cecxli*
      father-ERG Mzia-DAT light-CAUS-AOR:3SG fire(ABS)
      'Father made Mzia light the fire.' [kat]   (Harris, 1981, in H&MB, p. 12)

    b. *Raamanu   manga-gal-inda   Siite-yannu huduki-si-danu*
      Rama(NOM) monkey-PL-INSTR Sita-ACC   search-CAUS-3SG
      'Rama had the monkeys search for Sita.' [kan]   (Cole and Sridhar, 1977, in H&MB, p. 12)

    c. *Juzi-ka Juan-ta   ruwana-ta   awa-chi-rka*
      José   Juan-ACC poncho-ACC weave-CAUS-3SG
      'José made Juan weave a poncho.' [qvi]   (Cole, 1982, in H&MB, p. 12)

Other subject-adding constructions are structurally similar to the causative, such as the affective ('indirect passive') in Japanese [jpn]. A crucial aspect of the causative and similar constructions is the addition of a new EP which functions as a scopal operator with respect to the verb's own EP and takes as an argument the added participant. This is distinguished from the applicative (below), which is non-scopal and does not affect semantic roles.

3.2.2 Object-adding

Object-adding constructions can collectively be grouped under the term 'applicative,' which subsumes a broad variation in potential roles for the added structural argument. The prototypical applicative is the benefactive, as demonstrated in the Indonesian [ind] alternation in (7). In many languages (e.g., in the Bantu family, especially) applicatives can serve many other functions, including possessor-raising, instrumental, and locative applicatives.

(7) a. *Orang itu   masak ikan untuk perempuan itu*
      man   DEF cook fish for   woman   DEF
      'The man cooked fish for the woman.' [ind]

    b. *Orang itu memasakan   perempuan itu ikan*
      Orang itu me-masak-kan perempuan itu ikan
      man   DEF TR-cook-BEN woman   DEF fish
      'The man cooked the woman fish.' [ind]   (Chung, 1976, p. 58)

(8) a. *Ali memi telefisi   untuk ibu-nja*
      Ali TR.buy television for   mother-his
      'Ali bought a television for his mother.' [ind]

    b. *Ali mem-beli-kan ibu-nja   telefisi*
      Ali TR-buy-APPL mother-his television
      'Ali bought his mother a television.' [ind]   (Chung, 1976, in Wunderlich, 2015, p. 21)

4 Analysis

The overall approach I followed was to decompose the high-level, linguistically-significant valence-changing operations into their component operations on feature structures. These individual component operations can then be selected by the customization system and composed to achieve the high-level result. The components I selected to analyze and implement included addition and removal of subjects and objects, case constraints and alternations, and argument reordering. For the purpose of illustration, I focus here on object- and subject-adding operations.

4.1 Object addition

In adding an argument, there are several underlying operations in my analysis: (a) adding an argument to the COMPS list;[5] (b) constraining the added argument (or promoted subject), e.g. to be an NP or PP (HEAD *noun* or *adp*), or applying a CASE constraint; (c) appending the new argument's non-local dependencies to the rule mother's list;.[6] (d) contributing an added elementary predication (EP) via C-CONT; (e) linking the new EP's ARG1 to the daughter's INDEX; and (f) linking the new EP's ARG2 to the new argument's INDEX.

The addition of a new EP to the rule output is not as straightforward and requires some additional discussion. To motivate this analysis, consider the example of the benefactive from Indonesian in (8). In this example, the addition of the benefactive applicative suffix *-kan* in (7b) adds an argument position to the verb, which is filled by *perempuan itu* "the woman."

Notionally, the benefactive is adding a third semantic argument to the verb, which would add a hypothetical ARG3 to the EP contributed by the verb; however, this would seem to violate the principles of semantic composition in Copestake et al. (2005), namely, that composition consists solely of *concatenation* of daughter RELS values, not modification. More concretely, there is no EP-modifying operation available within the algebra of Copestake et al. (2001).

The solution is to have the lexical rule contribute a new EP, which takes both the EP contributed by the verb and the additional syntactic argument as semantic arguments. The predicate value for this new EP will provide the particular species of applicative (e.g., benefactive, as here). This new EP contributes its own event and takes as its arguments the respective indexes of the input and the added argument. In this analysis I treat the added arguments as non-scopal, with no intervening handle relationships; this contrasts with my analysis of subject addition below. The MRS resulting from this analysis is shown below in (9):

$$
(9) \quad \left[\text{RELS} \quad \left\langle
\begin{bmatrix} \textbf{\_memi\_v\_buy} \\ \text{ARG0} \quad \boxed{4}\ event \\ \text{ARG1} \quad \boxed{1} \\ \text{ARG2} \quad \boxed{2} \end{bmatrix},
\begin{bmatrix} \textbf{named} \\ \text{ARG0} \quad \boxed{1} \end{bmatrix},
\begin{bmatrix} \textbf{\_telefisi\_n\_TV} \\ \text{ARG0} \quad \boxed{2} \end{bmatrix},
\begin{bmatrix} \textbf{\_ibu\_n\_mother} \\ \text{ARG0} \quad \boxed{3} \end{bmatrix},
\begin{bmatrix} \textbf{benefactive} \\ \text{ARG0} \quad event \\ \text{ARG1} \quad \boxed{4} \\ \text{ARG2} \quad \boxed{3} \end{bmatrix}
\right\rangle \right]
$$

With all these elements combined, a complete rule implementing the benefactive can be implemented as illustrated in (10). This rule, however, in combining the distinct operations identified above, obscures common elements that can be reused for other similar object-adding operations. Reviewing the operations, it is evident that they vary along different axes, as summarized in Table 1.

This leads to a simplification and optimization: in the same way that the intransitive and transitive forms of subject removal can be viewed as variants of a single abstract analysis along the transitivity axis, these building-block operations can also be treated as being parameterized along their axes of variation and then combined to make the final rule type.

---

[5]Note that, cross-linguistically, the added argument can added either more- or less-obliquely to the verb's existing dependencies (i.e., at the head or tail of the COMPS list).

[6]To conserve space, NON-LOCAL features are omitted from the examples presented.

(10)
$$
\begin{bmatrix}
\textit{benefactive-lex-rule} \\[4pt]
\text{SYNSEM} \mid \text{LOCAL} \mid \text{CAT} \mid \text{VAL} \mid \text{COMPS} \quad
\left\langle \boxed{1},
\begin{bmatrix}
\text{LOCAL} & \begin{bmatrix}
\text{CAT} & \begin{bmatrix}
\text{HEAD} & \textit{noun} \\
\text{VAL} & \begin{bmatrix} \text{SPR} & \langle\,\rangle \\ \text{COMPS} & \langle\,\rangle \end{bmatrix}
\end{bmatrix}
\end{bmatrix} \\
\text{CONT} \mid \text{HOOK} \mid \text{INDEX} & \boxed{2}
\end{bmatrix}
\right\rangle \\[20pt]
\text{C-CONT}\quad
\begin{bmatrix}
\text{RELS} & \left\langle !
\begin{bmatrix}
\textit{event-relation} \\
\text{PRED} & \textit{"benefactive"} \\
\text{ARG1} & \boxed{6} \\
\text{ARG2} & \boxed{2}
\end{bmatrix}
! \right\rangle \\
\text{HCONS} & \langle ! \quad ! \rangle
\end{bmatrix} \\[16pt]
\text{DTR}\quad
\begin{bmatrix}
\textit{verb-lex} \\
\text{SYNSEM} \mid \text{LOCAL} & \begin{bmatrix}
\text{CAT} \mid \text{VAL} \mid \text{COMPS} & \boxed{1} \\
\text{CONT} \mid \text{HOOK} \mid \text{INDEX} & \boxed{6}
\end{bmatrix}
\end{bmatrix}
\end{bmatrix}
$$

Concretely, taking these operations in turn, the first operation (adding the argument) needs to have variants for adding an argument: (a) to intransitive or transitive verbs; and (b) at the front or end of the COMPS list. That is, the lexical rule type implementing each of the component operations can be viewed as the output of a function: $f : tr \in \{intrans, trans\} \times pos \in \{front, end\} \rightarrow lrt$.

To illustrate this variation, the rule type at (11) adds an argument to the (empty) COMPS list for an intransitive verb, and the rule at (12) adds an argument at the front of the COMPS list for a transitive verb and links the INDEX of that argument to its second semantic argument (ARG2).

(11)
$$
\begin{bmatrix}
\textit{added-arg2of2-lex-rule} \\[4pt]
\text{SYNSEM} \mid \text{LOCAL} \mid \text{CAT} \mid \text{VAL} \mid \text{COMPS} \quad
\left\langle
\begin{bmatrix}
\text{LOCAL} & \begin{bmatrix}
\text{CAT} \mid \text{VAL} & \begin{bmatrix} \text{SPR} & \langle\,\rangle \\ \text{COMPS} & \langle\,\rangle \end{bmatrix} \\
\text{CONT} \mid \text{HOOK} \mid \text{INDEX} & \boxed{1}
\end{bmatrix}
\end{bmatrix}
\right\rangle \\[14pt]
\text{C-CONT} \mid \text{RELS} \quad \left\langle ! \begin{bmatrix} \text{ARG2} & \boxed{1} \end{bmatrix} ! \right\rangle \\
\text{DTR} \mid \text{SYNSEM} \mid \text{LOCAL} \mid \text{CAT} \mid \text{VAL} \mid \text{COMPS} \quad \langle\,\rangle
\end{bmatrix}
$$

(12)
$$
\begin{bmatrix}
\textit{added-arg2of3-lex-rule} \\[4pt]
\text{SYNSEM} \mid \text{LOCAL} \mid \text{CAT} \mid \text{VAL} \mid \text{COMPS} \quad
\left\langle
\begin{bmatrix}
\text{LOCAL} & \begin{bmatrix}
\text{CAT} \mid \text{VAL} & \begin{bmatrix} \text{SPR} & \langle\,\rangle \\ \text{COMPS} & \langle\,\rangle \end{bmatrix} \\
\text{CONT} \mid \text{HOOK} \mid \text{INDEX} & \boxed{1}
\end{bmatrix}
\end{bmatrix}, \boxed{2}
\right\rangle \\[14pt]
\text{C-CONT} \mid \text{RELS} \quad \left\langle ! \begin{bmatrix} \text{ARG2} & \boxed{1} \end{bmatrix} ! \right\rangle \\
\text{DTR} \mid \text{SYNSEM} \mid \text{LOCAL} \mid \text{CAT} \mid \text{VAL} \mid \text{COMPS} \quad \langle \boxed{2} \rangle
\end{bmatrix}
$$

rule component	varies by
added argument	position (obliqueness), number of existing args
constraint on new argument	position (obliqueness), constraint (*e.g.* case, head)
non-local dependencies	position (obliqueness)
new EP's PRED value	predicate
new EP's ARG1	does not vary
new EP's ARG2	position (obliqueness)

Table 1: Rule component axes of variation (benefactive)

The remaining operation components can likewise be separated into independent rule types, isolated to a particular element and parameterized on its axis of variation. These "building blocks," as rule component supertypes, can then be assembled as inherited constraints on a complete applicative rule type, ready to be instantiated in a grammar. The partial inheritance tree showing these rule component supertypes for the notional benefactive full rule type described here is illustrated in Figure 2.

4.2   Subject addition

The canonical subject-adding operation is the causative, which introduces a new argument into the subject role and moves the erstwhile subject into another position. In contrast to the applicative, I treat the causative as a scopal predicate: the "causing" EP outscopes the underlying verb's EP and so provides the HOOK feature values for the entire VP.

Consistent with the strategy in Copestake et al. (2001), the scopal relationship is expressed by a handle constraint (HCONS) rather than directly, representing equality modulo quantifiers ($=_q$).

Similarly to my analysis of the applicative, the causative can also be decomposed into component operations, again parameterized along the axes of cross-linguistic variation.

5   Implementation in the Grammar Matrix

The Grammar Matrix customization system (Bender et al., 2010) combines a structured means of eliciting typological characteristics, validating responses for consistency, and using those choices to combine Matrix core grammar elements with stored analyses of various linguistic phenomena into a customized grammar. These stored analyses can include both static representations of cross-linguistically common phenomena as well as dynamically-generated implementations that embody language-specific variations.

My implementation of a library leverages the existing morphotactics machinery in the customization system (Goodman, 2013) by adding options to the questionnaire for grammar writers to attach valence-changing operations to lexical rule types, along with the relevant parameters (e.g., position of erstwhile subject) necessary to generate the operations. My extensions to the grammar customization scripts, in turn, use the selections in the choices file to generate the appropriate parameterized and common rule components, and then combine them into types to be instantiated.

While developing the library, two types of tests were used. Initially, I developed small, abstract pseudo-languages to exercise specific operations and combinations; I then attempted to model valence change in three natural languages, Lakota [lkt], Japanese [jpn], and Zulu [zul], and produced test suites of grammatical and ungrammatical examples. During this phase of development, I continued to revise my analyses and code to achieve full coverage of the examples. Once this phase was complete, I then froze library development and moved to the evaluation phase, described in the next section.

6   Evaluation

To evaluate the library as developed against a representative sample of the world's languages, I selected five held-out languages, from different familial and areal groups, that had not been used during development. Two languages were selected from descriptive articles intentionally held out, and the rest were selected by drawing randomly from a large collection of descriptive grammars, discarding those without valence changing morphology, until sufficient evaluation languages were collected.

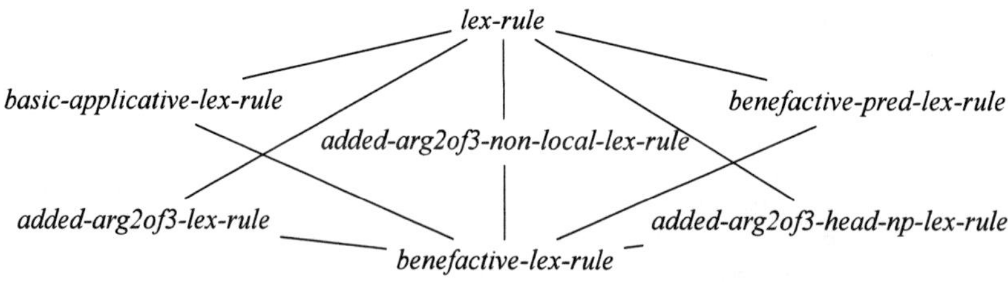

Figure 2: Example of rule component type hierarchy for applicative

I created test suites for each of these languages consisting of grammatical and ungrammatical examples of valence change, and attempted to model the corresponding phenomena using only the facilities available in the customization system questionnaire. I then attempted to parse the test suites using the customization system-generated grammars and recorded which grammatical examples were correctly parsed, which ungrammatical examples were erroneously parsed, and to what extent the parses generated spurious ambiguity. These results are summarized in Table 2.

Language	Family	examples		performance			
		positive	negative	parses	coverage	overgeneration	spurious ambiguity
Tsez [ddo]	NE Caucasian	11	8	10	91%	0%	0%
West Greenlandic [kal]	Eskimo-Aleut	15	14	12	73%	0%	0%
Awa Pit [kwi]	Barbacoan	7	7	5	71%	0%	0%
Rawang [raw]	Sino-Tibetan	11	6	6	55%	0%	0%
Javanese [jav]	Austronesian	13	8	12	92%	13%	0%
Total		57	43	45	79%	2%	0%

Table 2: Test languages test summary and performance

On the test suites for the five held-out languages, this approach as implemented in my library achieved an overall coverage of 79% and an aggregate overgeneration rate of only 2%. The language with the poorest coverage (55%), Rawang [raw], suffered almost entirely due to a relatively rich system of reflexive and middle constructions; my library lacked the ability to fill a valence slot while coindexing with an existing argument and so these examples could not be modeled. The sole example of overgeneration, from Javanese [jav], was similarly due to the inability of the current library to apply a HEAD constraint to an already-existing argument. Neither of these limitations appear to be fundamental, and so modifying the library to include these additional phenomena would be straightforward.

7   Conclusion

In this work I have presented an HPSG analysis of valence-changing verbal morphology, implemented in the LinGO Grammar Matrix, which I evaluated against several held-out languages. The results appear to support the hypothesis that a "building-block" based approach is an effective way to provide significant typological coverage of valence change. By developing and implementing this analysis within the larger Grammar Matrix project, these elements of valence change can be combined and recombined in different ways to test linguistic hypotheses and compare modeling choices, including the interactions of valence change with other phenomena. Although the scope of this work was limited to valence change expressed through verbal morphology, future work might include determining whether this approach can be extended to other phenomena, including, for example, periphrastic valence-changing constructions.

References

Emily M. Bender, Scott Drellishak, Antske Fokkens, Laurie Poulson, and Safiyyah Saleem. 2010. Grammar customization. *Research on Language & Computation* 8(1):23–72.

Emily M. Bender, Dan Flickinger, and Stephan Oepen. 2002. The Grammar Matrix: An Open-Source Starter-Kit for the Rapid Development of Cross-linguistically Consistent Broad-coverage Precision Grammars. In John Carroll, Nelleke Oostdijk, and Richard Sutcliffe, editors, *Proceedings of the Workshop on Grammar Engineering and Evaluation at the 19th International Conference on Computational Linguistics*. Taipei, Taiwan, pages 8–14.

Joan L Bybee. 1985. *Morphology: A study of the relation between meaning and form*. John Benjamins Publishing, Amsterdam.

Bob Carpenter. 1992. *The logic of typed feature structures*. Cambridge University Press, Cambridge, U.K.

Sandra Chung. 1976. An object-creating rule in Bahasa Indonesia. *Linguistic Inquiry* 7:41–87.

Peter Cole. 1982. *Imbabura Quechua*. Croom Helm, London etc.

Peter Cole and S. N. Sridhar. 1977. Clause union and relational grammar: Evidence from Hebrew and Kannada. *Linguistic Inquiry* 8(4):700–713.

Ann Copestake. 2002. Definitions of typed feature structures. In Stephan Oepen, Dan Flickinger, Jun-ichi Tsujii, and Hans Uszkoreit, editors, *Collaborative Language Engineering*, CSLI Publications, Stanford, CA, pages 227–230.

Ann Copestake, Dan Flickinger, Carl Pollard, and Ivan A. Sag. 2005. Minimal recursion semantics: An introduction. *Research on Language and Computation* 3(2):281–332.

Ann Copestake, Alex Lascarides, and Dan Flickinger. 2001. An algebra for semantic construction in constraint-based grammars. In *Proceedings of the 39th Annual Meeting of the Association for Computational Linguistics*. Association for Computational Linguistics, Stroudsburg, PA, USA, ACL '01, pages 140–147.

Joshua Crowgey. 2012. *The Syntactic Exponence of Sentential Negation: a model for the LinGO Grammar Matrix*. Master's thesis, University of Washington.

Jon Philip Dayley. 1989. *Tümpisa (Panamint) Shoshone Grammar*, volume 115. Univ of California Press.

R. M. W. Dixon. 1979. Ergativity. *Language* 55(1):59–138.

R. M. W. Dixon and Alexandra Y Aikhenvald. 1997. A typology of argument-determined constructions. In Joan Bybee, John Haiman, and Sandra A. Thompson, editors, *Essays on Language Function and Language Type*, John Benjamins, Amsterdam, pages 71–113.

R. M. W. Dixon and Alexandra Y. Aikhenvald. 2000. *Changing Valency*. Cambridge University Press.

Nora C England. 1983. *A grammar of Mam, a Mayan language*. University of Texas Press, Austin.

Antske S. Fokkens. 2010. Documentation for the Grammar Matrix word order library. Technical report, Saarland University, Saarbrücken.

Michael W. Goodman. 2013. Generation of machine-readable morphological rules from human-readable input. *University of Washington Working Papers in Linguistics* 30.

Alice C. Harris. 1981. *Georgian Syntax: A Study in Relational Grammar*. Cambridge University Press, Cambridge.

Martin Haspelmath and Thomas Müller-Bardey. 2004. Valence change. *Morphology: A handbook on inflection and word formation* 2:1130–1145.

Sándor Károly. 1982. Intransitive-transitive derivational suffixes in Hungarian. In Ferenc Kiefer, editor, *Hungarian Linguistics*, volume 4, pages 185–243.

Christopher D. Manning and Ivan A. Sag. 1998. Argument structure, valence, and binding. *Nordic Journal of Linguistics* 21(2):107–144.

Kelly O'Hara. 2008. *A morphotactic infrastructure for a grammar customization system*. Master's thesis, University of Washington.

Carl Pollard and Ivan A Sag. 1994. *Head-driven Phrase Structure Grammar*. University of Chicago Press.

Ivan A. Sag, Thomas Wasow, and Emily M. Bender. 2003. *Synactic Theory: A Formal Introduction*. CSLI, Stanford, CA, 2nd ed. edition.

Safiyyah Saleem. 2010. *Argument Optionality: A New Library for the Grammar Matrix Customization System*. Master's thesis, University of Washington.

Safiyyah Saleem and Emily M. Bender. 2010. Argument optionality in the LinGO Grammar Matrix. In *Proceedings of the 23rd International Conference on Computational Linguistics: Posters*. Association for Computational Linguistics, Stroudsburg, PA, USA, COLING '10, pages 1068–1076.

Willi Schaub. 1982. *Babungo*. Croom Helm, London etc.

Masayoshi Shibatani. 1990. *The languages of Japan*. Cambridge University Press.

Sanghoun Song. 2014. *A Grammar Library for Information Structure*. Ph.D. thesis, University of Washington.

Lucien Tesnière. 1959. *Eléments de syntaxe structurale*. Librairie C. Klincksieck, Paris.

Dieter Wunderlich. 2015. Valency-changing word-formation. In Peter O. Müller, Ingeborg Ohnheiser, Susan Olsen, and Franz Rainer, editors, *Word-Formation*, De Gruyter Mouton, Berlin/Boston, volume 3, pages 1424–1466.

Grammaticalization in Derivational Morphology: Verification of the Process by Innovative Derivatives

Junya Morita

Kinjo Gakuin University / 2-1723 Omori, Moriyama-ku, Nagoya City, Japan

`morita@kinjo-u.ac.jp`

Abstract

The present study investigates some creative aspects of derivational morphology in English and Japanese. Focusing on hapax legomena in large corpora, a strong indicator of online composition, relevant English and Japanese hapaxes are extracted from the British National Corpus and Balanced Corpus of Contemporary Written Japanese: agentive hapax nominals (e.g. *eyeballer*, *kakeochi-sha* 'one who elopes'), antiagentive hapax nominals (e.g. *directee*, *hi-seikyuu-sha* 'one who is demanded'), and hapax adjectivals (e.g. *tearable*, *tooki-kanoo(-na)* 'dumpable'). These innovations receive an in-depth analysis from morphological, semantic, and discursive viewpoints. The BNC/BCCWJ survey indicates that (i) semantic, functional, or morphosyntactic extension, a subprocess of grammaticalization, is constantly made under contextual pressure and (ii) it is primarily motivated by context-induced recategorization.

1   Introduction

While agentive and antiagentive derivatives are essentially non-deictic individual-level nominals (*employer*/*employee*), the *-er* derivative *secreter* in (1) functions as a deictic and stage-level nominal, which entails that 'one who concealed something treacherous at a certain point in the past.' The *-ee* derivative *packagees* in (2) signifies 'the ones who join a package tour,' but not 'the ones who are packaged into a tour'; the suffix *-ee* uncharacteristically joins to a noun and lacks a patient meaning. These words are coined on the basis of the prior utterance and are used once only in a large corpus, i.e. hapax legomena. What motivates these creative, context-sensitive grammatical shifts?

(1) "But it <u>looked very black against him</u> … He was a *secreter*." (BNC G3E:623)

(2) The plane is full of young English couples … When they land the young ones break lanes and stream off down the corridor, hustling for position. This crowd are experienced *packagees* … (BNC HGU:2840)

The aim of the present study is to elucidate some aspects of the semantic, functional, and formal extension of complex words by analyzing the innovative English and Japanese agentive/antiagentive nominals and deverbal adjectivals extracted from two large corpora, the British National Corpus (BNC) and Balanced Corpus of Contemporary Written Japanese (BCCWJ). After outlining the theoretical background (§2), we show three types of expansion of agentive/antiagentive nominals and deverbal adjectivals (§3) and explore their theoretical implications for grammaticalization (§4).

2   Theoretical Background

Bolinger (1972) shows that an intensifier such as *truly* is derived context-basedly from the corresponding "truth identifier" by grammatical shift. We can see in example (3) that the adverb *truly* shifts its function from a truth identifier in (3a), which refers to the truth of the whole sentence, to an intensifier of the adjacent adjective in (3b). Note that a truth identifier may not appear within a noun phrase. The prime motive of this grammatical shift is contextual "reinterpretation"—to reinterpret an expression not as a modifier of a phrase but as a modifier of its subphrase.

(3) a. He is *truly* a foolish person. (truth identifier)
    b. He is a *truly* foolish person. (intensifier)   (Bolinger, 1972:94)

Moreover, Clark and Clark (1979) discuss how a verb is innovatively zero-derived from a noun which is highly salient in a relevant verb phrase. In example (4), a novel verb is innovated in a context requiring the speaker's and hearer's mutual knowledge: Max has a queer habit of rubbing the back of a leg with a teapot. Conversion is thus crucially linked to contextual recategorization.

(4) Max tried to *teapot* a policeman.   (Clark and Clark, 1979:786)

Thus, an adverb or noun undergoes a contextual operation to induce the expansion of its meaning, function, and occurrence environment. This approach to linguistic potential forms the theoretical basis of this study.

3   Three Major Classes of Grammatical Expansion

Contextual operations can promote the semantico-functional and formal extension of a word formation device as well as the related extension of an existing derivative. To obtain a proof of such a creative facet of word formation, it is vital to examine hapax legomena, since hapaxes, words which occur only once in a large corpus, can be a reliable barometer of lexical inventions (Baayen and Renouf, 1996; Jackendoff, 1997:131-133).[1] Our target expressions are mainly extracted from BNC and BCCWJ; we have obtained 643 hapaxes of the suffix *-er*, 400 hapaxes of the Japanese counterpart (*-sha*), 83 word types of the suffix *-ee* including 17 hapaxes, and 54 word types of the Japanese equivalent (*hi-VN-sha*) including 12 hapaxes. The English nominal suffixes *-er* and *-ee* have been widely observed in the literature from a descriptive perspective: Jespersen, 1949; Marchand, 1969; Quirk et al., 1985. There are numerous treatments of the personal nominals in the generative literature, including Levin and Rappaport Hovav, 1992; Lieber, 2004; Baker and Vinokurova, 2009; Barker, 1988. Although rather fragmentary observations have been made on Japanese personal nominals (Nagashima, 1982; Kageyama, 1993), there has been no systematic analysis of them.

3.1 Semantic Extension

In the examples in (5) we can see contextual semantic extension. With an aid of contextual force, the suffix *-er* comes to stand for 'instrument' (*image-blocker*) as in (5a). Scalise (1984:45) points out that *-ee* normally affixes to verbs which allow animate objects, and hence **tearee* is ill-formed. However, the patient nominal *selectees* as well as *selectors* in (5b) imply non-human entities. The expansion to inanimate denotation of *selectees* is promoted by the prior antonymous expression (*selectors*). Interestingly, the contrast of *selectee* 'something that is selected' and **tearee* 'something that is torn' provides some evidence for the progression from animate noun to inanimate noun.

(5) a. ... the camera will not contain so much an image as an *image-blocker*, ie a mask or matte that blocks out part of the image behind it. (BNC FB8:241)
    b. Selectors may generally be identified by the fact that they presuppose one or more semantic traits of their *selectees*. (BNC FAC:1990)

The second case is the shift of the antiagentive suffix *-ee* to an agentive marker. Barker (1998:717) points out that *-ee* nouns entail the lack of volitional control over the relevant event. In example (6), the persons concerned merely attend a meeting. To emphasize the lack of volition, the typical agentive

---

[1]Hay (2003:79-81) refers to a number of psycholinguistic experiments which have shown that while complex words with high frequency are permanently stored in the mental lexicon, complex words with ultra-low frequencies of occurrence are generally composed by word-formation rules; the former type of words are retrieved from the lexicon without being accessed via formation rules (a memory-based procedure), whereas the latter follows a rule-based access procedure.

noun *attenders* or *attendants* is replaced with the *-ee* noun *attendees*.

(6) Some 30 named *attendees* heard a long and detailed speech from the Mayor in which … (BNC
AMY:144)

3.2 Functional Expansion

-Er derivatives usually express non-transitory properties of individuals (Baker and Vinokurova,
2009:531). Fiengo (1974:44) adduces good examples to show this: contrast *Jon is a* cheese-eater 'one
who (habitually) eats cheese' and ?*John was a* cheese-eater *once yesterday*. They may shift to stage-
level nominals, though. For example, the agentive noun *inscriber* in (7) has a stage-level property,
signifying 'one who inscribed the names at one point in time.' This novel word is directly derived from
the prior verb phrase *engrave our names in big letters upon the sand*. Discourse-dependent functional
extension can also be seen in the formation of *signee* in (8). It is noteworthy that the definition of the
term in the *Oxford English Dictionary* (2nd ed.) (OED) is 'one who *has signed* a contract or register.'

(7) We were on a beach, and someone—probably me in my cheerleader mode—suggested we engrave
our names in big letters upon the sand, then one of us would mount the promenade and photograph
inscription plus *inscriber*. (BNC EDJ:913)

(8) But on forty one minutes it was Milton who took the lead as new *signee* from A E R Harwell …
(BNC KS7:428)

Secondly, as seen in (9), the deictic formation of an agentive is possible: the transient name *time-
teller* is given to an entity (clock) which exists in the situation concerned. Recall that *time-teller* 'one
which/who *habitually* tells time' is not generally accepted. Similarly, as evidenced in (10), the patient
derivative *honorees* can be correctly used only when it refers to the participants in the situation of
utterance.

(9) It lacks but ten minutes to eight of the clock … With an oath the Weasel hurled the *time-teller* far
out into the heather … (BNC HA3:1724)

(10) "I feel very elated and honored," said Matlin, who is deaf. "I'm going to scream later." There
was another unusual double among the *honorees*: … (*Time*, February 23, 1987, p. 23)

3.3 Morphosyntactic Extension

As is commonly known, the agentive suffix *-er* essentially attaches to a verb or noun, and the
antiagentive suffix *-ee* principally joins to a verb. In certain contexts, however, these suffixes can be
added to other lexical categories. Barker (1998:716) points out that *-ee* is suffixed to nonverbal bases
(*giftee* 'one who receives a gift'), suggesting the categorial extension of its base. Furthermore, the base
of *-er* is categorially extended to adjective as in (11), where depending on the preceding predicate
adjectival *up to no good*, the same adjectival is incorporated into an *-er* word. Consequently, the
property of an entity is conceptualized in a lexical form.

(11) "I have decided you are up to no good. … But I prefer you to be up to no good in London. Which
is more used to *up-to-no-gooders*." (John Fowles, *The French Lieutenant's Woman*, p. 91)

Secondly, while word formation rules in general refer to no phrasal categories (*$*_N[large\ bank]$
er]), a relatively "small" phrase may be incorporated into a word, often under the conditions of
contextual connection. In (12), the human description which is deducible from the prior text ("one who
writes on one subject") is encapsulated into the momentarily constituted form *one-subject writer*.

(12) … South African Author Nadine Gordimer, 60, has emerged as the most influential home-grown
critic of her country's repressive racial policies. … Nor is Gordimer a *one-subject writer*. (*Time*,

July 23, 1984, p. 54)

And finally, Roeper (1987:295) comments as follows: *-er* takes only an [AG, TH] thematic grid in which the Theme role can be implicit; that is why **an intender to play baseball* is unacceptable, whose underlying verb takes an [AG, PROP] thematic grid. As shown in (13), however, the *-er* noun *tempter* may take a sentential complement in a proper context. Accordingly, *-er* undergoes recategorization so as to take the Proposition role. It can therefore be seen that nominalizers may context-dependently extend the inheritable complements of their bases as well as the categorial kind and size of them.[2]

(13) The Sun went to more extreme lengths in their massive coverage, <u>photographing Fairley's present wife under the caption "Georgina .... sought psychiatric help"</u> ... Directly underneath was *the tempter to move on to the special four-page pull-out section* ... (BNC CS1:1181)

3.4 Grammatical Expansion in Japanese

Contextual extension of personal nominals are recognized in Japanese as well. Let us first discuss it from a functional perspective. Stage-level agentive nominals can be seen in Japanese, as exemplified in passage (14).

(14) ... <u>sono futatsu-o ketsugoo suru mono-ga</u>   arawareru made Tokyo-wa
    the   two-Acc connection do   person-Nom appear   until Tokyo-Top
    toki-o   matte ita.   Sono *ketsugoo-sha*-ga   Tokugawa Ieyasu dearu.
    time-Acc wait Past-Prog the   connection-er-Nom   be
    'Tokyo was waiting the day when one who would connect the two things would appear. The connecter was Tokugawa Ieyasu.' (BCCWJ)

Here, linked to the antecedent phrase *sono futatsu-o ketsugoo suru mono*, the stage-level nominal *ketsugoo-sha* 'one who would connect (the two things) at a certain time in the past' is succinctly created as a thematic pro-form. It is thus recognized that contextually conditioned recategorization serves to facilitate the functional extension of a nominalizer.

Let us now turn to morphosyntactic extension. While Japanese antiagentive nouns are normally constructed by affixation of "*hi-...-sha*" to verbal nouns (VNs) (*hi-koyoo-sha* 'Passive-employment-er'), the base of the affix categorially spreads to non-VN, as exemplified by *hi-hoken-sha* 'Passive-insurance-er (=one who is insured).'[3] Additionally, the base of the suffix *-sha* is categorially expanded to (compound) adjective, as in *choosa-funoo-sha* 'investigation-impossible-er' (=one who is uninvestigable). Furthermore, phrase-incorporation can be observed in Japanese as well, as demonstrated in (15). An agentive name is given to a useful concept in the context of auction; the italicized agentive *sono jiten-sha* 'the timer' contains the phrase *sono jiten* 'the time.' Here, as elsewhere, contextual categorization is commonly accompanied by the morphosyntactic extension of a nominalizing suffix.

(15) <u>Ookushon-wa subete taimingu desu</u>. ... *Sono-jiten-sha* igai   daremo
    auction-Top   all   timing   be   the-time-er   except anybody
    nyuusatsu nai-mama kekkyoku owa-tta ...
    bid   not   eventually end-Past
    'Timing is the most important aspect of an auction. ... Nobody except the timer eventually bid at the auction ...' (BCCWJ)

3.5 A Difference in Semantic Expansion between English and Japanese

There is a crucial difference between English and Japanese: relevant semantic extension is likely to occur in English, whereas it is unlikely to take place in Japanese. Let us first consider the expansion

---

[2]Some of the complex words which are only temporarily acceptable in particular circumstances make their way into the lexicon; they may become institutionalized when they can be seen as useful enough to serve as "labels," i.e. as a basis for conceptualization. Since the conventionalized words no longer need contextual clues, it may be difficult to decide whether they are context-induced or not (cf. Morita, 1995:471).

[3]VN has a predicate function with argument structure and is accompanied by the light verb *suru* 'do' when used as a verb.

to impersonal denotation of agentive suffixes. The agentive hapaxes detected in BNC and BCCWJ are classified on the basis of their forms (derived words vs. compounds) and meanings (person-denoting vs. non-person-denoting), as displayed in Table 1.

		derived words	compounds	Total
English	[+personal]	130	411	541 (84.1%)
	[−personal]	12	90	102 (15.9%)
Japanese	[+personal]	123	276	399 (99.7%)
	[−personal]	0	1	1 (0.3%)

Table 1: Classification of agentive hapaxes in BNC/BCCWJ

Table 1 shows that English impersonal *-er* nouns (e.g. *weight-reducer*) are often created, while Japanese counterparts are rarely constructed; in English the number of inanimate agentive hapaxes comprises 15.9% of the whole agentive hapaxes, but it comprises only 0.3% of them in Japanese. Secondly, an antiagentive noun never shifts to an agentive in Japanese; unlike English patient derivatives, a *hi-VN-sha* 'V-ee' derivative is never found (in BCCWJ) extended to become an agentive (cf. **hi-kikan-sha* 'returnee').

We are now in the position to consider why we rarely see the comparable semantic expansion in Japanese. The Japanese agentive suffix *-sha* has the corresponding content word *mono*. They share the same ideographic (Chinese) character 者, meaning 'person'; this written form functions as a suffix when it is pronounced in a pseudo-Chinese manner (called *onyomi*), [ʃə], while it principally functions as an independent word when pronounced in a Japanese manner (called *kunyomi*), [mɔnɔ]. The suffix *-sha* is naturally developed from the cognate synonymous word *mono*. By the same token, the prefix *hi-*, pronounced in a pseudo-Chinese fashion, originally stems from the cognate synonym *koomuru*, which is pronounced in a Japanese fashion and means 'to suffer the action.' From the above observations, the lack of semantic expansion in Japanese is deducible from the fact that the Japanese affixes *-sha* and *hi-*, derived from Sino-Japanese words, continue to retain their original meanings ('person/be V-ed').

3.6 Deverbal Adjectivization

The preceding sections have been concerned with the extension processes of "personal nominalization." In this section, we will show that the same applies to deverbal adjectivization: *-able* derivation and its Japanese counterpart (*-kanoo* derivation). The data samples used for this section are extracted from BNC and BCCWJ; we have gained 595 word types in *-able* including 203 hapaxes and 271 word types in *-kanoo* including 50 hapaxes.

Let us first consider the semantic extension of *-able* adjectivization. *-Able* generally makes an adjective with a mixture of passive and 'ability' senses, 'can be V-ed.' (Quirk et al, 1985:1555). To obtain a proof of this general tendency, we have conducted a close inspection of the meanings of 203 *-able* hapaxes. Our BNC survey indicates that among the four submeanings of *-able*—(a) 'can be V-ed,' (b) 'should be V-ed,' (c) 'apt to,' and (d) 'suitable for'—the number of hapaxes with submeaning (a) accounts for 81% of the whole hapaxes recorded, entailing its dominance over rival senses. Examples (16)-(18) illustrate how the core or prototypical meaning is related to the peripheral meaning of (d).

(16) a. Knights too were <u>readily</u> *identifiable* … (BNC CTW:54)
    b. It has cushion covers that are <u>easily</u> *removable* for dry cleaning … (BNC A70:1804)

(17) a. The resulting straight thin poles were <u>readily</u> *saleable*. (BNC F9H:1619)
    b. a <u>very</u> *saleable* product (BNC CS5:596)/ <u>very</u> *collectable* coins (BNC G2Y:629)

(18) a. The Thames at Abingdon was barely *fishable* … (BNC A6R:1594)
    b. Scientists then set a goal: *fishable, swimmable* water that could support existing biota …
    (BNC B7L:669)

Derivatives ending in *-able* often occur with 'facility' adverbs such as *easily* and *readily*, as in (16a). The collocational behavior of these terms produces ambiguity, i.e., *removable* may be interpreted as 'can be removed' or as 'suitable for removing,' as seen in (16b). It should be noted that *-able* words in the latter sense are no longer related to the passive. This submeaning becomes conventionalized to act as an independent marker of the item's suitability for selling or collecting, as indicated in the examples of (17), where it fits well with the intensifier *very*. Since *-able* undergoes recategorization so as to convey an active import, a Locative subject and unergative verb can be involved in *-able* constructions, as (18) illustrates.

The second case of semantic extension is exemplified in discourse (19):

(19) As a piece of treasure of considerable historical importance, the Wolvercote Tongue was of course beyond price. In itself, however, as an artefact set with precious stones, it was, let us say, "*priceable*" … (BNC HWM:3054)

In *Webster's Third New International Dictionary*, *priceable* is defined as 'capable of being priced.' (It has no entry in OED.) *Priceable* in (19), however, denotes 'capable of being *highly* priced,' an intensive element being added to the original meaning. This is because the existing meaning of the word is extended to include an intensive feature on the basis of the property mentioned in the immediately preceding discourse. *Priceable* in quotation mark implies a special kind of meaning of the word.

Morphosyntactically, a condition of *-able* derivation may be overruled in certain circumstances. Since *-able* is essentially related to the passive, verbs which cannot be passivized may not be the bases of *-able* affixation (cf. *The accident was *survived* by Martin/ *John is *had* by Mary) (Chapin, 1967:56-58). In examples of (20), however, *-able* is added to verbs of this kind. Here, "peculiar" *-able* words are generated online with the aids of the related words in the syntactic environments of verb-object and coordination. Accordingly, a property of the relevant subject has become fruitfully conceptualized in a single lexical form.

(20) a. Martin survived an *unsurvivable* accident. (BNC A6W:586)
 b. It kept them apart, kept them foreign to each other, him *unhaveable*, her unhad. (BNC A0U:893)

The external argument of *-able* words is restricted to theme argument (Williams, 1981). As (21) illustrates, *-able* constructions are possible only when the Theme is externalized:

(21) a. Those things are promisable (theme externalized).
 b. *Those people are runnable (Actor externalized).
 c. *Those people are promisable (Goal externalized).   (Williams, 1981:93)

This syntactic constraint is relaxed in a certain limited way; as we have already seen in (18), Location argument can occur in the external position of an *-able* adjectival as a result of semantic extension. The same is true of example (22) below. The sentence of (22) is stated in a discourse of the row materials of boats. The relevant small clause implies 'plastic boats are much more suitable for escaping,' but not 'plastic boats can (much more) be escaped from,' with *-able* undergoing recategorization so as to express an active import. Here, the subject NP corresponds to the Source argument of the related base verb, with this argument being foregrounded and qualifying itself as the topic of property description. Thus semantic extension, together with the contextual pressure for foregrounding Location/Source, may help to expand the possible external argument from Theme to Location and to Source.

(22) … the development of high molecular density polyethylene has made plastic boats much more *escapable* ... (BNC G27:827)

We turn next to *-kanoo* adjectivization in Japanese (e.g. *pasuwaado-wa henkoo-kanoo-da* 'password is changeable'). First, as with the case of personal nominalization, the semantic extension of *-kanoo* derivatives does not take place; for example, *henkoo-kanoo(-na)* (change-able) 'can be changed' may not be extended to mean 'apt to change.' The suffix *-kanoo* preserves the original meaning for much the same reason as the one given for *-sha* and *hi-* nominalization; the suffix *-kanoo* shares the ideographic character 可能 'capable' with the adjectival content word *kanoo(-na)*, which helps to prevent semantic shift of the suffix.

In comparison, the morphosyntactic extension figures in *-kanoo* constructions. Although the suffix *-kanoo* generally attaches to a verbal noun (VN), it is not difficult to find examples where concrete nouns are the bases of *-kanoo*, as shown in (i) *kaku juuko-no yuka-wa dosoku-kanoo-da* (each apartment house-Gen floor-Top feet-in-(dirty-)shoes-capable-be) '(lit.) the floor of each apartment house is possible to walk on with your (dirty) shoes on' and (ii) *denshirenji-kanoo-na kobachi* (microwave-capable small bowl) 'microwavable small bow' (BCCWJ). Consequently, the range of possible categorial unit with which *-kanoo* combines is extended from a VN to an entity-denoting noun. It is noteworthy that lessening of selectional restrictions is characterized as a concomitant process typical of grammaticalization. The syntactic condition of "externalize the Theme" is generally valid for *-kanoo* adjectivization as well; an adjunct-related entity noun is unlikely to occur in the external position of a *-kanoo* predicate. There may be a case, however, where an entity noun of this kind appears in the external position concerned on the basis of contextual clues, as demonstrated in (23) and (24). Here Instrument/Means and Respect/Location arguments are highlighted as topics of characterizing predication. Notice that these arguments are externalized only if the relevant predicates are accompanied by the related adverbials.

(23) shiteiseki chiketto-wa   *(taishoo geemu nomi shiteiseki-de)   kansen-kanoo-da.
     reserved seat ticket-Top   relevant game only reserved seat-at watch-able-be
     '(lit.) The reserved seat ticket is watchable only at the reserved seat for the relevant game.'
                                         (BCCWJ)

(24) sono reesu-wa   ?(juubun)   gyakuten-kanoo-da.
     the   race-Top   sufficiently   reverse-able-be
     '(lit.) The race is sufficiently reversible.'
                                         (BCCWJ)

4   Implications for Grammaticalization

The phenomena discussed in §3 naturally conform to the system of grammaticalization. Grammaticalization is traditionally defined as "the increase of the range of a morpheme advancing from a lexical to a grammatical or from a less grammatical to a more grammatical status" (Heine et al., 1991a:3). Here we define it simply as extending the grammatical functions of a morpheme. Its primary means is to expand the use of existing forms for categorizing new concepts (Heine et al., 1991a:27; Lichtenberk, 1991:476). We will first illustrate semantic extension with English *-er* and *-ee* derivatives. The deverbal suffix *-er* chiefly attaches to action verbs (Marchand, 1969:273) and intransitive *-er* derivatives such as *runner* and *stander* typically involve the components of humanity, volitionality, and action (cf. "Ann *stands* in a nightgown"). It may happen that the feature [+volitional] turns into a central property in a certain context, that is, it is foregrounded, and additionally the feature [+human] is downgraded in prominence. Then it becomes possible to use an *-er* derivative for conceptualizing this situation, with the consequence that the word *stander* is recategorized, as exemplified in (25). In this case, the *-er* noun no longer refers to an entity but to a volitional activity (standing ovation). [4]

(25) He received 56 bouts of applause, including the interminable *standers*. (*The Guardian*, October 11, 1997, p. 10)

Similarly, the suffix *-ee* comes to stand for "agent.' Discourse (26) exemplifies the situation in

---

[4] Two main functions of morphological operations are recognizable: (i) to give a label or name to a useful category (labeling) and (ii) "to use morphologically related words of different syntactic categories," e.g. nominalization (syntactic recategorization), and these functions are not mutually exclusive (Kastovsky, 1986:594-596; Booij, 2005:13-14). All of the hapax nominals and adjectivals in this article are a case of labeling. Moreover, our central claim—contextual grammaticalization— accounts for a much wider range of phenomena, including syntactic recategorization; contextual grammaticalization may have direct connection to what is uttered in its preceding clauses and what an addresser assumes is known to the addressee.

which volitionality among the agentive features is lost and [−volitional] becomes a new focal feature. Then the suffix *-ee*, endowed with this feature, may be invoked for labeling this situation, leading to the coinage of *standee*. Moreover, this type of agentives may be impersonal as seen in (27), where the word *standees* is recategorized as denoting an unvolitional non-human entity.

(26) On a bus from Northallerton to Thirsk yesterday a sign stated that the vehicle could hold 24 seated passengers and six *standees*. (BNC K55:6600)

(27) "You know those life-size cardboard figures that stand around in video shops to advertise films?" she said. "They are called *standees*." (*The Independent*, April 15, 2004, p. 29)

The processes observed in (25) and (27) involve a conceptual transfer from the domain of animate beings to that of inanimate concepts, a specific aspect of grammaticalization (Heine et al., 1991b:151, 157). The grammatical extension of *-er/-ee*—from an agentive to a processual marker or from a patient to an agentive marker—is thus the result of context-induced recategorization. Table 2 presents a flow chart of the grammaticalization process described above.

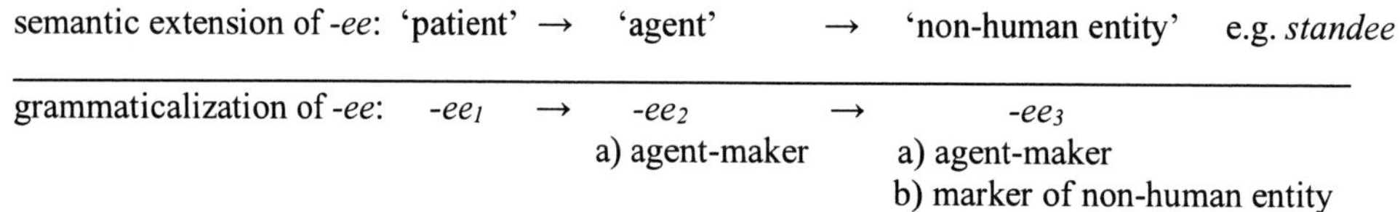

semantic extension of *-ee*: 'patient' → 'agent' → 'non-human entity' e.g. *standee*

grammaticalization of *-ee*: *-ee₁* → *-ee₂* → *-ee₃*
a) agent-maker   a) agent-maker
b) marker of non-human entity

Table 2: On the relation between the semantic extension and grammaticalization of *-ee*

The functional extension of agentive/patient affixes also goes along with grammaticalization. Discourse (28) clearly illustrates grammaticalization motivated by contextual recategorization.

(28) … it's the fact that when we tell people the truth, we do so by getting them to believe what we believe. But why do we do that? Why, for a start, do we want to be *tellees*, i.e. to adopt other people's beliefs? (BNC FBD:757)

The *-ee* derivative *tellees* in (28) denotes a complex entity of the patient which contains a proposition: 'one who adopts the speaker's belief when it is told.' This deictic, stage-level nominal implies 'one who is told to,' with the propositional complement of the base verb *tell* being contextually recovered. Significantly, the suffix extends its function from a mere nominalizer of simple verb to the nominalizer which combines with a larger conceptual unit in a discourse so as to give a label to a relevant entity. The "functional" grammaticalization of *-ee* is depicted in Table 3.

-ee₁ →   *-ee₂* e.g. *honoree* in (10) →   *-ee₃* e.g. *tellee* in (28)
a) marker of deictic, stage-level feature   a) marker of deictic, stage-level feature
b) function of giving a label to a larger conceptual unit in a discourse

Table 3: "Functional" grammaticalization of *-ee*

The same argument applies to the functional extension of the agentive nominal *inscriber* in example (7) as well as the antiagentive nominal *packagees* in (2) above.

As shown in (11), (12), (15), and (2) above, an established notion is temporarily formed for an addresser and the addressee at a particular time and the whole notion is categorized by encoding a prominent part of the notion. It is a personal nominalizer that plays a critical role in carrying out this function. The nominalizers at issue generally join to single words belonging to certain categories in accordance with the relevant morphological conditions. Yet, they may be added to categories different from the specified ones; *-ee* is suffixed to noun (*packagees* in (2)), *-er* is affixed to adjectival (*up-to-no-gooder* in (11)), and *-sha* is combined with non-VN (*sono-jiten-sha* in (15)). Moreover, the agentive suffixes *-er* and *-sha* may incorporate a phrase, as illustrated in (11), (12), and (15), resulting in morphosyntactic extension.

5 Conclusion

On the basis of close analysis of the spontaneous coinages discerned in large corpora, we have revealed some facets of the semantic, functional, and formal extension of English and Japanese agentive/antiagentive nominals and 'capable' adjectivals. We have then provided a unified account of them from the perspective of grammaticalization. Hopefully, the present study will shed new light on the origin of morphological potentialities. The refinement of extension conditions and the diachronic verification of grammatical expansion await further investigation.

Acknowledgments

I would like to express my gratitude to three anonymous referees for their valuable comments and suggestions on an earlier draft of this article. This work is partly supported by a Grant-in-Aid for Scientific Research (C) (No. 17K02697) from the Japan Society for the Promotion of Science.

References

Harald R. Baayen and Antoinette Renouf. 1996. Chronicling *the Times*: Productive lexical innovations in an English newspaper. *Language* 72:69-96.

Mark C. Baker and Nadya Vinokurova. 2009. On agent nominalizations and why they are not like event nominalizations. *Language* 85:517-556.

Chris Barker. 1998. Episodic *-ee* in English: A thematic role constraint on new word formation. *Language* 74:695-727.

Dwight Bolinger. 1972. *Degree Words*. Mouton, The Hague.

Geert Booij. 2005. *The Grammar of Words*. Oxford University Press, Oxford.

Paul G. Chapin. 1967. *On the Syntax of Word-Derivation in English*. MITRE, Bedford, MA.

Eve V. Clark and Herbert H. Clark. 1979. When nouns surface as verbs. *Language* 55:767-811.

Robert Wilson Fiengo. 1974. *Semantic Conditions on Surface Structure*. Doctoral dissertation, MIT.

Jennifer Hay. 2003. *Causes and Consequences of Word Structure*. Routledge, New York.

Bernd Heine, Ulrike Claudi, and Friederike Hünnemeyer. 1991a. *Grammaticalization: A Conceptual Framework*. University of Chicago Press, Chicago.

Bernd Heine, Ulrike Claudi, and Friederike Hünnemeyer. 1991b. From cognition to grammar: Evidence from African languages. In *Approaches to Grammaticalization* volume 1. Ed. by Elizabeth Closs Traugott and Bernd Heine, pages 149-187. John Benjamins, Amsterdam.

Ray Jackendoff. 1997. *The Architecture of the Language Faculty*. MIT Press, Cambridge, MA.

Otto Jespersen. 1942. *A Modern English Grammar on Historical Principles* VI. George Allen and Unwin, London.

Taro Kageyama. 1993. *Bunpoo to Gokeisei* 'Grammar and Word Formation.' Hituzi, Kasukabe.

Dieter Kastovsky. 1986. The problem of productivity in word formation. *Linguistics* 24:585-600.

Frantisek Lichtenberk. 1991. Semantic change and heterosemy in grammaticalization. *Language* 67:475-509.

Rochelle Lieber. 2004. *Morphology and Lexical Semantics*. Cambridge University Press, Cambridge.

Hans Marchand. 1969. *The Categories and Types of Present-Day English Word-Formation*. C. H. Beck, München.

Junya Morita. 1995. Lexicalization by way of context-dependent nonce-word formation. *English Studies* 76:468-

473.

Yoshio Nagashima. 1982. Gokoosei no hikaku 'Comparison of word constructions.' In *Nichieigo Hikaku Kooza* 'Lectures on Comparison between English and Japanese' volume 1. Ed. by Tetsuya Kunihiro, pages 227-285. Taishukan, Tokyo.

Randolph Quirk, Sidney Greenbaum, Geoffrey Leech, and Jan Svartvik. 1985. *A Comprehensive Grammar of the English Language*. Longman, London.

Malka Rappaport Hovav and Beth Levin. 1992. *Er-n*ominals: Implications for the theory of argument structure. In *Syntax and Semantics* 26. Ed. by Tim Stowell and Eric Wehrli, pages 127-153. Academic Press, New York.

Thomas Roeper. 1987. Implicit arguments and the head-complement relation. *Linguistic Inquiry* 18:267-310.

Sergio Scalise. 1984. *Generative Morphology*. Foris, Dordrecht.

Edwin Williams. 1981. Argument structure and morphology. *The Linguistic Review* 1:81-114.

Association for Computational Linguistics
209 N. Eighth Street
Stroudsburg, Pennsylvania 18360

ISBN 978-1-7138-0078-1